The Vine Project

SHAPING YOUR MINISTRY CULTURE
AROUND DISCIPLE-MAKING

COLIN MARSHALL
AND TONY PAYNE

D1004413

About the authors

Colin Marshall has spent the past 40 years training men and women in the ministry of the gospel, both in university and local church contexts. Since the publication of *The Trellis and the Vine* he has been heading up Vinegrowers, a ministry aiming to help pastors grow churches that are focused on disciple-making (see **vinegrowers.com**). Col is married to Jacquie, who has shared with him in this lifetime of ministry, and they have been blessed with three now adult children and four grandchildren.

Tony Payne has worked in Christian ministry, focusing on writing and publishing, for over 25 years. He is the author of many books, Bible studies and other resources, including *The Trellis and the Vine, The Course of Your Life,* and *Islam in our Backyard.* He is currently the CEO of Matthias Media, the Director of the Centre for Christian Living at Moore College, and a member of the staff team at St Paul's Anglican Church, Carlingford. With his wife, Ali, he has five children and two grandchildren.

The Vine Project

SHAPING YOUR MINISTRY CULTURE AROUND DISCIPLE-MAKING

COLIN MARSHALL AND TONY PAYNE

matthiasmedia

SYDNEY · YOUNGSTOWN

Matthias Media
(St Matthias Press Ltd ACN 067 558 365)
Email: info@matthiasmedia.com.au
Internet: www.matthiasmedia.com.au
Please visit our website for current postal and telephone contact information.

Matthias Media (USA)
Email: sales@matthiasmedia.com
Internet: www.matthiasmedia.com
Please visit our website for current postal and telephone contact information.

ISBN 978 1 922206 94 7

Cover design and typesetting by Lankshear Design.

Contents

Acknowledgements

Writing a book certainly focuses the mind. And writing a book about how to conduct ourselves as God's servants, in his church for the sake of Christ's name, really does focus the mind and the heart. Are we being true to God's revealed mind?

Tony and I have not written *The Vine Project* at our desks. The past six years since *The Trellis and the Vine* was published have been like one continuous conversation about the Christian life, church and ministry. It's been challenging, humbling, sometimes agonizing and mostly joyful. We're enormously thankful to the thousands of pastors and elders who have joined in that conversation at workshops, conferences and seminars all around the world.

We also want to acknowledge particular people who have invested time and thought in the conversation.

About 40 pastors took up my offer to be their ministry coach as they tried to implement the principles of *The Trellis and the Vine*. This firsthand experience of seeing very different churches grappling with new ways of thinking and behaving was invaluable.

A dozen pastors waded through the early versions of the material and gave detailed feedback and enough encouragement for us to keep going. This input has sharpened our understanding of ministry and has significantly shaped the final product.

Gary Bennetts, Stuart Holman and Greg Peisley spent a whole year using the early versions of this material, not only in their own churches but also as coaches in their neighbouring churches. Steve Lindemann equipped us to understand the process of culture change along the way. I looked forward to our monthly meetings as they helped us make the whole thing more usable (I hope).

Phil Colgan and Gary Koo, the pastors of the local churches where Tony and I are involved, have encouraged us to teach and experiment with these ideas because they are totally driven by the same convictions. We needed this space to work with people and groups as we wrote about ministry. Thank you, Phil and Gary.

We're also very grateful to the eight pastors who agreed to be interviewed at some length about their ministries, and to have excerpts from these conversations included in the book.

In recent days Andrew Heard and Craig Tucker have spent hours reading through our draft manuscript and sending back detailed feedback. They have been living this project for many years as church pastors who derive ministry practice from deep theological reflection. They will continue their sharpening critique of this book long after publication, for all our benefit. Two other friends call for special mention. One of our young theologically sharp writers, Guan Un, laboured long and fruitfully on the subject of discipleship to produce papers that shaped what you're about to read. And my colleague Craig Glassock is building the online support community that will be of great benefit to all who embark on the Vine Project. His passion for disciple-making knows no bounds.

We're also very much indebted to the team at Matthias Media (especially the managing editor, Emma Thornett), who have not only worked so hard to make this book a reality, but have exemplified its principles for nearly three decades in publishing ministry resources for disciple-making. In fact (as you will discover), we have been unable to resist referencing and commending Matthias Media resources at numerous points throughout the book. These are resources we know and trust—we hope you'll bear with our homegrown bias and enthusiasm.

And what can I say about Tony? Simply that the final text is his. Someone had to pull this six-year conversation into a coherent whole. It had to be someone who has bled these convictions for decades and someone who has been studying and writing about these things forever. When I read Tony's manuscript, I kept saying to myself, "Yes, that's exactly what we want to say, and what under God needs to be said at this hour".

To God be the glory.

CM, February 2016.

SETTING THE SCENE

The big question

We'd been talking together for the best part of a day. There were about 60 of us in the room, from a range of different churches in America's Midwest. And then one pastor stood up and asked the question that we have been asked countless times in the past six years.

"Look, I've read *The Trellis and the Vine*.[1] I thought it was great. It expressed what I have always thought and believed about Christian ministry. So bless you and thank you for writing it.

"But as I kept reading, I also had this sinking feeling in my gut. I just know that what actually happens in our church is a long ways from the kind of disciple-making ministry vision you outline and that I totally believe in. I'm not really sure how we came to be so far away from it. But the thing is: I don't really know where to start or how to make progress. It's like all the existing structures and ministries in our church are made of concrete.

"So here's my basic problem: *How can I change the whole culture of our church in the direction of disciple-making?*"

He was a Baptist from an average-sized church in Chicago, but he could have been a Presbyterian from Melbourne or an

---

1   Colin Marshall and Tony Payne, *The Trellis and the Vine: The Ministry Mind-Shift that Changes Everything*, Matthias Media, Sydney, 2009.

evangelical Anglican from Cape Town. In conversations, emails, workshops and conferences, we've been asked a version of this question more times than we can remember since *The Trellis and the Vine* became an unlikely international bestseller.[2]

I say unlikely because, as far as we were concerned, *Trellis and Vine* was an unexciting little book that consisted mostly of the blindingly obvious. We thought it would be read by a small number of loyal folk here in Australia, and perhaps prove to be a useful statement of ministry principles that could be passed on to the next generation.

However, sometimes the obvious is what people most need to hear (like when the child said of the emperor, "But he's got nothing on!"). Somehow, our restatement of the biblical principles of 'vine work' and ministry struck a chord with evangelical pastors and leaders all around the world.

One of the consequences was an immensely rich experience for which we are deeply thankful to God. Over the past six years, we have found ourselves speaking at conferences and running 'Trellis and Vine Workshops' all over the world. We have had the joy of spending thousands of hours talking about ministry with thousands of pastors and lay leaders, from churches of all different sizes, locations, denominations and cultures—from Cape Town to Chicago, from Singapore to Sydney, from Dublin to Dallas.

People came to these workshops and conferences with all kinds of questions and thoughts about the philosophy of ministry put forward in *The Trellis and the Vine*. Three kinds of questions were particularly common:

- What do you actually mean by 'discipleship' and 'disciple-making'? Are you basically arguing for more one-to-one work, or small group work? Or are you talking about more evangelism? Or all or none of the above?

---

2   If you've never heard of, let alone read, *The Trellis and the Vine*, don't worry. You might find reading it a useful exercise, but you don't need to stop now and do so. Most of the essential theological and ministry principles are restated somewhere in what follows. If you're curious, we've provided a basic summary of the argument of *The Trellis and the Vine* in appendix i.

- Where does preaching fit into what you're saying? Won't your emphasis on 'training disciples' lead to a devaluing of expository preaching ministry—which is something we've been fighting so hard to defend and strengthen over the past generation?
- Have you ended up making 'trellises' (i.e. ministry structures and supports) the bad guys of church life? Is it possible you have underplayed the systemic importance of how church life is structured and organized? And does prioritizing 'vine work' over 'trellis work' lead to a demeaning of the many people who spend so many hours faithfully working on the 'trellis'?[3]

We've been enormously blessed by the iron-sharpens-iron effect of talking through these questions repeatedly with many different brothers and sisters. In the chapters that follow we hope the fruit of these conversations is seen in an improved and sharpened presentation of the essential ministry principles first enunciated in *The Trellis and the Vine*.

However, the overwhelming reason that people came to talk with us over the past six years was to grapple with the dilemma raised by the pastor from Chicago. In many churches around the world, there is an immensely dissatisfying gap between what we hope and expect the gospel will produce as it bears fruit among us, and what we actually see day to day and Sunday to Sunday. To put it in the terms that we argued for in *The Trellis and the Vine*, we long for Great-Commission style 'vine work' to be the normal agenda and priority within our churches. We yearn for every member of our congregation to grasp this and to live it—to pray for and reach out to those around them to make new disciples, and to nurture and edify and encourage one another to maturity in Christ.

And yet, when we look at the gap between this exciting biblical vision and the reality of church life, our hearts sometimes sink. Our local congregations seem so complex, and so stuck in existing habits and ways of doing things. The existing structures and

---

3   Again, for a quick summary of what we mean by 'trellis work' and 'vine work' see appendix i.

'trellises' of our church almost seem to have a life of their own. They absorb or assimilate or repel our attempts at reform and change. Maybe this talk of 'vine work' and of every disciple being a disciple-maker works somewhere else (on university campuses maybe) but it doesn't seem to be catching on here. And if we're honest about the numbers, we aren't seeing much growth; and what little growth we see is largely the result of transfers rather than conversions.

We could multiply the examples, or tease out this sort of scenario at more length, but it would only inflame the sense of unease that many pastors, elders and core church members already feel. When we work hard but don't see growth, it hurts. It leads us to grapple with God's sovereignty (Why isn't he giving the growth?), to compare ourselves with others (What's wrong with me? Why they are doing so well?), and often to hop on the latest bandwagon program or ministry model hoping for success and growth at last.

As we've talked and thought constantly about these issues over the past six years, we've become convinced of the need to answer the question that the Baptist pastor from Chicago asked on behalf of nearly every evangelical church in the Western world: *How can we shift the whole culture of our church in the direction of disciple-making?*

That's the question that *The Vine Project* is aiming to answer.

It may seem counterintuitive to say so, but one of the reasons we're so keen to answer this question is that we know only too well of the enormous pressure that many pastors and church members are under. For many readers of this book, whether you are a keen lay leader or in full-time pastoral ministry, each week is a fresh struggle just to keep your head above water. We know this not only from our own life experience in ministry on church pastoral teams, but from the past six years of running workshops and coaching pastors and church leadership teams. We have constantly spoken with pastors and lay leaders who are grappling with energy-sapping, emotionally exhausting situations—everything from illness, grief and heartache in their own families to relational conflict, mental health issues and sexual abuse in the church family. We find ourselves waiting for that crisis-free 'normal' year where we can actually do some planning and make progress, but it never quite arrives.

For those of us who feel this way, working on a project to shift the whole culture of our church may feel completely beyond us. And for some of you, that may be quite right. It may not be the right time to start. You may want to read this book and hatch some plans for getting started properly a year or two down the track.

However, as we will argue below, disciple-making is really about calling people to faith and hope in Jesus Christ in the midst of this present evil age, with all its pressures. To become a church more focused on disciple-making is to become a fellowship that understands more clearly why life is often hard, and what resources God has given us to grow in faith and hope and love in the midst of the struggle. A disciple-making church is actually better able to handle the crises and pressures of everyday life.

What's more, one of the key pressure points for many pastors and church leadership teams is simply that there are too few shoulders being put to the wheel. We aren't training and mobilizing enough of our members to be fellow workers in the task, and so the pressure on the pastor and key leaders remains unrelenting. We need to build a larger team of engaged, equipped disciple-makers working together, and this is one of the key outcomes of *The Vine Project*.

In other words, one very important reason that we've written *The Vine Project*, and urge you to embark upon it as soon as you reasonably can, is that we know how tough church life and ministry can be.

An unusual book

It's a big question that we're seeking to answer (*how to shift your church culture towards disciple-making*), and the task is made less easy by the obvious fact that *each church needs its own answer*. Each church is at a different point on the spectrum, has different strengths and weaknesses, faces different obstacles, and, crucially, has different people whom God has blessed it with. Some of you may look at your church and see the need for root-and-branch reform; others may feel that you're broadly heading in the right direction but need an injection of growth and change. Some of you may even be at the point of planting a brand new church, and be in a position to start shaping the culture from scratch.

And yet despite our different starting points, the essential process of change, the tools of change, and the desired outcomes for change are common across all churches, because they have their roots not only in the way that groups of people (like churches) function and grow, but in the character and purposes and acts of God for his people.

That's why (somewhat unusually) we've called this book a 'project'. It's not a set of detailed answers or prescriptions delivered from on high to solve your problems. It's a set of processes, tools and guidelines for you to work through with a small team of like-minded fellow workers—starting from wherever you happen to be, with whatever strengths and weaknesses you happen to have.

This means that *The Vine Project* is *not a book just to read*, like all those other ministry books that you buy at conferences and read and feel mildly enthused by for a time, but which ultimately go to their home on the shelf with all the others. It's a project. It outlines a process to work through and talk over. It's a book that should lead to a plan and to actions taking place over time.

This is why it's a book that is likely to take you several years to finish—not, we hasten to add, because the content is vastly long or complex, but because the *process* it guides you through is not a quick fix. Church growth and change, like all Christian growth and change, takes time. It takes real-world implementation and patience. It is liable to false starts and hiccups. It needs constant monitoring and review and changes of direction to account for new or unexpected circumstances. At regular points in what follows, you'll be prompted to talk things over, evaluate your current circumstances, devise plans, take action, work on mini-projects, and so on. It's a process that will take months and years to complete. In fact, in some respects this is a book you'll never finish. We fervently hope that *The Vine Project* will not end up being just another of those ministry books that you browse through, pick up a few interesting insights from, and then cast aside.

This is also a book that you *cannot successfully read on your own*. Unless you gather a small group of godly, committed people to read this book with you, and to work through the process with you, then we're pretty sure it will do you and your church little good. Of course, we understand that in order to decide whether you want to gather such a group of people and launch into *The Vine Project* together, you may want to read through the book first yourself! But our point is simply that in order for what follows to lead to any actual growth or change in your church culture, you will need to work through it all with a team.

To make this process easier—of gathering a team and working through each phase of *The Vine Project* together over time—we're providing you with support. At **thevineproject.com** you'll find not only a growing library of videos, stories, articles and case studies, but also a community of other ministry teams who are all working on 'Vine Projects' in their own context. It's a place to ask questions, to learn from the experiences and insights of others, and to contribute your own.

Thevineproject.com is also where team members can download their free team manual. This manual (available in PDF and MS Word formats) contains all the discussion questions, evaluations, activities and mini-projects from this book, so that you can reformat them, print them out, scribble on them, type in answers, and so on.

We strongly encourage you to make the most of the support available at **thevineproject.com**. (For more information, see appendix ii or visit the website.)

How to make the best use of this book

It should be pretty clear by this point that this is a book to *use* and not just read, because answering the Big Question in your own context will require a thoughtful process over time, not a silver-bullet prescription from some ministry guru.

Here are a few pointers on how to make the best use of *The Vine Project*.

Firstly, the process we outline is not just for churches. It's for any ministry that has the potential to have its culture changed in the direction of disciple-making. For example, you may be reading this as a youth ministry leader, or as the leader of your church's men's or women's ministry. You may be the leader of a para-church mission group or fellowship of some kind. If you are leading a group of Christians, and have the authority and capacity to shape the direction and activities of that group over time, then *The Vine Project* is for you.

In fact, even if you are reading this as the senior pastor of a church, you may wish to run a pilot 'Vine Project' in just one part of your congregational life (say, in the youth ministry or in one of the congregations that make up your overall parish or church) before rolling it out more broadly.

Secondly, *The Vine Project* is not just for existing churches and fellowships. If you're about to start something brand new—whether a new church plant, or a new ministry of some other kind—working through *The Vine Project* is an ideal way to establish a strong disciple-making culture from the outset. Most of the suggested exercises and activities in *The Vine Project* assume an existing ministry in which you're seeking to bring a culture change—but nearly all of them are very easily adaptable to a new ministry starting from scratch.

Thirdly, whatever your context, the first step for you as a ministry leader of some kind is to read through the whole book yourself to get a sense of its theology and message, and of the process we're going to work through. This first read through has two main purposes:

- Obviously enough, you need to be convinced personally that you want to utilize this book, and its process, for bringing lasting culture change to your church or ministry. You need to be comfortable that you are on the same page as us theologically (at least in all the important areas, if not on every particular), and that our suggested process is one you're willing to commit to.
- You'll also start to get a sense, on this first read through, of who you might want to have on your Vine Project Team, as well as where you might want to modify or adapt or supplement the content for your own context—because we're pretty sure you'll want to. We have designed *The Vine Project* to be as flexible and applicable as possible to a multitude of different ministry contexts, but there will doubtless be topics you want to cover that are absent, as well as things we've covered that don't apply to you or that you'd want to handle differently. This first read through will no doubt generate a little list of these customizations that you'd like to make.

Fourthly, as we've already mentioned, a key aspect of *The Vine Project* is assembling a small team of fellow workers to work through the process together; to be the team of change agents who plan and initiate and exemplify and champion the change in culture that you're wanting to achieve. Who should be on this team?

- No more than ten people, and no fewer than four. It's a team that needs to function well as a group, with enough people to bring ideas and energy and capability to the task, but not too many that meetings are hard to organize or that group dynamics become difficult.
- You may look for people already in a position of leadership or oversight (like a body of elders or a parish council or similar authorized body) but it's also important to look further than your existing eldership in considering who to invite onto this team. Change requires fresh thinking, fresh energy, and a willingness to try something new—and this can be hard for an existing leadership team to embrace.

(After all, they are usually the ones most invested in everything that is currently in place.) You may put before your existing elders the idea of forming a new team to focus on *The Vine Project*—perhaps consisting of some existing key leaders (or elders), as well as some emerging leaders with potential.

- Whatever the mix of new and existing leaders in your team, or however they relate to your current structures, the really important thing is that they are F.A.T. (to use the old acronym)—Faithful, Available (at least potentially) and Teachable. You want people who are Faithful to the gospel in their convictions and in their lives. This is not the time or place for new converts (no matter how gifted and impressive they are), or for powerful, influential people who are really not solidly converted, mature, gospel-hearted people. You'll want people whom you can call upon to be Available to work with you and each other, and to keep working together over a significant period of time. This may mean freeing them from other responsibilities—in fact, it will almost certainly mean this, given the way F.A.T. people usually get involved in church life. There may be some pain associated with this—with pulling a leader out of an existing ministry, and thus creating a hole—but unless you have a team of people who are available to meet together fairly regularly, and to put in some work together to bring change, then the whole exercise will probably end up being an unproductive talkfest. And finally, you don't need people who have arrived and already know how to do everything, or who have strong hobbyhorses that they are continually riding. You want people who have a humble Teachable heart, who know they still have a long way to go, and who are keen to keep making progress as disciples of Christ.

Fifthly, once you've gathered a team, one of your first tasks will be to draft a rough plan together as to how you are going to work through the five phases of *The Vine Project*. How often are you going to meet initially, and for how long each time? At what pace do you want to work through each phase? We've put together a suggested plan of attack (at the end of the next chapter), but feel free to modify this according to your circumstances.

And *finally*, to make best use of this book, and to answer the Big Question most effectively for your own context, keep bathing the whole process in prayer. We'll keep reminding you about this at various points, because we strongly suspect that you're like us and every Christian leader we've ever known—prayer gets squeezed out by the pressures and busyness of church life. All Christian ministry, including the project on which we're about to embark, should take its cue from Paul's summary of his ministry in Colossians 1:28-29:

> Him we proclaim, warning everyone and teaching everyone with all wisdom, that we may present everyone mature in Christ. For this I toil, struggling with all his energy that he powerfully works within me.

We need to keep praying for Christ's energy to work powerfully within us, for his Spirit to guide us as we think and plan, and for God to give the growth as we devise new ways of planting and watering.

Changing the culture

I (Tony) arrived at an evangelical Anglican church in Sydney as an 18-year-old, fresh into town from the country, enthusiastic and clueless in equal measure, a converted Christian from a high-church charismatic Anglican background (there's a strange mix).

The culture shock was disorienting and exciting all at once. Everything about my new church in Sydney was different: the way everyone dressed for church; the lack of ritual and ceremony; the kind of songs we sang; the evident commitment of those who attended; the way people hung around after church, talking for hours; and of course the preaching, which involved expounding and explaining and applying the text of the Bible in a way that I had never heard. It wasn't just that I was exposed to new ideas and teachings. The way they did things was different; the whole culture of the church was different.

I particularly remember on my first few visits being totally shocked by something that I don't think most of those present even noticed. For most of the service I had no idea who the pastor was. He didn't sit in a special chair up the front. He wasn't dressed in special robes. And when the time came for the sermon, some guy dressed the same as the rest of us got up from a random chair in the congregation and walked up the front to the pulpit. At this point I had to assume that he was the pastor, and after being there for a few weeks I came to know that he was—and that he exercised a strong and effective leadership within the congregation. But that small detail (of the pastor/preacher sitting in the body of the congregation and wearing normal clothes) communicated something very powerful to me. It said: *They think about the minister differently here.* He is a leader, but he's also profoundly one of us. He isn't a mediatory priest who stands up the front between us and God and administers sacred mysteries for our benefit. His main job is to open and expound the Bible—and that's where the authority lies.

For a young and somewhat confused Anglo-Catholic this was revolutionary, and in a good way. Over time I came to understand more deeply the theological convictions that lay behind this seemingly small and simple difference (in where the pastor sat and what he wore). And I came to see that the very different 'culture' of the two churches was not simply the result of the difference between younger and older, or between city and country, or between informal and formal (although all these factors of course had their influence on what was done and how). Underneath it all, two quite different theologies were at work. The welter of different habits, norms, practices, languages, forms, structures, traditions and relationships stemmed from a different set of convictions and beliefs. And the range of different practices in turn expressed and reinforced those convictions and beliefs— or in some cases, as is inevitable, clashed with the stated convictions and beliefs (because no church is perfectly consistent or without contradictions and problems).[1]

In fact, my experience of these two very different churches illustrates a foundational (if rather obvious) truth about church

---

1   What in fact various practices and activities actually communicate will vary from place to place, depending on what we might call the 'prevailing cultural vocabulary'. So we're not saying that having the preacher/pastor dress in normal clothes and sit in the congregation is an unchangeable law as of the Medes and the Persians! All the same, in the social and ecclesiological climate of Sydney in the 1980s, it communicated an important and powerful message.

culture: what we routinely *do* communicates, reinforces and shapes who we are, often far more than what we teach.

You see, the Anglo-Catholic tradition of my youth had all the right words. We steadfastly used the Anglican *Book of Common Prayer* (BCP) week by week, which is one of the most gloriously Reformed and evangelical documents of the English Reformation. The BCP is riddled with the gospel and with the great doctrines of justification by faith alone through grace alone in Christ alone. It's an evangelical book through and through. And we repeated its words so regularly that we all knew them by heart.

And yet the set of practices, habits, structures and rituals that made up our regular church life were not Reformational or evangelical at all—just the opposite, in fact. The 'priest' (as he was called) was up the front dressed in the elaborate sacrificial robes of Catholicism. The service was a religious ritual filled with symbolic acts (like the use of incense) rather than an act of fellowship or mutual edification. Holy communion was practised in a manner that made it very clear that this (rather than the word of God) was the chief way in which we were to be spiritually fed. The gospel was never clearly explained in the 15-minute largely moralistic sermons. There was no expectation that the Bible would be read or studied by the congregation, either by themselves or in groups. There was no evangelism—in fact, no expectation that non-Christian people needed conversion.

The whole apparatus of church life not only shouted an anti-evangelical theology but also schooled us in it, week by week. The culture—the whole way we did things right across the spectrum of our church life—spoke so loudly and persistently that the gospel words of the BCP were never 'heard' and embraced, even though we faithfully mouthed them every single Sunday.

The same is true with respect to disciple-making, and any other conviction or practice that we want to see take root and grow in our churches. You can uphold the conviction personally and in your mission statement, and you can say the words, but if the whole way you do things communicates, expresses and reinforces a different set of convictions, then you will make little progress.

Imagine, for example, that an ecclesiastical miracle happened and you were appointed as the new pastor of the ritualistic church I grew up in—you being thoroughly Reformed and evangelical in your theology. How would you bring about deep and lasting change to a thoroughly Anglo-Catholic congregation?

I suspect the first thing you might change would be the preaching. You would start to preach the gospel and the Bible, and pray that the powerful word of God would begin to change hearts and lives. And you would do that persistently and patiently.

But also imagine that while doing so, you never changed any of the rituals, activities, structures and traditions of the congregation—not even carefully over time. You simply continued to dress in the same robes and conduct the service and the holy communion in the same way as the previous pastor. You initiated no structures or activities to promote Bible reading and study, and continued to do no evangelism. Do you think the culture of the church would change? Perhaps, over some considerable time, there would be some movement. The prayerful preaching of the word would have its effect. But we might also safely predict that if the activities, structures and traditions of the congregation never changed—if there was, in other words, no corporate repentance—then the effect of biblical sermons would be much the same as the effect of the biblical words of the *Book of Common Prayer*. They would be heard and acknowledged, but absorbed, assimilated and contradicted by the countervailing weight of the existing culture—of what you actually did, day by day and week and by week. Or to put it another way: we need to be doers of the word and not just hearers only.[2] Where there is no repentance, there is no change.

The culture of a church—or any organization, come to that—is a heavy and powerful drag against any attempt for meaningful change. (By 'culture', just to clarify, we mean 'the whole way we do things around here'—the complex and deep-rooted matrix of beliefs, practices, shared language, traditions and preferences that

2   Jas 1:22

a group of people have developed over a period of time.)[3] The culture will usually shape what people actually do in any given circumstance, often more so than their stated beliefs. For example, in many evangelical churches if you were to ask congregation members whether they believed that the church should reach out to the lost and that Christians should share their faith with others, most would say yes. When the pastor concludes his sermon with an exhortation to more evangelism, they will nod and feel slightly guilty. And yet if the established culture of their church does not promote, exemplify and practise this sort of active evangelism, both corporately and individually, then very little evangelism will ever take place. If evangelistic enterprise is not in fact a normal part of 'the way we do things around here', then exhortations from the pulpit for more evangelism will usually come to nothing. The exhortation will hit the solid mass of the culture and bounce off.[4]

The trellis strikes back

As we've talked with many pastors over the past six years about their attempts to put a 'Trellis and Vine' or disciple-making ministry philosophy into practice in their churches, it has become apparent to us that 'culture' is a significant and under-addressed

3   The word 'culture' is not easy to define. In fact, Raymond Williams rates it as "one of the two or three most complicated words in the English language" (see R Williams, *Keywords*, Flamingo, London, 1983, p. 87). It can be used to describe the intellectual or artistic productions of a society, or of a subgroup within a society (e.g. 'high culture'). Quite often, it is used to refer to the customs, habits, norms, social arrangements, and way of life of a particular group of people, and the artefacts and products that they produce (e.g. '21st-century French culture', or 'the corporate culture of IBM'). We're using it more in this latter sense, to describe 'the whole way we do things around here'.

4   There is an extensive literature around 'culture' and its place within organizations, most of it from the world of management. A helpful summary article is John Katzenbach and Ashley Harshak, 'Stop blaming your culture', *Strategy+Business*, vol. 62, Spring 2011 (viewed 13 December 2015): http://strategy-business.com/article/11108. For a different angle that makes many interesting points, see James D Hunter's *To Change the World: The Irony, Tragedy and Possibility of Christianity in the Late Modern World*, OUP, New York, 2010, especially Essay 1, 'Christianity and world-changing'. One of Hunter's insights is that ideas on their own rarely change a culture.

issue. What we have seen most often is pastors seeking to bolt a few new programs or initiatives onto the existing culture—things like:

- preaching a sermon series on 'disciple-making'
- starting some one-to-one Bible reading with people, or giving out copies of David Helm's book *One-to-One Bible Reading: A Simple Guide for Every Christian*[5]
- adding 'disciple-making' to the goals for the year
- trying harder with welcoming newcomers
- running a training course on how to share your faith with outsiders.

What usually happens is that after six or twelve months of trying to inject one or more of these new elements into church life, the enthusiasm starts to wane, and the weight and momentum of the existing culture squashes any progress that has been made. It's like trying to turn around an ocean liner with a few strokes of an oar. The pastor is left muttering, "This 'trellis and vine' business might work well somewhere else, but it's not working here. Maybe it's time I tried something else."

And so the cycle continues. A new model or idea will come along next year, the same attempt will be made to inject something new, and the prevailing culture will swallow it, belch, and move on in its slow irresistible way.

To stretch a familiar metaphor to the limits of its usefulness, we might say that the prevailing culture of a church is made up of both 'vine' and 'trellis' elements—that is, both the conviction-based activity of every Christian speaking the word of God to others at every level by the power of the Spirit (vine), and all the structures, programs and committees of your congregational life (trellis). What we're saying about 'culture' is that there's little point teaching some new convictions or initiating some new kinds of vine work unless you're also prepared to reform and

5 David Helm, *One-to-One Bible Reading: A Simple Guide for Every Christian*, Matthias Media, Sydney, 2011.

optimize the trellis that supports it and gives it structure and shape. Both must be done as part of a total package.

Although we did make this point in *The Trellis and the Vine*, we don't mind admitting that the overall emphasis of the book may have masked its importance. Many readers we've spoken to gained the impression that we basically think 'vine = good' and 'trellis = necessary evil'. This is certainly not what we think or meant to convey, and no doubt the fault is ours.

Ministry trellises are not the bad guys of church life. The point we were making in *The Trellis and the Vine* is that it is very possible, and in fact very common, to have a multitude of programs and activities and administrative structures—that is, a large, well-maintained and impressive trellis—without very much actual vine work going on at all—that is, without many people actually speaking and proclaiming the message of the Bible at every level in church life and in the world.

But the problem is *not* that trellises are somehow inherently a hindrance to vine work. It's that often they aren't designed and run to facilitate and optimize the vine work. To use corporate-speak, they are not 'aligned'. They just exist. And, as we've been discussing, they often carry and express and reproduce a culture that resists our efforts to bring real change. Trellises can powerfully support and enable disciple-making ministry to take place; but they can also work *against* this kind of ministry growing and flourishing in your midst.

Which brings us back to the Big Question this book is seeking to answer: *How do you shift the culture of a church in the direction of disciple-making?* Come to that, how do you work on the culture of a church to change it *any* direction?

The answer is that you can't.

You can't change the culture by working on the culture, because culture is a description of what you have become. It's a way of summarizing the whole way you do things, the multifaceted web of tacit beliefs and practices, formal and informal, that make up who you are and how you roll.

You can't work on 'culture', as such. It's the product of years and decades of idea-driven practices and practically expressed ideas. What you *can* work on and change are the elements that produce culture:

- the deeply held beliefs and convictions that drive and underpin your culture (not all of them always openly expressed)
- the activities, practices and structures that express and embed those beliefs at every level of church life.

You can work to bring change to the way people *think*, and to how those convictions are *practised* in behaviour and structures and habits—and over time you will look back and say that you have generated a new 'culture'. There will be a new set of core beliefs and default reactions; a new set of habits and rituals; a new set of behaviours that will come to be seen as normal and expected; a new set of structures and systems that support these new behaviours; a new shared language; a new set of memories about the things we've done together, the successes and the failures.

To illustrate what this change process looks like in practice, we've interviewed a number of pastors who are engaged in this culture-change process in a range of different ministry contexts.[6] You'll find excerpts from these interviews dotted at different points throughout the book (and you'll find the full versions at **thevineproject.com**).

However, at this point we'd like to tell the culture-change story of a secular organization—a sporting club—because it nicely illustrates the kind of process we're going to talk about.

~

In late 2004 Jim was appointed as Head Coach in one of Sydney's semi-professional cricket clubs. The club's performances during the previous season were well below expectations. Within two years of Jim's appointment they had won

---

6   We've fictionalized the names and details of the people and churches in these stories to protect those involved—both from the pride of being profiled as a 'successful' church, and from the temptation to sugar-coat the reality (if they knew that their church members or friends might read it). Apart from that, we have let those involved speak for themselves.

several team championships and the club championship. This is an interview with Jim about how he set about transforming the club's culture over several years.

What was the state of the club as you started out?

We had excellent facilities and equipment, a solid playing roster, and a small core group of committed administrators and volunteers. I was also starting out with the respect of the players because I had fairly recently enjoyed success as a leader at the club.

We had virtually the same roster and resources as the previous season, so it was clear that other things needed to change if results were to improve over the next few years.

The players' on-field performances were unsatisfactory, but there were also underlying problems that needed addressing. Expectations and policies around team commitment and selection were ad hoc and inconsistent, and there was little to no intentional leadership development. At the same time we were doing almost nothing to improve our psychological skills. It's widely accepted that cricket is 90% mental and 10% physical, so we needed to make this a non-negotiable part of our training sessions.

How did you go about changing things?

The big thing for me was to develop a culture of teamwork rather than individualism. If every member were committed to our goals, the results would follow.

I believed four important things:

- Firstly, *players want to be part of something bigger than their own performance.* Like baseball, cricket is an individual game within a team game. I had to shift the normal thinking that the value of an individual's contribution can be measured in runs and wickets.
- Then I was convinced that, given they commit so much time to training and playing, *players want to enjoy these things, along with the social side of the club.* So having fun needed to be a key driver in all we did.
- It also seemed pretty obvious to me that *everyone wants to feel valued.* So the challenge was to help the players

to value the contribution of every club member, from the canteen lady to the club president. We developed a basic checklist that captains went through with the players at the end of each match. One of the items on that list asked them whether they had thanked any club volunteers during the previous week. Players pretty soon got the message about what we were going to value in our club.

- Lastly, I was convinced that the best use of my time was to *invest in leaders and develop new ones.* In cricket the team captain is the one who makes the decisions, and who guides and directs his team's fortunes on match day. I needed to pour myself into developing the team captains (six of them), and work with them to identify some potential leaders that they could develop in turn.

Did you set any performance goals?

We settled on the challenging goal of winning the club championship within two years. Every role and job description in the club was linked to the end goal. We also developed a philosophy of 'club first, team second, player third'. In team sport this can be a nuanced thing at times. But we made sure the general philosophy was reinforced in what we did, and we made sure it was visible around the club.

Did you do anything else to start shifting the culture of the club?

We did plenty of things. One that springs to mind was the way we tried to shift the thinking from individualism to teamwork. In Australian sport we like to talk about the 'one percenters'— the little things team members do that contribute to victory. I felt this was a bit too clichéd so I borrowed from an old Christian adage. We adopted the phrase, "If you were arrested for being a team player, what evidence would be used against you?" Every week as part of our club meetings, players had to stand up and say, "Billy should be arrested for being a team player because he was seen doing *x*".

It was really slow going at the start. I had to give them lots of examples, and even ask players a week ahead to be on the lookout for things to share at club meetings. After a bit of pushback over the early months, the players really got into it and started noticing all the little things—even things I had never thought of—that go into being a great team player. Those weekly sessions became a lot of fun, but more importantly they kept reinforcing our standards and values.

The investment in our leaders really paid off. In a sporting club, the culture can shift quite quickly once people see the leaders change and set a new tone. The challenge is to continually reinforce the things you want to see, both subtly and overtly, so that in time they become the default culture.

~

How much time, effort, thought, energy and sweat, how many tears, setbacks, successes, failures, joys and sorrows do you think will be required to bring about this kind of wide-ranging, deep-rooted change to any organization—let alone a long-standing church culture?

It won't be a quick process—that's why this book is part of a *project* to work through over years rather than another ministry book to read and put back in its place on your shelf with all the others.

It will require more time and effort and gifts than any one person has—that's why this is a project to embark on with a *team* of godly, committed, gospel-hearted fellow workers who can encourage each other and keep each other going.

And of course it's a work that none of us are remotely competent to do—that's why we depend on God. Like the apostle Paul, we gratefully say:

> Not that we are sufficient in ourselves to claim anything as coming from us, but our sufficiency is from God, who has made us sufficient to be ministers of a new covenant, not of the letter but of the Spirit. For the letter kills, but the Spirit gives life. (2 Cor 3:5-6)

A process for change

So where does one start?

As Craig Hamilton points out in his book *Wisdom in Leadership*, most ministers have a tendency to start in one of two places:

> It often seems like there are two ways to live when it comes to being in Christian ministry. You're either a Bible person or a leadership person. You read theology books or you read leadership books. You read books by Don Carson and John Stott or you read books by Bill Hybels and John Maxwell.
>
> And that's a problem.
>
> It's always felt like a problem to me because I'm a Bible guy. I've always been a doctrine guy. Let's talk about models of the atonement and *perichoresis* and *enhypostasis* and *anhypostasis* and the *ordo salutis* and all kinds of other Latin words. Let's talk about preaching and texts and contexts and subtexts. That's who I've always been, and I'm still that guy.
>
> And yet, as a leader in different settings over the years, I observed that when groups of people get together they function in certain predictable ways. I knew it was true that I could lead a group well or I could lead a group badly. And even if I had all kinds of amazing and life-changing things to teach, and even if I explained them as clearly and persuasively as I could, I still had to help groups of people organize and achieve things.
>
> I realized the either/or was a false choice—that all this talk about leading people well wasn't necessarily godless, faithless pragmatism. Rather, it was about living with wisdom and loving my neighbour. And both of those things are in the Bible and God seems to think they're good ideas. So I came to see that if I really wanted to be a Bible guy I probably also needed to be a leadership guy, because it's both/and.[7]

---

7   Craig Hamilton, *Wisdom in Leadership: The How and Why of Leading the People You Serve*, Matthias Media, Sydney, 2015, p. 11.

If you're a 'Bible guy' you'll probably want to start to change your culture with the theological and biblical convictions that you want your people to hold, and chances are you may never get beyond there. If you're a 'leadership guy' you'll probably be impatient to square away the theological stuff quickly in order to get into the nitty-gritty of strategic analysis and planning.

In the process we're about to outline, it's emphatically both/ and. The theologically driven convictions and beliefs are vital and foundational—we need to take the time to dig into them, to sharpen them, and to live and breathe them. But the practices, programs, activities and structures that express and embody and facilitate the living out of our convictions are just as vital. This means long-term work is needed at this point. Let us encourage you not to give up in the midst of it—because you will be tempted to.

The process we're about to put forward is hardly revolutionary or controversial. It's a pretty standard procedure that any organization might undertake in bringing about significant organizational or cultural change. It has five phases:

- **Phase 1: Sharpen your convictions**—dig into the Bible and its theology to clarify what you believe about disciple-making and ministry.
- **Phase 2: Reform your personal culture**—make sure that your convictions have penetrated the culture of your own life; that you are demonstrating your convictions by how you live and minister to others.
- **Phase 3: Loving, honest evaluation**—undertake a clear-eyed thoughtful examination of everything that happens in your church to see how well (or poorly) it accords with your convictions: in what areas does your culture best reflect your convictions, where is it weakest, and where is the greatest potential for growth and change?
- **Phase 4: Innovate and implement**—work out what you want to stop doing, start doing, and keep doing; plan new pathways for disciple-making and work out how to implement these over time.

- **Phase 5: Maintain momentum**—monitor and review how the project is unfolding; look at obstacles and work out how to overcome them; build momentum and keep it rolling.

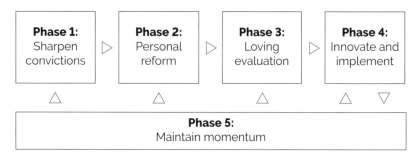

Each of these phases will take some time to complete. In fact, some of them (like Phase 2) will, by definition, never be completed.

However, there is a logic to how the phases follow each other and build upon each other. We would urge you strongly not to skate past any of them too quickly, but to take the time to do the work thoroughly and thoughtfully. Turning an ocean liner around takes hefty quantities of both energy and time. But once you've put in this energy and time, and established a new direction (and a new destination), the momentum can work in your favour.

Different churches and ministries will work through these phases at different rates. You'll need to work out a plan that suits your own context (and no doubt modify that plan as you go along).

Below is what we would regard as a standard sort of time frame for the mythical 'average' church. It assumes that you get together with your chosen fellow workers as a 'Vine Project Team' regularly for a two-hour meeting, and also schedule in some extended meetings at different points—for example on Saturday morning, or at a weekend retreat.

Phase	Content	Approximate time
Launch and setting the scene	Launch the team (preferably with a meal or social component); discuss 'Changing the culture'; come up with a plan for your team meetings	Extended meeting (with meal)
1 Sharpen convictions	Read and discuss Conviction 1	1 meeting
	Read and discuss Conviction 2	1 meeting
	Read and discuss Conviction 3	1 meeting
	Read and discuss Conviction 4	1 meeting
	Read and discuss Conviction 5	1 meeting
	Summarize and integrate	Extended meeting
2 Personal reform	Read and discuss Phase 2	1 meeting
	Discuss and pray about personal plans	1 meeting
	Implement personal plans	3 months minimum (continue to meet to discuss and review your personal plans)
3 Loving evaluation	Read Phase 3 and do Evaluation Exercise 1	1 meeting
	Other evaluation exercises	Extended meeting
	Summary/conclusions	1 meeting
4 Innovate and implement	Read and discuss intro; Focus Area 1	Extended meeting
	Focus Area 2	Extended meeting
	Focus Area 3	Extended meeting
	Focus Area 4	Extended meeting
	Integrate and finalize plans	Extended meeting
5 Maintain momentum	Read and discuss Phase 5	1 meeting
	Review plans; decide on ongoing meeting schedule	Extended meeting

When you join the community at **thevineproject.com** you'll find more information designed to support you in launching your own Vine Project.

DISCUSSION

1. If you had to summarize your church culture in a two- or three-word slogan, what would it be?

2. See if you can identify the key habits and activities and traditions that express and reinforce the culture of your church.

3. Which of the five phases of the process we're about to embark on do you think you will find most difficult? Why?

4. What are you looking forward to in working through the process we've outlined?

PHASE 1 //
SHARPEN YOUR CONVICTIONS

Introduction

W
e've been suggesting that bringing effective, long-lasting change to the culture of your church will involve both the convictions (or theology) that you hold and prayerfully teach, and the structures, habits, practices, programs and relationships that express and support those convictions.

Both aspects are important, and of course are linked. Convictions will lead to certain practices; practices will be based on and express certain convictions. And together, convictions and practices generate a culture—a 'way we do things around here'.

The two main problems nearly every church culture faces are:

- lack of shared clarity on core convictions (i.e. we don't all have a clear shared understanding of who we are and what we're trying to do together under God)
- lack of alignment between convictions and practice (i.e. a bunch of miscellaneous things happen around the church that no longer reflect our convictions, if they ever did; or, worse, that reflect and reinforce different convictions that are alien to us).

Now in case you're worried that we're going all business-speak at this point, and that soon we'll be talking about strategic intent, asset leverage and KPIs, all we're saying is that we have to address both our beliefs and our practice, both our convictions and our structures, if we're going to see real change. This is hardly controversial.

Nor is it very radical to say that a good place to start in the process is with our convictions; with the heart and soul; with what we really believe. We need to have a high degree of shared clarity about what we believe if we're ever going to bring real change to the whole culture that expresses and embodies those beliefs.

Without taking the time and space to argue for it here, we are going to proceed on the assumption that the clarity we're looking for should be sought in the Bible—rather than through a negotiated settlement of the various opinions that we might happen to hold. We're not looking for clarity and agreement at any cost. What we're after is a sharp, clear, shared understanding of the scriptural truth about Christian life and ministry, to serve as a solid foundation and framework for our entire church culture.

Five convictions

The five convictions we're about to explore capture what we take to be the heart of biblical discipleship, disciple-making and ministry.

It hardly needs saying, but we don't for a minute believe that our way of putting it is the only way of putting it. In fact, an essential element of this first phase of the process is that you come up with your own way of expressing and communicating the deep, shared convictions that should drive everything you do. Nor do we think that we've stopped learning and growing in our own understanding of these matters. In many ways, the convictions that follow are a restatement (using a different structure) of the theologically driven ministry principles we articulated in *The Trellis and the Vine,* reflecting all that we've learned over the past six years of widespread discussion and reading and rethinking. We look forward to that process continuing!

All that being said, we obviously think the following five convictions are a true and helpful rendering of what the Bible says about discipleship, disciple-making and ministry. Like any set of foundational principles, they seek to say everything that is necessary to say in order to be a basis for action together. And each principle strives to be discrete and complete in itself (that is, not simply repeating some aspect of one of the other principles).

The five convictions are built around five key questions related to 'discipleship' and 'disciple-making', namely:

- Why make disciples?
- What is a disciple?
- How are disciples made?
- Who makes disciples?
- Where to make disciples

By answering each of these questions, biblically and theologically, you should be able to construct a coherent vision of what disciple-making is, and what it means for your church. (The summary chapter and diagram at the end of the five convictions should also help you do that.)

Let us start, then, with the 'why' question.

Conviction 1: Why make disciples?

Why is it important to make disciples?[1]

We could answer that question and save ourselves some time, I suppose, by simply quoting Matthew 28:19 and saying, "Because Jesus told us to".

And that's certainly true. With all the authority he possesses as the risen Lord of heaven and earth, Jesus did indeed charge his disciples to go and make disciples of all nations.

However, in his generosity and gentleness towards us, God has done more than give us a bare command ("Just go do it, and stop complaining"). He has revealed much, much more.

He has let us in on why 'making disciples' is so important and so urgent. In fact, he has let us in on a secret that explains the nature and destiny of everything in our world, including us and our lives, and our churches, and more besides.

In many ways the Bible is the story of this secret being revealed. The entire first half of the Bible sets up the problem and the promise of a solution—but a solution that is hidden in the impenetrable

---

1   Perhaps it would be more logical to ask 'What is a disciple?' before we ask why we should make them, but for reasons that should become obvious as you read on, we've decided to start with the 'why' question. We will come to 'what' in our second conviction.

clouds of the future. The prophets and wise men of the Old Testament spoke of this future, and longed to know it and to see it, but never more than glimpsed it at a distance.[2]

This mystery that the Old Testament longingly tries to see, the New Testament proclaims as having burst into the open in the Lord Jesus Christ. God's age-long worldwide purpose for his world is now available for all to see and touch and hear:

> That which was from the beginning, which we have heard, which we have seen with our eyes, which we looked upon and have touched with our hands, concerning the word of life—the life was made manifest, and we have seen it, and testify to it and proclaim to you the eternal life, which was with the Father and was made manifest to us—that which we have seen and heard we proclaim also to you... (1 John 1:1-3)

The apostles go around proclaiming this extraordinary news—that the life that was with the Father, that was from the beginning, that brings eternal life, has now been "made manifest" in the person of Jesus.

This revelation of God's secret is like the 'Aha!' moment at the end of the mystery story, when all the clues and pieces of the puzzle come together. Now, at last, we can see what the plan was all along.

In this first conviction, we're going to explore and clarify just what this extraordinary plan of God is—because it will help us to grasp more clearly and powerfully why 'making disciples' is of such urgent importance.

Redeeming a people for his Son

What is God's plan for us and our world?

There are many passages scattered across the New Testament that answer this question, and although the answers they give

2   1 Pet 1:10-12

employ different words and metaphors, the substance of them is remarkably similar.

Let us take just a few examples, starting towards the end of the New Testament and working backwards.[3]

In Revelation 7, the apostle John catches sight of a numberless multitude, from every nation and people group and language imaginable, all standing before the throne of God and before the crucified and risen Christ, who is pictured simply as the Lamb. And this vast throng, whose dazzling robes have been whitened by the blood of the Lamb, cry out in celebration: "Salvation belongs to our God who sits on the throne, and to the Lamb!"[4]

Well might they celebrate, because they will serve there in the throne room of God, and be sheltered by his own presence. The ravages and frustrations of earthly life—hunger, thirst, scorching heat, tears—will be no more, but instead they will be tended by the Lamb, who is at the same time their shepherd:

> Then one of the elders addressed me, saying, "Who are these, clothed in white robes, and from where have they come?" I said to him, "Sir, you know". And he said to me, "These are the ones coming out of the great tribulation. They have washed their robes and made them white in the blood of the Lamb.
>
> "Therefore they are before the throne of God,
>> and serve him day and night in his temple;
>> and he who sits on the throne will shelter them
>>> with his presence.
> They shall hunger no more, neither thirst anymore;
>> the sun shall not strike them,
>> nor any scorching heat.
> For the Lamb in the midst of the throne will be
>>> their shepherd,
>> and he will guide them to springs of living water,
> and God will wipe away every tear from their eyes."
>> (Rev 7:13-17)

3   We will only briefly summarize the main points of these passages; in your discussion (see the guide at the end of this conviction), take the time to read and explore them for yourself.

4   Rev 7:10

Note the elements in this picture of the ultimate future: the crucified and risen Christ is there, ruling with God; by his death he has cleansed and gathered together a people from every nation around the throne of God; and the ravages of sin and evil and death are no more.

The book of Revelation lays open to us other similarly breathtaking scenes of God's ultimate purpose for his creation, but let us flip back a few pages to the book of Hebrews, where chapter 12 shows us another picture of God's final plan for all things. Again, it's a vast assembly. This time the venue is described as the heavenly Jerusalem, with innumerable angels in attendance, along with all those who are enrolled in heaven and the spirits of the righteous made perfect. Again, there are two figures at the centre—God the judge of all, and Jesus, the mediator of a new covenant whose sprinkled blood speaks a better word than the murdered blood of Abel.

Again, note the elements: God, his risen Son, the joyful gathering of the people who have been sprinkled by his blood, and the contrast with evil and death:

> For you have not come to what may be touched, a blazing fire and darkness and gloom and a tempest and the sound of a trumpet and a voice whose words made the hearers beg that no further messages be spoken to them. For they could not endure the order that was given, "If even a beast touches the mountain, it shall be stoned". Indeed, so terrifying was the sight that Moses said, "I tremble with fear". But you have come to Mount Zion and to the city of the living God, the heavenly Jerusalem, and to innumerable angels in festal gathering, and to the assembly of the firstborn who are enrolled in heaven, and to God, the judge of all, and to the spirits of the righteous made perfect, and to Jesus, the mediator of a new covenant, and to the sprinkled blood that speaks a better word than the blood of Abel. (Heb 12:18-24)

A few more pages back brings us to Paul's little letter to Titus, which focuses mostly on how God's people are to live now—in church, in their households, in society—given their place in God's unfolding plan. Towards the end of chapter 2, there's a short description of what that plan is, revolving around the two 'appearings' of Jesus Christ.

The first was when he appeared as the grace of God to bring salvation for all people and to train us to live no longer in ungodliness and worldly passions but in a godly, self-controlled way in this present age. The second appearing is the one we're still waiting for:

> For the grace of God has appeared, bringing salvation for all people, training us to renounce ungodliness and worldly passions, and to live self-controlled, upright, and godly lives in the present age, waiting for our blessed hope, the appearing of the glory of our great God and Saviour Jesus Christ, who gave himself for us to redeem us from all lawlessness and to purify for himself a people for his own possession who are zealous for good works. (Titus 2:11-14)

The end to which the plan is heading once again involves a people who have been redeemed from evil by the gracious self-giving of Jesus Christ—a people in this instance who are purified and eager to do good.

Let's make another stop on our flip backwards through the New Testament, this time in the opening chapter of Colossians. Here Paul reminds his readers that God has enacted a revolutionary change in their lives. He has rescued and redeemed them from the dark country in which they were enslaved, forgiven their sins, and given them an inheritance in the light-filled kingdom of his beloved Son.[5] And this Son, this majestic preeminent figure, is at the centre of the picture once again. Or rather, he is at the beginning and the middle and the end of the picture:

> He has delivered us from the domain of darkness and transferred us to the kingdom of his beloved Son, in whom we have redemption, the forgiveness of sins.

5   Col 1:13-14

He is the image of the invisible God, the firstborn of all creation. For by him all things were created, in heaven and on earth, visible and invisible, whether thrones or dominions or rulers or authorities—all things were created through him and for him. And he is before all things, and in him all things hold together. And he is the head of the body, the church. He is the beginning, the firstborn from the dead, that in everything he might be preeminent. For in him all the fullness of God was pleased to dwell, and through him to reconcile to himself all things, whether on earth or in heaven, making peace by the blood of his cross. (Col 1:13-20)

In the Son all things were created, in him all things hold together, and in him all things find their purpose and fulfilment. And again, as in the other passages we've looked at, God has gathered a congregation of people from every nation—a church—of which Jesus is the head.

We could keep going, and find similar teachings in numerous other places. We could look at the extraordinary opening chapter of Ephesians, with its cosmic story of God's plan from before time began to choose and redeem and forgive and adopt a holy people for himself through the blood of Jesus Christ—a plan for the whole world, both Jew and Gentile, that in the fullness of time will come to its end when all things are united under Christ.

Or we could scale to the mountain top that is Romans 8, and from there see the magnificent vista of God's eternal plan: to send his Son in the flesh to save his people from condemnation; to give them his Spirit as a guarantee that they are now his adopted children as they await the renewed creation to come; to predestine and call and justify and glorify all those whose he has chosen to be remade in the image of this Son. This is like Titus 2—the new people that God is gathering will have a new character. The scarred and disfigured image they bear will be remade so that it is like Jesus himself, who is the true and perfect image of God.

Out of this present darkness

A common thread running through most of these extraordinary passages is that the people God is gathering into his kingdom are *from every nation*. To our modern ears, this idea sounds rather lovely—that all the peoples of the earth might finally be brought together, and might celebrate together, despite all the linguistic and cultural differences that separate us; a kind of heavenly United Nations in which all the rich diversity of humanity is represented.

This, after all, is how most of us in the post-enlightenment West have been taught to think about the diversity of human language and culture—as a gorgeous human tapestry, with each people group contributing its own unique and wonderful colours and threads. And indeed, we do find all the goodness and beauty that God has woven into his creation present in every corner of it.

But in the Bible's depiction of history and of God's plan, the scattered diversity of the nations has a dark underbelly. It is a consequence of the judgement of God at Babel.[6] According to Paul in Acts 17, it is meant to induce a humble searching after the true God who has scattered us.[7] The gathering of all nations around the throne of God in Revelation is not so much a celebration of cultural diversity as a celebration of how God has overcome the one foundational problem that all the nations share—that "all have sinned and fall short of the glory of God, and are justified by his grace as a gift, through the redemption that is in Christ Jesus".[8]

To put it in a way that the New Testament frequently does, what all human cultures and nations profoundly share is that we dwell in darkness.

We see this very powerfully in Ephesians, which, perhaps more than any other New Testament book, revels in the radical unity that humanity now enjoys—because the barrier between Jew and Gentile has been broken down, and together we have access to the one Father, and are citizens and members of the one household of God.

6   Gen 11:1-9
7   Acts 17:26-27
8   Rom 3:23-24

But Ephesians is equally insistent that the reason we are now so united in Christ is that we were also united in sin:

> And you [i.e. you Gentiles] were dead in the trespasses and sins in which you once walked, following the course of this world, following the prince of the power of the air, the spirit that is now at work in the sons of disobedience—among whom we all [i.e. we Jews as well] once lived in the passions of our flesh, carrying out the desires of the body and the mind, and were by nature children of wrath, like the rest of mankind. But God, being rich in mercy, because of the great love with which he loved us, even when we were dead in our trespasses, made us alive together with Christ—by grace you have been saved—and raised us up with him and seated us with him in the heavenly places in Christ Jesus, so that in the coming ages he might show the immeasurable riches of his grace in kindness toward us in Christ Jesus. (Eph 2:1-7)

A few chapters later, Paul calls this lost, captive state we were in simply "darkness": "at one time you were darkness, but now you are light in the Lord".[9] This incredible world we live in, which the generous creator God has filled with beauty and goodness and relationships and love—this world is also rightly described as "this present darkness".[10]

This is an important aspect of the 'why' of disciple-making. God's plan is a rescue mission for people trapped in an awful and inescapable darkness. The world we live in is not neutral territory. It is not a bright, sunny place where nice people just get on with their lives and work and interests, and where Christians are people who happen to have a particular interest in going to church.

Of course, it can feel that way sometimes—especially for those of us blessed to live in quietly prosperous parts of the Western world. We live and breathe among a throng of educated, healthy,

9 Eph 5:8

10 Eph 6:12; note also Jesus' words in John 12:46: "I have come into the world as light, so that whoever believes in me may not remain in darkness"; see also Colossians 1:13.

peace-loving citizens, living a seemingly light-filled life of stimulating work, abundant food, fine entertainment, and beloved friends and family. Our TV screens reassure us that this is the case, and that the occasional irruption of darkness into our comfortable lives is only an abnormal and anomalous glitch. Normal transmission will be resumed as soon as possible.

But the daily immersive exposure to this view of the world often changes our perception of "this present darkness". It's like the dimmer switch is turned up; the darkness doesn't seem so dark, and people don't seem so lost in it.

This has multiple effects and consequences for our Christian lives, but perhaps the most serious is how drastically it saps the urgency out of making new disciples of Christ. We so easily settle into a comfortable week-by-week church existence, where we are happy to be together and to help each other grow as disciples of Christ, and (to be frank) are reasonably content with the world around us continuing on its way to hell in a hand basket. We stop appreciating how deep is the prevailing darkness, how lost and blind are our neighbours and friends and community, and how desperate and sad is the plight of the millions who "remain in darkness".[11]

William Booth's famous (and shocking) *A Vision of the Lost* springs to mind. It's worth reading in full, but here is a taste:

> I saw a dark and stormy ocean. Over it the black clouds hung heavily; through them every now and then vivid winds moaned, and the waves rose and foamed, towered and broke, only to rise and foam, tower and break again.
>
> In that ocean I thought I saw myriads of poor human beings plunging and floating, shouting and shrieking, cursing and struggling and drowning; and as they cursed and screamed they rose and shrieked again, and then some sank to rise no more.
>
> And I saw out of this dark angry ocean, a mighty rock that rose up with its summit towering high above the black

11 John 12:46

clouds that overhung the stormy sea. And all around the base of this great rock I saw a vast platform. Onto this platform, I saw with delight a number of the poor struggling, drowning wretches continually climbing out of the angry ocean. And I saw that a few of those who were already safe on the platform were helping the poor creatures still in the angry waters to reach the place of safety.

On looking more closely I found a number of those who had been rescued, industriously working and scheming by ladders, ropes, boats and other means more effective, to deliver the poor strugglers out of the sea. Here and there were some who actually jumped into the water, regardless of the consequences in their passion to "rescue the perishing". And I hardly know which gladdened me the most—the sight of the poor drowning people climbing onto the rocks reaching a place of safety, or the devotion and self-sacrifice of those whose whole being was wrapped up in the effort for their deliverance.

As I looked on, I saw that the occupants of that platform were quite a mixed company. That is, they were divided into different "sets" or classes, and they occupied themselves with different pleasures and employments. But only a very few of them seemed to make it their business to get the people out of the sea.

But what puzzled me most was the fact that though all of them had been rescued at one time or another from the ocean, nearly everyone seemed to have forgotten all about it. Anyway, it seemed the memory of its darkness and danger no longer troubled them at all. And what seemed equally strange and perplexing to me was that these people did not even seem to have any care—that is any agonizing care—about the poor perishing ones who were struggling and drowning right before their very eyes... many of whom were their own husbands and wives, brothers and sisters and even their own children.[12]

12 The full text of William Booth's *A Vision of the Lost* is available online here (viewed 20 February 2016): https://salvationarmy.org.au/Global/State%20pages/Victoria/Crossroads/Spiritual%20Care/vision%204%20lost.pdf

Make more disciples

The New Testament story is the same, again and again. This present world is in urgent need of deliverance from the darkness of sin, suffering, evil and death; and God is doing just that: he is rescuing a people from every nation by the death and resurrection of Jesus Christ—people who are being transformed to be like Jesus, and who are gathered in celebration around Christ's throne in a new creation where evil and death are no more.

If we needed more imperatives alongside the explicit one in Matthew 28, this picture surely provides them. The multitudes all around us in this present darkness are in desperate need of rescuing, and God's history-wide plan is to do just that—to deliver and transfer redeemed sinners into the kingdom of his Son.

This understanding of God's worldwide and history-wide plan gives us a different perspective on 'disciple-making'. It's like a zoomed-out picture that explains what's really going on.

Think about it for a moment. What do you think is really going on when your unbelieving friend Fred becomes a disciple of Jesus, and joins a church?

According to the world, what is happening is that for a range of personal and situational reasons, Fred is turning to religion and spirituality to fill certain needs in his life—for meaning, for belonging, for comfort, for certainty, to be the best possible version of himself, and more. The world may see this as a positive development for Fred or not, but however they evaluate it, it will be in terms of the various ways in which 'faith' helps people improve their lives.

According to some Christians, what is going on is not much different from the world's description, with the exception that the God Fred is turning to really is there, and really will help Fred improve his life. That is, the key outcome of Fred becoming a Christian is a better life for Fred—more meaningful, more up-right and loving, more rounded and spiritual, possibly even more successful in helping Fred to become the Fred that he was always meant to be.

According to many other Christians, this focus on Christianity improving our lives now is a bit tawdry and unspiritual. They would say what is really happening is that God is giving Fred something much better and more valuable than any life improvement he might imagine, and that is a new personal relationship with God through Jesus—a relationship that gives him salvation and peace with God now, and entry into heaven when he dies.

Now this last description is getting closer, and is in fact perfectly true. But it needs to go further. When we zoom even further out and look at what is happening to Fred with the benefit of what we have just seen in the Bible, we can say that what is going on is not *just* about Fred, or in fact even *primarily* about him. What is happening, amazingly, remarkably, is that God is continuing to move all of history—in this case the little fragment of human history that is Fred—towards its final goal. With the conversion of Fred, God is laying one more brick in an eternal spiritual temple founded on Christ, and glorifying to Christ.[13] Jesus is building his church,[14] his congregation, his assembly, his great gathering of redeemed humanity that will one day throng around him in a new heavens and earth—and he is doing it one Fred at a time.

This is why we want to make more and more disciples of Jesus Christ: *because God's goal for the whole world and the whole of human history is to glorify his beloved Son in the midst of the people he has rescued and transformed.*

We could represent this diagrammatically like this:

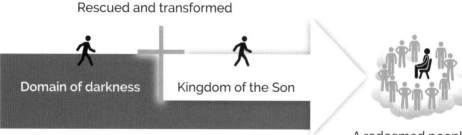

A redeemed people
gathered around the risen Christ

13 1 Pet 2:4-5
14 Matt 16:18

PHASE 1: SHARPEN YOUR CONVICTIONS

Like all attempts to represent these sorts of ideas visually, we acknowledge that there will be shortcomings and simplifications in our diagram. We'd love you to improve on it (and please get in touch to share your improvements). We will keep adding components to this diagram in the following pages as we work through the five convictions.[15]

~

This must be our first and foundational conviction, because it frames and determines everything else. It reminds us that making disciples is not primarily a human activity with goals that we set (although it is those things in a subsidiary sense). Whatever happens in Christian ministry and in church, and whatever happens in our neighbourhoods and families and workplaces, is part of what God is doing to move all things inexorably towards their goal and end—which is Jesus Christ.

BEFORE YOU START
Remember that the team manual is available for download free of charge at **thevineproject.com**. In it you'll find space to write or type your thoughts and answers for every discussion point, question, and activity in this book. For more information regarding the online support, see appendix ii or visit the website.

DISCUSSION

Here are some suggestions to help you work through the content of this section as a team.

For this and each of the following convictions:

- In advance of meeting together, each member of the team should read the text expounding the conviction,

---

15 We have tried to represent the now-not-yet tension of this present evil age by 'inserting' the kingdom of the Son into the 'domain of darkness'. The domain of darkness still exists, even as people are being transferred out of it into the kingdom of the Son. It will only be finally destroyed on the last day, when the new creation dawns.

marking it up along the way. Underline things you think are particularly important; put question marks next to things you aren't sure are right, or which you don't fully understand. This is a book that you hereby have permission to scribble on.

- When you get together, start by sharing your scribblings. What did you find particularly striking or helpful or challenging? Where were your question marks?
- Work through as many of the following suggested discussion questions, Bible passages and activities as you think useful.
- Conclude each discussion with prayer.

1. Read at least four of the following passages (that we touched on above):

Revelation 7:9-17   Colossians 1:13-20
Hebrews 12:18-24   Ephesians 1:1-14
Titus 2:11-14   Romans 8

In each passage, particularly note what you learn about:

a. the end towards which God is moving everything (including us)
b. the place of Jesus Christ in God's plans
c. the significance of Jesus' death for God's plans
d. humanity's place in God's plans
e. why making disciples is important.

2. Why do you think many churches lose motivation and urgency for making more disciples of Jesus? (How would you describe your own urgency for the task? And that of your church?)

3. See how many different ways you can truthfully finish this sentence:

We make disciples because...

Conviction 2: What is a disciple?

Disciples, discipleship, discipling, disciple-making.
These words are such an established part of conversation about ministry and church life that we rarely pause to consider what we actually mean by them.

Take, for example, this collection of recent quotes, in which 'discipleship' and 'disciple-making' seem to mean a range of different things:

> While listening to Dr Hendricks speak, I sensed that discipleship might be something I could do, unlike more public types of ministry because you didn't have to preach or do anything public.[1]

> What would happen to the church of Jesus Christ if a majority of those who claim to follow Christ were nurtured to maturity through intimate, accountable relationships centered on the essentials of God's word? Self-initiating, reproducing disciples of Jesus would be the result.[2]

1   Dennis McCallum and Jessica Lowery, *Organic Discipleship: Mentoring Others into Spiritual Maturity and Leadership*, rev. edn, New Paradigm, n.p., 2012, p. 15.
2   Greg Ogden, *Discipleship Essentials: A Guide to Building Your Life in Christ*, expanded edn, IVP, Downers Grove, 2007, p. 9.

Discipleship is all about living life together rather than just one structured meeting per week.[3]

Many churches have used various types of small groups as part of their discipleship strategy (home groups, life groups, fellowship groups, community groups, etc.).[4]

Mark calls the Church to abandon its imperialistic dreams on the one hand, and its passive noninvolvement on the other, and to become for the world what Jesus was for the world. That is what discipleship, following Jesus, really means.[5]

We need more of the engine that Jesus used to change the world, the engine he instructs us to use. This engine will not create perfect churches, but it will create *effective* churches.

It's relational discipleship.[6]

These quotes are representative of much of the conversation that swirls around 'discipleship' today, including the many discussions we've had with pastors since *The Trellis and the Vine* was published. Our abiding impression has been that although many people use the language of discipleship and disciple-making often, not many people are particularly clear what they mean by it. Their (sometimes implicit) definitions are often too narrow in scope or too vague about what is involved.

Generally speaking, most people assume that discipleship is a personal, relational and intimate kind of thing; something that happens in our private lives or in small groups, perhaps in contrast to other aspects of church life that are more public or

---

3 Francis Chan with Mark Beuving, *Multiply: Disciples Making Disciples*, David C Cook, Colorado Springs, 2012, p. 11.

4 Randy Pope with Kitti Murray, *Insourcing: Bringing Discipleship Back to the Local Church*, Zondervan, Grand Rapids, 2013, p. 107.

5 NT Wright, *Following Jesus: Biblical Reflections on Discipleship*, Eerdmans, Grand Rapids, 1995, pp. 49-50.

6 Jim Putman and Bobby Harrington with Robert E Coleman, *DiscipleShift: Five Steps That Help Your Church to Make Disciples Who Make Disciples*, Zondervan, Grand Rapids, 2013, p. 22; emphasis original.

programmatic. Most tend to roughly equate being a 'disciple' with a general idea of 'following Jesus'. And nearly everyone agrees that effective discipleship and disciple-making are hugely important and are a (or the) vital factor in rejuvenating churches and changing the world.

But why 'disciple' is the category or language we should use to talk about these things is not so obvious, and certainly not when we see how the New Testament uses the word (which we'll come to below).

Of course the thing with words—like 'disciple' and 'discipleship'—is that they shift and morph over time, as we use them in different ways and with reference to different things-in-the-world. This is not a problem. It's just the reality of language as a living, dynamic gift of God.

But it can sometimes be a problem when we take a Bible word—like 'disciple'—and use it in a different way from how the Bible uses it, or to mean something other than what the Bible means by it. It's a problem not because absolute precision in language is such a virtue in itself, but because it can lead us to miss out on the riches of what the Bible is actually saying. We see a particular word in our English Bibles (like 'disciple'), and the meaning, references and connotations of how we currently use the word in English come to our minds. We naturally assume that this is what the Bible is talking about at this point—but it may not be. The biblical author may have a somewhat different set of things in mind, and so we miss the force or implications of what is being said. Worse, we can misread what is being said, and bring all the weight of a biblical imperative to bear on something in our church experience that is not necessarily what the Bible is talking about at all.

All of which means that a vital step in clarifying our convictions about discipleship and disciple-making is to clarify what we mean by these important terms.

What is a disciple?

There's not much controversy or difficulty about the meaning of the word translated 'disciple' in the New Testament (the Greek word *mathētēs*). It basically refers to a learner or student, someone who is apprenticed to a teacher to learn from him.[7]

Put simply, a disciple is a learner; discipleship is 'learnership'.

We see this clearly enough in the way the Gospels use the word. A disciple aims to learn the ways and practices and wisdom of his teacher:

> "A disciple is not above his teacher, but everyone when he is fully trained will be like his teacher." (Luke 6:40)

> And they said to him, "The disciples of John fast often and offer prayers, and so do the disciples of the Pharisees, but yours eat and drink." (Luke 5:33)

Whether it's the disciples of John, the Pharisees or Jesus, the basic point is the same—the 'learners' stand in relation to their teacher (or teachers), whose teachings and way of life they seek to learn and adopt.

Certainly they are learning intellectual content—a way of thinking and perceiving the world, a body of knowledge and understanding. We often see Jesus teaching his 'learners' this content in the Gospels:

> Seeing the crowds, he went up on the mountain, and when he sat down, his disciples came to him.
> And he opened his mouth and taught them, saying...
> (Matt 5:1-2)

But in the case of Jesus' disciples, the outcome of this learning was not simply the mastery of a certain body of knowledge—what we would today associate with classroom or academic learning. What the 'learners' were learning from Jesus was a way of life based on an understanding of certain truths about reality (as were the disciples of John and of the Pharisees, for that matter). The

---

7   This is reflected in the origin of our English word 'disciple'—the Latin *discere*, 'to learn'.

goal was for them not only to know what their teacher knew, but also to be like their teacher, to walk in his ways. They weren't learning a subject; they were learning a person, if we can put it like that—his knowledge, his wisdom, his whole way of life.

This is in part why 'learners' often followed their teacher around. They not only listened to the teacher's words, but saw his words in action in his life, and sought to learn that way of life by being with him constantly. Following him and being with him was also the routine way that the teaching was conveyed and mastered. We see this in the Gospels as the 'learners' often ask Jesus questions, pose dilemmas, and get him to clarify and elaborate on his public teaching.

Perhaps this is one reason that the concept of 'following' has come to dominate most people's thinking about discipleship. If asked to give a simple definition of what a disciple is, many would answer, "Someone who follows Jesus". From what we have seen so far, it would perhaps be more accurate to say, "Someone devoted to learning Jesus".

However, even though 'discipleship' is not identical with 'following', the two are closely related in the Gospels—for at least two reasons.

The first is related to the kind of learning that the 'learners' (i.e. disciples) were committing themselves to. You could hardly learn from the Master, and adopt the way of life he taught and exemplified, if you weren't regularly with him—watching, listening, practising, asking questions, and so on. Jesus wanted his learners to walk with him, and to learn to be like him.

But the significance of following Jesus goes deeper than that in the Gospels, because of who Jesus was and where his 'learners' were following him to. Jesus repeatedly tells people that following him is an exclusive, life-and-death commitment. To go with him means to leave everything else behind, including your very life. As he puts it so starkly in Luke's Gospel:

> "So therefore, any one of you who does not renounce all that he has cannot be my disciple [learner]." (Luke 14:33)

To 'learn' Jesus—to submit yourself to his teaching, to walk in his ways—will mean leaving behind all your current loyalties and commitments. It will mean walking the road to Jerusalem with him, and facing up to the cross that is waiting there. As Jesus makes very clear, saving our old life is not an option; it's only by losing our lives that we save them.[8] Or to put it in the language of Paul, it is only by being crucified with Christ that we can rise to a new life in him.[9]

'Following' Jesus in the Gospels is very much like repentance. It is abandoning my current existence and heading off in a new direction, to learn a whole new life from a new Master, and to be part of the new kingdom that he will bring.

Two potent symbols

This is perhaps why baptism is such an appropriate symbol for initiation into being a 'learner'. Baptism was how disciples were typically 'made', as John's Gospel shows us in passing:

> Now when Jesus learned that the Pharisees had heard that Jesus was making and baptizing more disciples than John... (John 4:1)

Baptism was a symbol of repentance, of washing away the old and starting afresh, of dying and rising again. A new 'learner' was baptized as a vivid way of declaring that he had decisively turned away from his old understanding and life, and had now embarked on the new life that he would learn from his teacher.

Of course, in the case of being initiated into learning Jesus, that repentance was not just a turning away from one's former life, but a recognition that one's former life had been lived in selfishness and rebellion towards God. Repentance was also a plea for forgiveness—for a washing clean of all those thoughts,

8   Mark 8:34-36
9   E.g. Rom 6:1-8; Col 2:11-15

actions, attitudes and character traits that were contrary to the new kingdom Jesus embodied and taught.

Jesus is not just any teacher, and in repenting and following him you are not becoming just any 'learner'. To become a 'learner' of Jesus requires a repudiation—a radical unlearning—of our former rebellious way of life. It means being forgiven for the offence that our life has been before God, and submitting ourselves to a divine Teacher who speaks the very words of the Father.

This may be somewhat different from how we have learned to think about 'learning'. We tend to see learning through the lens of modern education, in which we move from a state of ignorance to being 'educated'—that is, acquiring information or knowledge or skills we previously lacked. The problem that 'learning' addresses is a lack of knowledge, almost as if there is a blank slate needing to be filled.

But the people Jesus calls to be 'learners' don't have a blank slate. Their slate is very full—of foolish, darkened, enslaved thinking that is opposed to learning Jesus at every point. Becoming a learner of Christ therefore requires a radical change. It requires a great work of God to rescue us from the dark domain in which we were enslaved, and to transfer us into the kingdom of his beloved Son.[10] From our side, it requires repentance—that is, a dying to the web of lies that our lives once were built on.

It's not really a surprise, then, when we arrive at Matthew 28, that baptism is an integral part of Jesus' grand commission to make 'learners' of all nations. But we'll return to Matthew 28 shortly.

The other potent symbol of becoming a 'learner' is the yoke. We see it in Jesus' words in Matthew 11:

> "All things have been handed over to me by my Father, and no-one knows the Son except the Father, and no-one knows the Father except the Son and anyone to whom the Son chooses to reveal him. Come to me, all who labour and are heavy laden, and I will give you rest. Take

10 Col 1:13-14

my yoke upon you, and learn from me, for I am gentle and lowly in heart, and you will find rest for your souls. For my yoke is easy, and my burden is light." (Matt 11:27-30)

To 'take the yoke' is a metaphor for service and submission and obedience, for accepting the authority of another—like oxen, who are yoked together to plough in the service of their owner; or slaves, who bear the yoke of their master.

'Taking the yoke' is a way of talking about 'learnership'—the submitting of oneself to learn from and follow the ways of a master or teacher.[11] This is essentially what a 'disciple' was in New Testament times: someone who submitted to the authority of a teacher, in order to learn from him and become like him.

Jesus gives two reasons in this passage why he is the obvious person to learn from. The first is the stunning claim that all things have been handed over to him by the Father—that he is the Son and heir of God (much as we saw in Conviction 1). He, and only he, has exclusive access to the foundational knowledge of all things. He is the only one who knows the Father, and who can therefore reveal the Father to others. If you want to learn what God is really like—in fact, if you want to get to know God the Father himself—the Son is your only option as a teacher.

Now a claim like this doesn't sound like the words of someone who is "gentle and lowly in heart", and whose yoke would be easy and light. And yet that is the stunning and confounding contrast that Jesus constantly presents, and which the scribes and Pharisees so comprehensively fail to grasp. The all-conquering, kingdom-bringing, Father-revealing Son of God is born in a backwater, in a stable, and grows up in obscurity. He comes not with sword and military might, but with teaching and healing and compassion. He enters Jerusalem not on a warhorse but on a donkey. And when he is finally lifted up in his great hour of glory, his throne turns out to be a cross on which he dies a forsaken

---

11 The Greek word for 'learn' (*manthanō*) in verse 30 is the verb form of the noun we normally translate as 'disciple' (*mathētē*).

death for the sins of his enemies.[12]

He comes to bring rest and peace and salvation. This is why his yoke is a blessed relief from the hard and heavy burden that the scribes and Pharisees placed on the shoulders of their 'learners'. Theirs was a school of grinding external self-justificatory law-keeping, based on the traditions of men rather than true knowledge of the Father.

Which leads us to the second reason that taking on the yoke of Jesus is so attractive: it's not a school where you pass on merit. Or rather, it's a school where the pass mark is 100% but where the final exam is done by the teacher.

The yoke of Jesus is total submission to his authority as the Teacher. But it is not a burden; it is liberation. His yoke brings a paradoxical freedom—freedom from the heavy burden of sin through forgiveness; and freedom to now learn a whole new way of living that is fit for the kingdom of God.

These two symbols—baptism and the yoke—say a lot about the kind of learning that the learners of Jesus were undertaking. It required a radical break from the past and initiation into a new relationship with the Teacher; it was a form of service and submission that was in fact rest and freedom; it involved a whole new way of life in learning to be like the Teacher.

~

Perhaps we could sum up what we have seen so far by saying that a 'disciple' is someone engaged in transformative learning.[13]

This is a kind of learning where the student's understanding of reality is changed and keeps changing, leading to a transformed experience and life. Our understanding and life changes decisively as we repent and submit ourselves to a new teacher, who reveals the Father to us, and reveals ourselves to us. And our understanding

12 In Isaiah 50, the Servant who knows "how to sustain with a word him who is weary" (v. 4) is the one who himself was not rebellious, and yet who was treated with disgrace (vv. 5-6).

13 'Transformative learning' is a term used in educational theory, and about which there is some debate. In borrowing the term, we certainly don't intend to enter that debate (it is not our expertise).

keeps being renewed continually over time, as it deepens and widens and begins to be expressed in our actions and lives; as we unlearn old ways of thinking, and as we continue to rearrange our mental furniture in light of the new Owner who has come into the house.

We'll look further in Conviction 3 at how exactly this change of thinking takes place through the work of God's word and Spirit, but for the moment we need to notice that the effect of this transformed understanding is a corresponding transformation of our whole person—of our identity and experience and life and action. Being a 'learner' of Jesus necessarily involves learning truth and content conveyed in words, but it must also involve the learning of a new way of being and living.

The Great Commission itself reminds us of this. The eleven first learners are charged by Jesus to make learners of all peoples, initiating (or baptizing) them into relationship with Father, Son and Spirit, and teaching them to keep all of Jesus' commandments.[14]

We often don't take much notice of that little word 'keep'. The learners are to be taught not only to *know* the commandments of Jesus. The 'learning outcome' is that they *keep* or observe or obey the commandments of Jesus. They are to learn the new way of life that the Lord Jesus Christ commands his subjects to live, which is summarized and encapsulated in the 'love' commandment— to give ourselves sacrificially for the benefit of others, as Christ has done for us.

In fact, whereas we often think of learning in terms of our own personal growth and advancement—of becoming a better me in some way—to learn Christ is to be increasingly focused on others rather than ourselves. It's to lay down our lives for others, as Christ laid down his, in weakness and suffering and death.

This is what a 'learner' of Jesus is learning: a transformed existence based on a transformed relationship with God in Christ.

It hardly seems necessary to point out that 'disciple' (or 'learner') is therefore just another name for 'Christian'—for

---

14 Matt 28:16-20

someone who has renounced the lie that used to be at the centre of their lives, who has recognized the dark and lost state they were living in, and who has turned to Christ in faith as their Master, Saviour and Teacher—to learn to be like him, to learn to keep all his commandments, and to live out that commitment daily and weekly and yearly for the rest of their lives.

In this sense 'learnership' cannot be thought of as a *subset* of the Christian life, or as a *stage* in the Christian life. It is simply one way to describe the totality of the Christian life.[15] To be a 'learner' of this kind is simply to be a Christian.

The same is true of church. As we'll discuss further below, a church can very fruitfully be thought of as a 'transformative learning community'—that is, a gathering of people who are all learning Christ together. 'Making learners' of Christ is not something that a church takes care of in adult Sunday School, or by putting on a Wednesday night program, or by encouraging people to meet in one-to-one Bible reading pairs—although of course all of these activities may indeed help people to learn Christ. Everything we do as God's gathered people (as 'church') should be an exercise in the transformative learning of Christ.

But we will come to back to this in due course.

The disappearing learner?

One of the curious little mysteries of the New Testament is that there seem to be no 'disciples' after the book of Acts.

Throughout the Gospels and in Acts, the noun *mathētēs* ('disciple' or 'learner') appears often as a description of those who have devoted themselves to being learners under Christ. But after a final mention in Acts 21:16, the word promptly disappears. In all the remaining 22 books of the New Testament, no-one is described as a 'learner' or 'disciple'.

---

15 Not the only way of course, but a very useful way.

Now is this a bit odd, not least because Jesus specifically told his learners (disciples) to go and make more learners (disciples). And it's not as if they got to Acts 21 and then gave up on the task. It's obvious from the epistles that what the apostles did to make learners in Acts (i.e. to preach the gospel in the power of the Spirit, to baptize people into Christ, and to teach them to keep all his commandments), was what they and the whole apostolic band continued to do everywhere.

In fact, the verb form of 'disciples'—*manthanō*, 'to learn'—does appear quite often in the epistles, in connection with the gospel truth that Christians have learned, and the lifestyle or action that goes along with it. Here's a sample:

> I appeal to you, brothers, to watch out for those who cause divisions and create obstacles contrary to the doctrine that you have **been taught [learned]**; avoid them. (Rom 16:17)

> For you can all prophesy one by one, so that all may **learn** and all be encouraged... (1 Cor 14:31)

> What you have **learned** and received and heard and seen in me—practise these things, and the God of peace will be with you. (Phil 4:9)

> Not that I am speaking of being in need, for I have **learned** in whatever situation I am to be content. (Phil 4:11)

> ...Of this you have heard before in the word of the truth, the gospel... since the day you heard it and understood the grace of God in truth, just as you **learned** it from Epaphras our beloved fellow servant. (Col 1:5-7)

> They have become callous and have given themselves up to sensuality, greedy to practise every kind of impurity. But that is not the way you **learned** Christ!—assuming that you have heard about him and were taught in him, as the truth is in Jesus, to put off your old self, which belongs to your former manner of life and is corrupt through deceitful desires, and to be renewed in the spirit

of your minds, and to put on the new self, created after the likeness of God in true righteousness and holiness. (Eph 4:19-24)

And let our people **learn** to devote themselves to good works, so as to help cases of urgent need, and not be unfruitful. (Titus 3:14)

Perhaps Christians as 'learners' didn't disappear from the rest of the New Testament after all.

It is very striking how these few brief quotes line up with what we see of 'learnership' in the Gospels and Acts. It clearly involves content—that is, words being spoken and taught, and then received and learned. But it also involves learning from a teacher's actions and example, and seeking to do likewise (as in Phil 4:9). It involves being taught not just information but a totally new repentant way of life—to kill off the old 'me' and with a renewed mind embark on a whole new existence (as in Eph 4:19-24).

And of course, in looking at these few occurrences of the word 'learn', we haven't surveyed the multiplicity of other terms and phrases that convey the same concepts—that the Christian life is a matter of understanding and embracing a new vision of reality, a new truth, a new word that has been announced, proclaimed, taught, modelled and passed on; and that it is also a matter of responding to that liberating word in ongoing repentance and faith that is lived out in every sphere of our lives.

'Learning Christ' is a reality that the New Testament attests to repeatedly and powerfully.

However, it is worth asking whether 'learnership' has waned (if not disappeared) in many modern churches. And by this we don't mean that there is less one-to-one ministry than there should be, or less small group ministry, or that every church should have a 'learnership pastor'.

What we mean is that in our observation of churches, and in our conversations with pastors all over the world, the culture that exists in many churches is no longer a culture of transformative learning, if it ever was. The whole 'way we do things around here' is not focused on transformative learning through the word of God in the power of the Spirit of God.

Would you describe your church's culture in this way? Would you describe your own life in this way, come to that? What other cultures and frameworks tend to be operating instead?

We'll talk more about this in Phase 3 as we assess our current culture against our convictions. But let us not get ahead of ourselves.

What is a disciple? *A forgiven sinner who is learning Christ in repentance and faith.*

We could add one small detail to our diagram to represent this—namely an 'L' (learner) sign above the person who has been transferred out of darkness and into the kingdom of the Son, and who now continues that transformational learning in every sphere of life, especially in the 'transformational learning community' that we call 'church'.

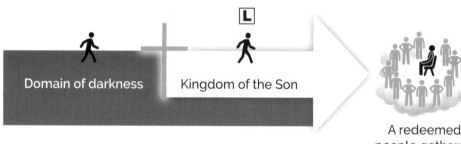

Rescued and transformed

L

Domain of darkness   Kingdom of the Son

A redeemed people gathered around the risen Christ

The next step is for you to reflect on the content of this conviction, to test it against Scripture, and to formulate your own way of expressing it.

DISCUSSION

As well as your own notes and scribblings, here are some discussion starters to get you talking.

1. Read these well-known passages where Jesus explains what it means to be his disciple: Matthew 10:16-33; Mark 8:31-38; Luke 14:25-33.

   a. What do disciples need to learn about Jesus?
   b. What are the consequences of learning Christ in this way?
   c. Why is it inconsistent to 'learn Christ' and not subject our whole life to his will?
   d. What alternative masters does Jesus highlight?

2. Discuss each of the following common views of discipleship. What truth (if any) do they express? Where are they wrong or inadequate?

   View 1: Discipleship is a second stage of Christian experience that happens sometime after conversion. You can be a Christian but it's only the really dedicated, committed people who are disciples.

   View 2: Discipleship is an intentional ministry strategy or program—like one-to-one mentoring, small group ministry, or a 12-week discipleship program.

   View 3: The essence of discipleship is personal accountability to a discipler. Discipleship is about the kind of trusted relationship where someone keeps us accountable about quiet times, church attendance, or avoidance of particular sins, like pornography.

   View 4: Preaching is not really about discipling people. It's more to do with proclamation, teaching and exhortation.

3. Compose your own concise statement of what it means to be a disciple of Jesus. (You might find this statement useful later on in Phase 3, in assessing how effectively the various ministries of your church are 'making disciples'.)

Conviction 3: How are disciples made?

Having lifted our eyes to the panorama of God's momentous plans for gathering his people in Christ ('Why make disciples?') and then done some careful thinking about what a disciple actually is (a 'Christ-learner'), we now come to the 'how' question: *By what method or means is God rescuing and gathering his people into the kingdom of his Son?*

It's supremely important that we pose the question in this way, with this grammar—that is, with God as the active subject of the sentence. In thinking about means and methods, and especially about the part that human efforts and activities play in the process of making disciples, we must constantly keep asserting the primacy of God's will and action. We will come back to this as we proceed, but let this be the first of many such reminders: you may plant, and I may water, but it is God who gives the growth.[1]

Our hope is that you find the explanation below of how to make disciples to be totally conventional and unremarkable—actually no, we hope you *do* find it remarkable, but not because it is new. We haven't found the holy grail of disciple-making methodology, nor do we think such a missing secret or key exists.

---

1   1 Cor 3:6

The means we will be highlighting are those that God has given from the very beginning, but which for various reasons we often neglect or misunderstand or misuse. We will do our best to expound and explain those methods clearly, sharply and with a fresh (and we hope refreshing) perspective, but we make no claim to be innovators.

Let us make a start, then, by dipping into some key Bible passages.

~

The logical place to start is no doubt with the Great Commission in Matthew 28, but it really doesn't go into much detail about *how* disciples are made. As we've already noted, all nations must be initiated as 'learners' of the risen authoritative Lord Christ (baptism), with an expectation of ongoing teaching to keep all of his commandments, and a promise that Jesus himself will be with us to the end of the age. Beyond that, there's no detail as to the methodology involved.

The picture gets filled out somewhat in Luke 24, where we read a different (or additional) version of the Great Commission in Jesus' words to the assembled disciples in the upper room. Jesus opens their minds to understand the Scriptures, and shows them that the task they are about to be sent out to accomplish has always been God's plan. What was written in the Law and the Prophets and the Psalms must be fulfilled:

> Then he opened their minds to understand the Scriptures, and said to them, "Thus it is written, that the Christ should suffer and on the third day rise from the dead, and that repentance and forgiveness of sins should be proclaimed in his name to all nations, beginning from Jerusalem. You are witnesses of these things. And behold, I am sending the promise of my Father upon you. But stay in the city until you are clothed with power from on high." (Luke 24:45-49)

There are three necessities that have been "written": that the

Christ should suffer, that he should rise from the dead, and that repentance and forgiveness should be proclaimed in his name to all nations, starting from Jerusalem. As in Matthew 28, the worldwide authority of the crucified and risen Christ means that repentance and forgiveness (i.e. becoming his disciple) applies to all nations. The task for the disciples is to declare that news to the world in Spirit-empowered proclamation.

This of course is what we see happening in Acts. The Spirit descends in power upon the whole gathering of disciples at Pentecost, and their mouths are opened to declare the great deeds and works of God to the nations.[2] Peter stands and explains that what is happening is just what the Scriptures (and Jesus himself) foretold: that the Davidic Messiah has died and risen on high to be the Lord of all, that he has poured his Spirit upon his people, and that now is open season for repentance and forgiveness of sins. The crowd are cut to the heart, and many respond.[3]

This initial pattern continues throughout Acts. The disciples of Jesus, led by the apostles (including the new boy Paul, who joins the ranks in chapter 9), fan out from Jerusalem to Judaea and Samaria and to the rest of the world with the momentous news of Jesus Christ. The summary of what happened in Derbe in Acts 14 is a typical example:

> When they had preached the gospel to that city and had made many disciples, they returned to Lystra and to Iconium and to Antioch, strengthening the souls of the disciples, encouraging them to continue in the faith, and saying that through many tribulations we must enter the kingdom of God. (Acts 14:21-22)

The gospel is preached, disciples are made, and then they are strengthened and encouraged to continue in the faith to the end. This is the story of Acts—although whether it should be called the 'Acts of the Apostles' or the 'Acts of God' is an interesting question. Throughout Acts, although the gospel word is proclaimed

2   Acts 2:1-11
3   Acts 2:14-41

by and through the disciples of Jesus (in obedience to his commission), there are also several references to God's word having a vitality and power of its own:

> And the **word** of God continued to increase, and the number of the disciples multiplied greatly in Jerusalem, and a great many of the priests became obedient to the faith. (Acts 6:7)

> But the **word** of God increased and multiplied. (Acts 12:24)

> And the **word** of the Lord was spreading throughout the whole region. (Acts 13:49)

> So the **word** of the Lord continued to increase and prevail mightily. (Acts 19:20)

Likewise, Acts leaves us in no doubt that the power behind the proclamation and spread of the word is God's own power by his Spirit. At every point in the narrative, the Spirit is active—whether in giving boldness to the disciples to speak in the face of opposition,[4] or falling upon those to whom they speak,[5] or directing the path of the mission,[6] or giving joy to the disciples in the midst of suffering.[7]

The making of disciples is *God's work*, achieved as his word and Spirit work through the activity of the disciples and in the hearts of those they speak to.

When we come to the New Testament letters, written to the churches established by the ministry of the apostles in Acts, we find a continuation of these methodological themes. To illustrate, we're going to take a whirlwind tour through 1 Thessalonians, but the same exercise could be fruitfully done with any of the New Testament letters.

How did the Thessalonians become 'learners of Christ', both initially and in their ongoing walk with him?

4   Acts 4:31
5   Acts 11:15
6   Acts 16:6-7
7   Acts 13:52

- Paul proclaimed the gospel to them, "not only in word, but also in power and in the Holy Spirit and with full conviction".[8]
- The response of the Thessalonians tells us something not only about the effect of the proclamation on them, but also about its content. After they heard Paul and were convicted by the Holy Spirit, they "turned to God from idols to serve the living and true God, and to wait for his Son from heaven, whom he raised from the dead, Jesus who delivers us from the wrath to come".[9]
- None of this was easy. Paul, Silvanus and Timothy "had boldness in our God to declare to you the gospel of God in the midst of much conflict";[10] and a mark of the genuineness of the Thessalonians' conversion was that they "became imitators of us and of the Lord, for you received the word in much affliction, with the joy of the Holy Spirit".[11]
- Paul and his colleagues loved and cared for the Thessalonians, being gentle with them like a mother,[12] and encouraging them like a father[13] to walk in a manner worthy of God.[14] They shared "not only the gospel of God but also our own selves, because you had become very dear to us",[15] which in context meant a very practical hard-working concern by Paul to earn his own living while he "proclaimed to you the gospel of God".[16]
- Paul sends Timothy to "establish and exhort you in your faith, that no-one be moved by these afflictions".[17]
- Paul continues to give thanks for them, and to pray earnestly for them that God would increase their love, and establish their hearts blameless before God when Jesus returns.[18]

---

8 1 Thess 1:5; cf. 2:13
9 1 Thess 1:9-10; cf. 5:9-10
10 1 Thess 2:2
11 1 Thess 1:6; also 2:14
12 1 Thess 2:7
13 1 Thess 2:11-12
14 1 Thess 2:12
15 1 Thess 2:8
16 1 Thess 2:9
17 1 Thess 3:2-3
18 1 Thess 3:8-13

- Paul then exhorts them to continue "more and more" to live a life of holiness and love, pleasing to God, according to the instructions (or 'commandments') he had given them through the Lord Jesus.[19]
- Paul then points forward to the hope of the resurrection and the return of Jesus, not only so that they won't be misled or uninformed about these matters, but also so that they can continue to encourage and build one another up in these truths.[20]
- The letter closes with final exhortations to do good and to hold on to the good, to rejoice and to pray constantly, and with a prayer that God would keep them blameless at the coming of Jesus Christ.[21]

The elements here are those that we find repeated throughout the New Testament:

- the word or gospel of God concerning his Son, proclaimed and taught, both initially and continuously[22]
- the work of God by his Spirit to bring conviction, to change the heart, and to bring forth the fruit planted by the word—which can be summarized as 'repentance and faith' (again, as an initial response and then continuously day by day)[23]
- the agency of God's people in speaking the word, in exemplifying and modelling the Christ-learning life, in praying for God to work by his Spirit, and in mutual encouragement, exhortation and edification[24]
- the struggle, conflict and suffering that attends this whole process, because it is taking place over time within "this present darkness"; that is, the ongoing proclamation and practice of 'learning Christ' is constantly threatened from without by opposition, and from within by erroneous

19 1 Thess 4:1-12
20 1 Thess 4:13-5:11
21 1 Thess 5:12-28
22 Luke 24:45-47; Rom 10:14-17; 1 Cor 1:17-18, 15:1-11; 2 Cor 4:5-6; Col 1:3-8; 2 Tim 4:1-2
23 John 16:7-11; Acts 1:8, 2:1-4; Gal 5:16-24; Eph 1:13-14; 1 Thess 1:4-5; 2 Tim 1:13-14
24 Rom 15:14; 1 Cor 14:1-3, 26; Eph 4:7-16; Phil 1:3-4; 1 Thess 4:18, 5:12-14; Titus 2:3-5; 1 Pet 2:9-12

teaching and our own wayward hearts (hence the need for constant ongoing proclamation, prayer, repentance and faith).[25]

To put it in the briefest way possible, disciples are made *by the persevering proclamation of the word of God by the people of God in prayerful dependence on the Spirit of God.*

Now we would be surprised if many of our readers found this short summary particularly controversial or novel.

However, we would also be surprised if many of our readers felt that they therefore had disciple-making under control. Our problem is not that we have never heard of these basic methods of disciple-making ministry, nor even that we don't practise them, at least to some extent. Our problem is very like the problem the Thessalonians faced with respect to the Christian life: a constant tendency to lose sight of what's important, to be distracted by false or half-true alternatives, and to grow weary or lose our way in the face of multiple pressures.

In many ways our message in this book is like Paul's to the Thessalonians: we know these truths aren't new to you; we know you have been putting them it into practice (at least to some extent); now we urge you to do so "more and more".

This "more and more" will require an honest look at what you're currently doing, to see how well it reflects your convictions about basic disciple-making methodology. That will be our task in Phase 3.

But before we get there, we need to sharpen and hone our understanding of these core principles about how disciples are made, so that we can bring a keen-edged understanding not only to evaluating what we are currently doing, but also to planning for change.

Let's sharpen what we mean by these key components in the making of Christ-learners, under four headings, each starting with P.

---

25 John 15:18-19; Acts 4:29-31; 2 Cor 4:7-12; Eph 6:10-20; Phil 1:27-30, 3:7-16; 1 Thess 1:6-7, 2:14-16; 2 Tim 2:14-19, 3:10-13; Heb 3:12-14

1. Proclamation of the word of God

In the New Testament, the proclamation of the word is the basic means for creating and growing 'Christ-learners'. You could even say that there is only one central activity in making disciples—the speaking of the word of God[26]—and that all the other elements describe in what Spirit, by which people, and in what manner that speaking is done.

Volumes could be (and have been) written on this subject,[27] but here we will have to confine ourselves to five brief points:

- *The content* of the 'word' is essentially the plan and promise of God centred on Jesus Christ (i.e. what we explored in Conviction 1). We could try capturing it in one long sentence like this: *God has fulfilled his age-long plans for his creation through sending his Son, born in the line of David, to die for sins and rise again as the Saviour, Lord and Christ of all the world, so that people dwelling in darkness from every nation might now hear his call to repentance and faith, be forgiven, reconciled and justified, and live a life that increasingly seeks to obey all his commandments, as they await the sure hope of entering his eternal kingdom.*

  That's one way of saying it. Or you might prefer Paul's two-word summary ('Christ crucified'),[28] or his 10,000-word summary (the epistle to the Romans).

- This word of God *doesn't consist of two different words*—an evangelistic word for non-Christians, and an edifying word

---

26 We use 'speaking' as a general catch-all word—in the New Testament there is a wide range of overlapping and related terms that describe different purposes or styles of speech that are directed towards learning Christ (evangelizing, teaching, exhorting, proclaiming, encouraging, admonishing, instructing, reminding, rebuking, and so on).

27 Peter Adam, *Speaking God's Words: A Practical Theology of Preaching*, IVP, Leicester, 1996; Peter Jensen, *The Revelation of God*, IVP, Leicester, 2002; Matt Chandler, Josh Patterson and Eric Geiger, *Creature of the Word: The Jesus-Centered Church*, B&H Publishing, Nashville, 2012; DB Knox, 'What must not change in a changing ministry' and 'The priority of preaching' in *D Broughton Knox Selected Works*, vol. 2, *Church and Ministry*, ed. Kirsten Birkett, Matthias Media, Sydney, 2003, pp. 211-20; Christopher Green and David Jackman (eds), *When God's Voice is Heard: Essays on Preaching Presented to Dick Lucas*, IVP, Leicester, 1995; Peter G Bolt (ed.), *Let the Word do the Work: Essays in Honour of Phillip D Jensen*, Australian Church Record, Camperdown, 2015.

28 1 Cor 2:2

for Christian disciples. The word that is proclaimed at the beginning is the same word that is proclaimed in the middle and at the end, and every day in between. This gospel word concerning God's grace to us in his Son is what crashes into our lives and turns us around, and it is also what continues to teach, instruct and admonish us to godliness and faith every day as we await his return.[29] Of course, we will understand the word more deeply as we go along. We will grasp with greater clarity how black is the darkness we were rescued from, how mind-blowing are God's eternal purposes worked out over generations through Israel, how sure and glorious is our hope, how wonderful is the justification and reconciliation that came by Christ's blood, and how liberating and challenging is the life we are now called to live in 'keeping all his commandments'. But (as DB Knox used to say) even though the gospel of Christ is a well that you can always dig a little deeper, it is still the same well, dug in the same place.

- This one message about Jesus Christ, in all its dazzling facets, is *the message of the Bible*. We preach the gospel by expounding the Bible.[30] The Bible is our authoritative and sufficient source for truly and faithfully knowing the word and speaking the word. This is the word that must be proclaimed—not a set of inspirational thoughts about how to improve your life, not the thoughts that a springboard verse triggers off in our heads, and not a fresh revelation that we think God has given us. If we believe that the Bible's word is the powerful speech of God, then in many respects what we want to see flourish in our church culture is as many instances as possible of the Bible being spoken, read, studied, preached, explained, taught, discussed, memorized, prayed over and meditated upon.

---

29 Titus 2:11-14

30 See Phillip D Jensen and Paul Grimmond, *The Archer and the Arrow: Preaching the Very Words of God*, Matthias Media, Sydney, 2010, chapter 3.

- *There are many ways and modes* in which this biblical word can be spoken.[31] It can be by letter (as much of the New Testament is); it can be in a private home late at night;[32] it can be in a synagogue or a marketplace,[33] in the open air[34] or in a lecture hall;[35] it can be in the form of public reading and preaching in church,[36] or in the form of conversation in a private vehicle.[37] Of all these different modes in which the word can be spoken, the preaching and teaching of the word in the gathered congregation has a particularly central and foundational place—and we will say more about this in the two convictions that follow.[38] But for now it is important to notice that the contexts in which the word might be spoken are broad and multifaceted. One symptom of a congregational culture that is weak in 'disciple-making' is that there are few contexts or instances beyond the Sunday sermon in which the Bible's word is regularly being spoken.

- *Not all instances of the word being spoken require the Bible itself to be open.* When we sit on our young son's bed, and encourage him to trust Jesus in the midst of his anxieties or fears, we're engaged in a form of teaching or proclamation. We could have taught him by opening Philippians 4:6-7 or 1 Peter 5:6-7 or Psalm 27, and at some time or place it would be important to do so. Indeed, if we had not been regularly reading, studying, speaking and hearing the Bible's word, we would not have known what to say to our son. But whenever we do with words what the biblical authors are doing with words, we are speaking the Bible's message. When we proclaim a certain truth (about God or Christ or the future or ourselves), or repeat

---

31 See Peter Adam's material on this in *Speaking God's Words*, pp. 59-70.

32 Acts 20:7-9

33 Acts 17:17-18

34 Acts 16:13-14

35 Acts 19:9

36 1 Tim 4:13

37 Acts 8:29-35

38 Phillip Jensen and Paul Grimmond provide an insightful treatment not only of the centrality and importance of expository preaching, but of the Christ-centred content of that preaching. See Jensen and Grimmond, *The Archer and the Arrow*, especially chapter 2.

a certain promise, or urge a certain manner of living, or provide encouragement on the basis of God's faithfulness, or whatever it might be, we 're-speak' the word that God has spoken in the Bible.[39] This is the very essence of how we learn Christ.

Since no book is complete without a Martin Luther quote, let us close this brief section on the centrality of the proclaimed word with the words of the great Reformer:

> One thing, and only one thing, is necessary for Christian life, righteousness and freedom. That one thing is the most holy Word of God, the gospel of Christ, as Christ says, John 11[:25], "I am the resurrection and the life; he who believes, though he die, yet shall he live"; and John 8[:36], "So if the Son makes you free, you will be free indeed"; and Matt. 4[:4], "Man shall not live by bread alone, but by every word that proceeds from the mouth of God". Let us then consider it certain and firmly established that the soul can do without anything except the Word of God, and that where the Word of God is missing there is no help at all for the soul. If it has the Word it is rich and lacks nothing since it is the Word of life, truth, light, peace, righteousness, salvation, joy, liberty, wisdom, power, grace, glory, and of every incalculable blessing...
>
> ...
>
> You may ask, "What then is the Word of God, and how shall it be used, since there are so many words of God?" I answer: The Apostle explains this in Romans 1. The Word is the Gospel of God concerning his Son, who was made flesh, suffered, rose from the dead, and was glorified through the Spirit who sanctifies. To preach Christ means to feed the soul, make it righteous, set it free, and save it, provided it believes the preaching.[40]

---

39 Timothy Ward argues that contemporary speech-act theory can help us understand how the reading or proclamation of the Bible's word is a 're-performing' of what God is doing through the word of Scripture in its original context. See Timothy Ward, *Words of Life: Scripture as the Living and Active Word of God*, IVP Academic, Downers Grove, 2009.

40 Martin Luther, 'The Freedom of a Christian', in J Dillenberger (ed.), *Martin Luther: Selections from his Writings*, Anchor Books, New York, 1962, pp. 54-5.

2. Prayerful dependence on the Spirit of God

We don't know of any church that uses 1 Peter 1:10-12 as its motto verse, which is not surprising given what a long, complicated sentence it is. But it's also a shame, because these verses have it all: the salvation plan of God announced by the prophets, its fulfilment in the sufferings and glories of the Christ, and the proclamation of all this in the gospel. Peter particularly emphasizes the initiative and work of God's Spirit throughout it all—"the Spirit of Christ" spoke through the prophets to predict "the sufferings of Christ and the subsequent glories" (v. 11) and "the Holy Spirit sent from heaven" spoke "through those who preached the good news to you" (v. 12).

As we've noted already more than once, God is the one who not only hatches the great plan of salvation in Christ, but sets it in motion, steps into creation himself to die and rise, and pours out his own Spirit to empower the spread of his word and to bring change and growth into our lives. God is the worker; we are his assistants and agents (as we'll see further below).

The New Testament characteristically speaks of this active work of God as the work of his Spirit, who is called variously "the Spirit of God",[41] "the Spirit of the Lord",[42] "the Spirit of your Father",[43] "the Spirit of his Son",[44] "the Spirit of Christ",[45] "the Holy Spirit",[46] or simply "the Spirit".[47] At every point in the making of Christ-learners, God is active by his Spirit:

- he speaks by his Spirit through the mouths of the biblical authors to give us his word[48]
- he regenerates and renews our hearts by his Spirit so that

---

41 1 Cor 2:11
42 Acts 5:9
43 Matt 10:20
44 Gal 4:6
45 Rom 8:9
46 Luke 11:13
47 Rom 8:5
48 Acts 1:16; 4:24-25

we grasp hold of his offer of salvation and are justified freely by his grace[49]

- he gives his Spirit to us as a guarantee of our future hope and citizenship in the kingdom of God[50]
- he transforms us by his Spirit, and brings forth the fruit of righteousness in our lives[51]
- he pours out his Spirit on the disciples to open their mouths to speak his word[52]
- he gives boldness by his Spirit for them to continue speaking his word[53]
- by his Spirit he is present with us, gifting and enabling us to speak the word in love to one another for mutual edification.[54]

We have only scratched the surface here in describing how vital (in every sense of that word) is the work of God's Spirit in making learners of Christ. When we speak the word—in whatever context or in whatever manner—we are like the sower of Jesus' parable.[55] We cannot control or determine what sort of soil the word falls into. Very often our words seem to bounce off the hard surface of people's foreheads, or penetrate only very slightly and temporarily into their hearts.

But when God's Spirit is present in our hearers to soften the heart, to open the eyes, to make the soil fertile, then the words we speak become for our hearer the words of eternal life. It was like this for the Thessalonians who received Paul's preaching "in the Holy Spirit and with full conviction"[56] and who thus recognized the words they were hearing "not as the word of men but as what it really is, the word of God, which is at work in you believers".[57] This in turn is why Paul so characteristically thanks *God* for the

---

49 Titus 3:4-7; John 3:1-8
50 Eph 1:11-14
51 2 Cor 3:17-18; Gal 5:16-24
52 Acts 2:6-11, 17-18
53 Acts 4:31
54 1 Cor 12-14
55 Mark 4:1-9
56 1 Thess 1:5
57 1 Thess 2:13

faith and love and hope that he sees in God's people, and keeps praying to *God* for an increase in their spiritual understanding, maturity and fruitfulness.[58]

This points to the key indicator for this conviction within our own lives and churches: our level of trust in this principle will be demonstrated by our constant dependent prayer for God to give the growth.[59] Prayerlessness, like Wordlessness, is a classic symptom of a sick disciple-making culture.

3. People are God's fellow workers

It seems too obvious to say that *God's people* are the agency by which the word is proclaimed in prayerful dependence on the Spirit. Who else is it going to be?

But it is important to clarify and sharpen what we mean by saying this,[60] because it will become very important in the evaluation and planning that is to come. Briefly then:

- The first two points (above) make it clear that 'making disciples' is God's work. It's his plan, his salvation, his grace, his word, and his Spirit. But God uses means or agents to do his work. In particular, he works through his people. It's not that God does some of the work, and then leaves the rest of it to us (or vice versa). God works sovereignly in, under and through our actions with his own action, to achieve his own purposes. In doing so, God doesn't violate our will, or render our action any less our action. When we do something (i.e. some 'planting and watering'), we are really doing something—but God works in and through that activity to bring growth in a way that we cannot control. It's 100% us, and 100% God.[61]

58 Colossians 1:3-5 and 9-12 provide one example of this common Pauline pattern.

59 1 Cor 3:6

60 So important, in fact, that we will come back to aspects of this in more detail in Conviction 5.

61 This way of expressing the interaction of human action and divine action is sometimes called 'compatibilism'. For a clear exposition and defence of this view see DA Carson, *How Long, O Lord? Reflections on Suffering and Evil*, 2nd edn, Baker Academic, Grand Rapids, 2006.

- This is important to grasp, because it saves us from proudly overvaluing our efforts. We are just slaves and nobodies, planting and watering, and praying for God to give growth.[62] However, it also saves us from undervaluing the importance of our efforts, as if faithfulness, diligence and skill in planting and watering are optional. We are *God's* fellow workers. If our work for him is careless or faithless then the results will not be good, either for us or for the church.[63]

- Which people does God use to make learners of Christ? God uses his covenant people, his congregation, his saints. There is a big biblical theology theme at work here that would be worth unpacking at length, had we the time and space. God chose Israel to be for him "a kingdom of priests and a holy nation",[64] a vocation at which they failed spectacularly. The prophets looked forward to a time when Israel *would* be a light to the nations,[65] and in the New Testament we see that day dawning. Christ's new covenant people are the holy nation, the royal priesthood, who declare the excellencies of God to the world.[66] They are a redeemed people, small and great, young and old, on whom the Messiah has poured out the long-promised Spirit so that they might prophesy and tell forth the great deeds of God.[67]

- The practical outworking of this important theme is that in the new age of the Spirit, *all* God's people have their mouths opened to speak God's word by his Spirit—to one another and to the world. They will do so in different ways, in different contexts, taking up different opportunities, with different levels of gift, and indeed different levels of responsibility (some will be pastors and teachers)—but that

---

62 This is Paul's point in 1 Corinthians 3:5-8.
63 This is what Paul goes on to say in 1 Corinthians 3:10-17.
64 Exod 19:6
65 Isa 42:6, 49:6, 60:3
66 1 Pet 2:9-10
67 Acts 2:11, 16-18

God's word would be proclaimed on the lips of all his new covenant people is a given in the New Testament.[68]

- This word is not only proclaimed by all; it is of course lived out and exemplified by all—and this too is how learners learn. As we noted in Conviction 2, 'learning Christ' is not an academic or theoretical discipline but a new way of life that seeks to keep the commandments of Christ. The theme of imitation, modelling and example as a means of learning and growth is a common one in the epistles. Paul not only regards himself as an example to learn from, but also sees the cycle of learning and imitation continuing among his readers.[69] The word is proclaimed by people who show its truth and character by living it out, thus instructing and encouraging others, who in turn embrace the word and live it out.

- As God's people prayerfully proclaim God's word by God's Spirit, the godly fruit that is produced in people's lives can be summarized as *love*.[70] Love is the new commandment that Christ-learners are learning. As we respond to the gospel, and pass from death to life, the new transformed life that we live has love as its characteristic virtue and motivation. Love drives us to think of others, to care for others, and to sacrifice our own interests for the sake of others. Love motivates us to reach out to others with the gospel, and to see church as an opportunity not just for personal growth but also for the up-building of those around us.[71] Love also shapes the *manner* of our speaking and encouraging and teaching of others— not overbearing, impatient or impersonal, but the kind of

---

68 This diversity-within-unity is the big idea of 1 Corinthians 12-14, which we will come back to in Conviction 4. We will also take some further space to assemble the evidence for this crucial principle, as well as explore how we should rightly understand the 'democratized' word ministry of all Christians with respect to the roles and responsibilities of pastors, elders and teachers.

69 Phil 3:17; 1 Thess 1:6-7; Titus 2:1-10. We will say more about this in Phase 2, when we discuss reforming our own personal culture.

70 Col 3:12-14

71 Again, this is the argument of 1 Corinthians 12-14. The famous chapter 13 on love drives the teaching in chapter 14—that is, because of love we will seek not our own interests, nor even our own edification, but the edification of those around us.

gracious, nourishing, encouraging teaching that parents give to their children.[72] And love compels us to persevere in laying down our lives and suffering whatever may come, for the sake of seeing people come to Christ and learn Christ. This takes us to the fourth aspect of how disciples are made.

4. Persevering, step by step

Does becoming a 'Christ-learner' take place in one momentous step, or in a series of incremental steps over time?

The answer is 'both', and it is very important to say so.

On one side, we must remember that being delivered from darkness and transferred into the kingdom of the Son is a mighty alien act of God. It blasts into our lives from outside, turning darkness into light, slavery into sonship, and death into life. These are not things that happen by degrees.[73] The salvation that God has won for us in Christ is already fully and completely achieved—and indeed the New Testament repeatedly warns against the insidious suggestion that we need to do something more to work our way towards salvation, through ritual acts or exalted experiences or legalistic law-keeping. This is the message both of Colossians (all the fullness of God is in Christ and you have been filled in him, so don't let anyone fool you) and of Galatians (you have been set free in Christ as a son, so don't let anyone enslave you again in law-keeping).

But the other side is also important to maintain. Although we have already been decisively raised with Christ and guaranteed an eternal inheritance with him, we nevertheless live out our new lives in the midst of this present darkness, like a colony of the

---

72 1 Thess 2:7-12

73 We must also be aware that this binary light-and-darkness view of the world is horribly offensive in Western culture, and will only be more so as our society becomes increasingly politically correct. However, if we don't retain a clear theology of conversion, we will give up calling unbelievers to repentance. We will end up treating everyone as if they are already in the light, or possibly in a civilized grey zone somewhere in the vicinity of light.

next age. We strive more and more to cast off what belongs to our former life (to "put to death the deeds of the body" as Paul puts it),[74] and to clothe ourselves in the new garments that befit our new self, which is being "renewed in knowledge after the image of its creator".[75]

The Christian life is lived in this sense of groaning, persevering anticipation. The victory is already won in Christ. We are already blameless and righteous and sanctified in his sight, washed clean, granted citizenship in heaven. And yet in faith and hope we seek more and more to live a life of love as we await the final consummation—the resurrection of the dead, when our struggle with the world, the flesh and the devil will finally be over.

Paul captures this beautifully in Philippians 3. Having affirmed in the strongest terms that his own works and law-keeping are all rubbish, and that righteousness comes only from trusting in Christ, he nevertheless speaks of 'straining forward' towards the goal:

> Not that I have already obtained this or am already perfect, but I press on to make it my own, because Christ Jesus has made me his own. Brothers, I do not consider that I have made it my own. But one thing I do: forgetting what lies behind and straining forward to what lies ahead, I press on toward the goal for the prize of the upward call of God in Christ Jesus. (Phil 3:12-14)

The Christian life happens in one enormous, momentous step from death to life; it also takes place step by step, as we learn to observe all of Christ's commandments, as the suffering we endure for Christ produces in us endurance, character and hope.[76] As we put it in Conviction 2, the kind of learning we are engaged in is *transformational*—both in a decisive, once-off transformation

---

74 Rom 8:13; cf. Col 3:5f

75 Col 3:10; the new clothes are described in the verses that follow, especially 12-14.

76 Rom 5:3-4. Just as underplaying the binary nature of conversion will diminish the call to repentance, so downplaying the persevering, transformational nature of Christian living tends to promote an unengaged, 'cheap grace', decisionist Christianity—I've punched my ticket to heaven; I can sit back now and smell the roses.

(from death to life), and in a day-to-day transformation by the constant renewing of our minds.[77]

We dwell on this point because it helps us to name an important aspect of the methodology by which disciples are made: *Christ-learners are 'made' patiently and perseveringly over time.* Disciple-making deals in the messy realities of weariness and faint-heartedness, and our constant struggle against sin.[78] It takes account of the reality that Christians will be at different stages in 'putting off and putting on'—some will be new to the faith, some weak, some stronger, some immature, some in relational conflict, some struggling with a particular temptation or desire, some threatened by a particular false teaching, and so on.

The New Testament itself demonstrates it. We could say confidently that the New Testament has a single unified Christ-centred message, but we could also affirm that it applies that message (particularly in the epistles) to a wide variety of problems, situations, challenges and issues. The New Testament is a discipling handbook for the multifaceted landscape in which we learn Christ—there isn't a circumstance or issue or struggle we encounter that it does not teach us about in some place or other.

This is also true of those who are outside the kingdom, who still live in the domain of darkness. At one level, the situation is binary. They are as totally lost and doomed as the Christ-learner is totally found and saved. And our message to unbelievers is always a single unified message (i.e. it is some aspect of the gospel). And yet unbelievers, too, will be at different stages of life, in different circumstances, with different objections and struggles and sins. Some will be very stubborn and hard of heart,[79] while others will be much closer to the kingdom;[80] some will be without God and without hope in the world,[81] while others will have all

---

77 Rom 12:1-2
78 Heb 12:3-4
79 Rom 2:5; Acts 19:9
80 Like the scribe in Mark 12:34.
81 Eph 2:12

the form of morality and religion but none of its true power.[82] We could modify our diagram again to represent all this:

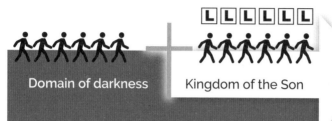

Rescued and transformed

Domain of darkness   Kingdom of the Son

Help those around you take a step to the right through the four Ps

A redeemed people gathered around the risen Christ

In other words:

- By the cross of Christ we are rescued out of the domain of darkness into the kingdom of the Son, and have an eternally secure inheritance in Christ that is already ours.
- Our daily 'walk' is now in the light rather than in the darkness, as we live out day by day who we really are (as citizens of Christ's kingdom). We are all at different points on that walk, and need to keep pressing on to what lies ahead. *The movement is always to the right,* as it were. Christ-learners are transformed as they grow to maturity in Christ.[83]
- Those who remain trapped in the domain of darkness are also at different points and have different issues. Some are 'far away' and hard of heart; others are 'closer', in that they are hearing the gospel and considering the gospel of Christ.
- Thus, the goal of every form of Christian ministry could be summarized simply as seeking to help each person, wherever

82 Matt 23:1-28; 2 Tim 3:5
83 We will come back to this 'moving to the right' image in Conviction 4, but we might as well get the standard joke out of the way at this point—that growth in Christ does not entail us becoming more politically right wing!

they happen to be, to take a step to the right—to come closer towards hearing the gospel and being transferred out of the domain of darkness into the kingdom; and then to press forward towards maturity in Christ in every aspect of their lives.

- The means by which God moves people to the right are: Proclamation, Prayerful dependence on the Spirit, People as his fellow workers, and Persevering in it, step by step.[84]

This has important implications for the methodology by which people become Christ-learners and grow as Christ-learners.

For a start, it's inevitably and enduringly *personal*. Each person has their own struggles. Each person lives at a different address in either the domain of darkness or the kingdom of light. Just as it is important to affirm how *corporate* church life is—we are united together in love as one body—it is just as important to say that the body is made up of many individually different members.

This is the constant risk with all systemic or programmatic approaches to Christ-learning—that we flatten out the process and treat everyone engaged in that program as being at the same point and requiring the same input. This is not a reason to forswear all attempts to organize ourselves or devise systems or run programs— that would be all but impossible in any case. In fact, in Phase 4 we will spend some considerable time and energy organizing ourselves. But as we do so, this is a risk to be managed and mitigated against. Our programs and activities should function to help each person press forward from the point where they are.

To borrow more education-speak, Christ-learning is *differentiated learning*. It meets each individual learner where they are, and seeks to move them forward. There are of course many things we learn all together and are encouraged in all together (especially in church each Sunday), but the personal implications and applications of these truths need to be talked through and prayed through with each person. So as the mythical Fred becomes a Christ-learner, he should have his or her own personal tutor or tutors—one or more people who actually know Fred and what his

---

84 In later chapters we will summarize this as '4P ministry'.

struggles are, who discern what teachings Fred hasn't grasped yet, who stick with him over months and years, who help him to stay strong, to keep making progress in godliness, to keep pressing and straining forward.

The archetypal Reformed pastor Richard Baxter was very strong on this. He insisted on the necessity of the 'personal conference' alongside public preaching. In his view, a pastor who did not combine his sermons with regular personal instruction or catechization of his flock was neglecting a vital duty.[85]

We would push Baxter's point a little further (in light of what we have seen above) and say that this particularly connects with the role of all God's people in proclaiming the word of God to others. Not many of us will be public preachers in pulpits, and not many of us will be public evangelists in the marketplace, but all of us can be 'private tutors' to the multitude of individual people (Christian and non-Christian) we know and interact with day by day—in our families, in our workplaces, in our neighbourhoods, in small groups of Christian disciples, and so on.

We will talk more about the relationship between public preaching and the word ministry of all God's people in the two convictions that follow, but for now let us just notice one of the liberating side benefits in thinking in this way about the persevering, step-by-step nature of Christian growth (and thus of Christian ministry).

If the goal of Christian ministry can be envisaged simply as helping any individual person we know to take one step to the right (towards Christ or towards maturity in Christ), then this is a task that each and every Christian can embrace with confidence. If we call upon the average church member to take up arms as a gospel minister or a disciple-maker or an evangelist, then (rightly or wrongly) many will feel sufficiently threatened to run in the opposite direction. But what if we were to say the following instead? "Why don't you pray for the person next to you (wherever that might be), and see if by your word and example you can encourage

---

85 See Richard Baxter, *The Reformed Pastor*, 5th edn, Banner of Truth, London, 1974, pp. 174-6, 196.

them to take one step—even one small step—to the right?"

This is far more concrete, more immediate and more achievable for the average person. With confidence that God will work through his word and Spirit, even slowly and gradually over time, we can all do our part in helping everyone around us take a step forward in Christ.

Mobilizing our efforts to train and equip as many of our members for this sort of ministry is a key step in creating a new culture of Christ-learning in our midst.

DISCUSSION

1. We've used four Ps to summarize the means God gives us for making disciples. See if you can come up with your own simple way to communicate it. For example, try to craft a summary by using:

   a. four Ss
   b. the letters of the word SPUR
   c. anything else you can come up with.

2. All diagrams are inadequate in some way. See if you can find any ways of improving or tweaking the diagram so that it does a better job of communicating the essence of Christian ministry:

Rescued and transformed

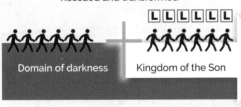

Help those around you take a step to the right through the four Ps

A redeemed people gathered around the risen Christ

3. Take one of the following shortish New Testament epistles, and read through it asking the following question: *By what means or in what manner does this letter say that people become Christians and grow as Christians?* Note down everything you find, and use it to support or modify or improve our argument above about how disciples are made.

Ephesians   1 Timothy
Philippians   Titus
Colossians   1 Peter
1 Thessalonians

4. Think of someone you know who is finding life hard in this fallen world, and pray about what you could do to help them 'take a step to the right' toward Christ. How could you demonstrate your love for them? What story could you tell from your life that would point them to Christ? What could you say to them about the truth of Christ? What Scripture passage could you share with them (in person, by email, by card)? What might stop you from taking any action?

Conviction 4: Who makes disciples?

So far we've looked at what a disciple really is, why 'making' them is so important, and what methods or means God has given us to do so.

In this fourth conviction, we want to zoom in on one aspect of the 'how' of disciple-making—namely, *which people exactly* are involved in the task, and how we are to understand their different roles and gifts.

We've already discussed this briefly in Conviction 3, where we argued that *God's people* are his agents in prayerfully and perseveringly proclaiming the word. Moreover, we suggested that it wasn't just the most committed of God's people, or an elite class of God's people, but *all* of God's people who are granted the joy and privilege of 'making disciples'. To take it back to Matthew 28, the commission to make disciples is a commission for all disciples.[1]

---

1 Having said this, it is also important that we preserve the unique place of the eleven disciples (or 'apostles') in God's disciple-making purposes. They are the ones who received the commission in the first instance to call all people to obey what Jesus had taught them. In God's providence, it is in the apostles' written word that we find the teaching of Jesus. This apostolic gospel, enshrined in Scripture, is our link to Jesus' word and his mission. We become disciples by hearing and obeying Jesus' teaching, mediated to us through these specially commissioned apostles. As disciple-makers we simply repeat the apostles' teaching over and over again.

In discussing this issue with many pastors around the world over the past several years, a few key points or questions came up repeatedly.

- Firstly, it was hard to find anyone who disagreed in principle with the idea that disciple-making was for all disciples. In fact, for most pastors, this is the dream—somehow to persuade the bulk of their congregation members that the work of ministry, whether in reaching out to unbelievers or edifying believers, is something for *all of us* to be involved in. Pastors also frequently reported that many of their regular mature members took the same view: that the work of the church is a team sport, and we should all do our best to 'get involved' rather than just be passengers, even if their actual success in achieving or mobilizing that involvement was patchy.

- However, in a vast number of places, 'getting involved' consisted mostly of some kind of administrative or practical help—being on a roster, organizing or running something, helping with property or other practical tasks, and so on. In other words, in many churches that we spoke with, 'every member ministry' was a common and accepted concept, so long as 'ministry' was defined as any general act of service or help rendered for the sake of the church—rather than as something that might look like the four Ps (of Proclamation, Prayer, People and Perseverance).

- This is where it got a little sharper, and where many pastors wanted to talk more—not only to interrogate the biblical evidence for equipping potentially every member as a speaker of the word of God, but to understand what that might *look like in practice*. What would a church culture be like in which a growing number of the members saw themselves as prayerful speakers of the word to those around them? And what might motivate and equip more of the congregation to dive in and have a go at helping others to learn Christ?

- This led to the other common (and important) question: if it is granted that all of us are engaged in the four Ps together, what of diversity and the doctrine of gifts? What about those who just don't seem remotely ready or capable of speaking the word of God? And how should we understand the task and responsibility of pastors, elders and teachers? In particular, does promoting a more widespread word ministry throughout the congregation in some way devalue or undermine the important place of expository preaching from the pulpit?

In this fourth conviction, we will look at these important questions under four headings:

- What the Bible says about all Christians speaking the word
- What does it look like in practice?
- Overcoming inhibitions
- The expository pulpit and the expository church

What the Bible says about all Christians speaking the word

When we turn to the Bible to direct and shape what we do, we find that God speaks to us in a variety of ways—such as by direct instruction and command, by narrative example and illustration, by proverbial wisdom, or by a principle that teaches us about the nature of things or our place in God's purposes (and thus what sort of action is desirable or required).

For example, if someone were to ask us to justify why the Bible regards adultery as being wrong, we would say: because of the seventh commandment; because of the multiple examples of the evil and destruction that adultery brings (e.g. David and Bathsheba); because of the wisdom literature's frequent pithy warnings on the subject; and also because adultery offends against the Bible's overall teaching about the good of marriage, sexuality and relationships.

Much the same is true of what the Bible says about the nature and purpose of Christian speech, and in particular the 'edifying' speech we engage in for the purpose of seeing others come to know Christ and be built up in him. It's not a matter simply of a few proof texts or commands (although we'll come to those). It fits into the larger picture of God's purposes for us as 'speakers'.

At the most basic level, God gave us mouths with which to speak because he created us as personal beings who are able to express thoughts and intentions and promises to one another (and to the personal God who made us). Words allow us to do things in relationship with others that we couldn't otherwise do—to thank, to ask, to comfort, to confess, to forgive, to celebrate, to praise, to mourn, to inform, to teach, and so on. Words reveal the heart.[2] Words are the currency of relationship.

Of course, our capacity for speech (like every created part of us) is corrupted and distorted by our sin and rebellion against God. We do evil with our speech, both in rejecting God and in harming others—we blaspheme, lie, curse, hate, deceive, manipulate, flatter, slander, pour forth obscenity, and much else besides.[3]

Correspondingly, our speech (like every aspect of our lives) is transformed by the saving work of God. By the work of God's Spirit, we are set free to confess that Jesus is Lord, to praise his name, to give voice to our faith in prayer and thanksgiving, and to bring life and encouragement to others through what we say to them.[4]

In his little book on gospel speech, Lionel Windsor points out that this is a common pattern in the Bible. God not only gives sinners the gift of salvation, but also "puts a speech or song in their mouths, and tells them to speak over and over again about how amazing his salvation really is".[5]

The most pointed example of this is prophecy. When God's Spirit comes upon someone in the Old Testament, what normally

---

2   "The good person out of the good treasure of his heart produces good, and the evil person out of his evil treasure produces evil, for out of the abundance of the heart his mouth speaks" (Luke 6:45).

3   In his catalogue of human sin in Romans 3, Paul tellingly quotes the psalms: "Their throat is an open grave; they use their tongues to deceive. The venom of asps is under their lips. Their mouth is full of curses and bitterness" (Rom 3:13-14).

4   1 Cor 12:3; Rom 10:9-10; Heb 13:15; Eph 6:18, 5:18-20

5   Lionel Windsor, *Gospel Speech: A Fresh Look at the Relationship between Every Christian and Evangelism*, Matthias Media, Sydney, 2015, p. 24. Windsor especially draws attention to Deuteronomy 32, Isaiah 59 and Psalm 51 as examples of this common movement or pattern.

happens next is that they prophesy—that they speak forth the word that God has given them to say.[6] In Numbers 11, Moses expresses the wish that God would do this not just for the 70 elders but for all of his people: "Would that all the LORD's people were prophets, that the LORD would put his Spirit on them!"[7]

What Moses says here, almost in exasperation, prefigures a hope that would become more urgent as the sorry history of Israel unfolds—namely, that when the time finally came for God to redeem and renew wayward Israel, he would pour out his life-giving, prophecy-generating Spirit not just upon some select leaders or representatives, but upon *all of them*, from the smallest to the greatest.

This of course is the promise that Peter quotes to explain to the crowd the extraordinary events of Pentecost, where people from all over the world were hearing the Spirit-filled disciples "telling in our own tongues the mighty works of God".[8] This democratized outpouring of Spirit-filled speech, says Peter, is only what was foretold:

> "But this is what was uttered through the prophet Joel:
>
> "'And in the last days it shall be, God declares,
> that I will pour out my Spirit on all flesh,
> and your sons and your daughters shall prophesy,
>   and your young men shall see visions,
>   and your old men shall dream dreams;
> even on my male servants and female servants
>   in those days I will pour out my Spirit, and
>   they shall prophesy.'" (Acts 2:16-18,
>   quoting Joel 2:28-29)

Three sometimes overlooked points are worth noting here:

- First, it was the whole company, and not just Peter or the eleven, who were "filled with the Holy Spirit and began to

---

6 E.g. Num 11:25; 1 Sam 10:10; 1 Chr 12:18; 2 Chr 24:20
7 Num 11:29
8 Acts 2:11

speak in other tongues as the Spirit gave them utterance".[9]

- Second, the passage draws an equivalence between telling out "the mighty works of God" (v. 11) and the democratized prophecy promised by Joel.[10]
- Third, the outpouring of the Spirit and its effects are sure evidence that the crucified and risen Jesus is indeed both Lord and Christ, Messiah.[11]

The age of the Messiah has dawned, in which the Spirit is poured out on all his people, and the clear evidence of this (according to Peter) is the extraordinary phenomenon they are witnessing—the outbreak of prophecy on the lips of all God's people.

In other words, the remarkable events at Pentecost indicate that a new state of affairs is now in place. Those who repent and put their faith in Jesus the Christ will all be filled with the promised Holy Spirit (as Peter affirms to the crowd at the end of his sermon).[12] This would lead us to expect a corresponding flowering of Spirit-inspired utterance among God's people—and this is indeed what we see unfolding in the rest of the New Testament. In Acts and in the epistles we see a flourishing of gospel-driven, Spirit-empowered speech not just via the apostles and evangelists and pastors and elders, but in the mouths of believers generally.

Here is a selection of the evidence, either as examples of this kind of speech taking place, or as apostolic commands for it to take place.

---

9   Acts 2:1-4; this fact has not always been noticed in the midst of debate about the nature of speaking in tongues. That *all* of them received the Spirit was in sharp contrast to the experience of Israel in the age before the Messiah, where the Spirit had been poured out only on chosen prophets and intermittently on kings and others.

10 That is, Peter explains what is happening in verse 11 by saying that this is what the prophet Joel said would happen when the Spirit was poured out—that God's people would prophesy.

11 This is the climactic point of Peter's sermon: "Being therefore exalted at the right hand of God, and having received from the Father the promise of the Holy Spirit, he has poured out this that you yourselves are seeing and hearing... Let all the house of Israel therefore know for certain that God has made him both Lord and Christ, this Jesus whom you crucified" (Acts 2:33, 36).

12 Acts 2:38-39

- In Acts 4:31, the disciples who were meeting with Peter and John prayed for an increase in boldness to speak the word, with the result that "the place in which they were gathered together was shaken, and *they were all filled with the Holy Spirit and continued to speak the word of God with boldness*". As at Pentecost, the filling of the Spirit empowers the whole group to speak boldly and openly.

- When the church is scattered throughout Judea and Samaria in Acts 8, the apostles stay in Jerusalem but "those who were scattered went about preaching the word".[13] Philip is the example provided, a man "of good repute, full of the Spirit and of wisdom", who had been given the duty in Acts 6 of distributing food.[14] Philip's designated role in the church may have been focused on practicalities but he cannot stop proclaiming Christ, both publicly in Samaria[15] and privately in the chariot of the Ethiopian eunuch.[16] Interestingly, like Peter in Acts 2, the Spirit-filled Philip expounds the truth of Christ through the Spirit-inspired Scriptures.[17]

- Paul looks forward to visiting the Romans so that "we may be mutually encouraged by each other's faith, both yours and mine".[18] Later in the epistle he again affirms their competence for mutual instruction: "I myself am satisfied about you, my brothers, that you yourselves are full of goodness, filled with all knowledge and able to instruct one another".[19]

- The argument of the extended passage in 1 Corinthians 12-14 is essentially this: that by our common baptism in the Spirit, we are all members of one body, and should seek the common good through the diversity of our gifts; in fact, because of the driving importance of love (in chapter 13), all Christians should seek one kind of gift in particular—to

13 Acts 8:4
14 Acts 6:2-6
15 Acts 8:4-6
16 Acts 8:26-35
17 Acts 8:35; cf. Acts 2:16, 25, 34
18 Rom 1:11-12
19 Rom 15:14

speak intelligible words from God (i.e. prophecy) that build up those around them. Perhaps the summary verse is this: "What then, brothers? When you come together, each one has a hymn, a lesson, a revelation, a tongue, or an interpretation. Let all things be done for building up".[20] The whole section assumes that a rich, Spirit-filled, diverse, unified and orderly speaking of the word of God, motivated and regulated by love, is the norm for Christian fellowship.

- In Ephesians 4, however we might understand the "work of ministry" for which the saints are to be equipped (v. 12), the outcome is communal *speech*—that "speaking the truth in love, we are to grow up in every way into him who is the head, into Christ, from whom the whole body, joined and held together by every joint with which it is equipped, when each part is working properly, makes the body grow so that it builds itself up in love".[21]

- In Ephesians, as in 1 Corinthians, it is love that describes both the motivation and manner of the speaking. This points to an important truth—that the more Christians grow in Christlike love, the more they will seek to do good to others by the words they speak. Or to put it in terms of the language we have been using: the more that Christ-learners move 'to the right', the more they will want to speak the word to those on their left (whether younger or less mature Christians, or unbelievers).

- In Colossians, Paul summarizes his own ministry as proclaiming Christ, "warning everyone and teaching everyone with all wisdom".[22] Later in the letter he uses similar terms to urge the Colossians to do much the same: "Let the word (Greek: *logos*) of Christ dwell in you richly, teaching and admonishing one another in all wisdom, singing psalms and

---

20 1 Cor 14:26

21 Eph 4:15-16. Also see later in the chapter: "Let no corrupting talk come out of your mouths, but only such as is good for building up, as fits the occasion, that it may give grace to those who hear" (Eph 4:29).

22 Col 1:28

hymns and spiritual songs, with thankfulness in your hearts to God".[23] Paul subsequently asks the Colossians to pray that God would open a door for him to preach the word (*logos*), and then urges them to make their word (*logos*) to outsiders gracious, seasoned with salt, and suitable for answering everyone.[24] Again, the picture is of a variety of ministries based on the one word of Christ (teaching, admonishing, singing, preaching, speaking, answering), conducted both by the apostle and by the Christian brethren he is writing to.

- Then there are the straightforward commands of 1 Thessalonians—"encourage one another with these words";[25] "encourage one another and build one another up, just as you are doing";[26] "we urge you, brothers, admonish the idle, encourage the fainthearted, help the weak".[27] Or the similarly direct instructions in Hebrews—"exhort one another every day, as long as it is called 'today', that none of you may be hardened by the deceitfulness of sin";[28] "let us consider how to stir up one another to love and good works, not neglecting to meet together, as is the habit of some, but encouraging one another, and all the more as you see the Day drawing near".[29]

The sweep of the Bible's teaching on this subject culminates in the book of Revelation, where God's redeemed people gather round his throne, crying out and singing and speaking forth his praises. It's as if perfected humanity in Christ has only one word left to say:

> After this I looked, and behold, a great multitude that no-one could number, from every nation, from all tribes and peoples and languages, standing before the throne and before the Lamb, clothed in white robes, with palm

23 Col 3:16
24 Col 4:2-6
25 1 Thess 4:18
26 1 Thess 5:11
27 1 Thess 5:14
28 Heb 3:13
29 Heb 10:24-25

branches in their hands, and crying out with a loud voice, "Salvation belongs to our God who sits on the throne, and to the Lamb!" (Rev 7:9-10)

There is ample and strong evidence, in other words, that speaking the word of God to others for their salvation and encouragement is an expected and necessary component of the normal Christian life. Correspondingly, a healthy church culture is one in which a wide variety of word ministries are exercised by a constantly growing proportion of the membership.

What does it look like in practice?

We would be surprised if the biblical evidence we have just outlined would be hotly contested by many of our readers. However, it is one to thing to stand and salute these convictions; it is quite another to fall into step and march behind them into battle.

For many pastors we have spoken to, one significant issue is that (for whatever historical, traditional or local reasons) a culture of widespread and wide-ranging lay word ministry is simply outside their experience. They aren't sure what it *looks like* or how it might fit into the patterns of ministry and church life they are used to. And they aren't sure whether it would *work* where they are, with the people they have.

Let us try to clarify, then, some aspects of what democratized proclamation looks like in practice.

- Firstly, one thing it *doesn't* look like—and that is an unregulated, chaotic outbreak of ignorant, false or foolish teaching, with every man and his dog setting up his own 'pulpit' (as it were) to spread his or her own particular take on doctrine. Indeed, alongside the many examples above of Christians being urged to speak in the New Testament, we could also have looked at numerous other texts in which Christians are commanded *not* to speak (such as to spread division or false teaching, or to dispute about foolish or inconsequential matters).[30] It's very important that the word we all speak is the one, true word of Christ, and that we do so in a manner that builds others up (as opposed to satisfying our pride or desire for self-expression). (We'll say more on this in the material below on the relationship between pastoral leadership and every member word ministry.)

- As we noted in Conviction 3, 'proclamation' of the word of Christ comes in many forms.[31] It is grounded in and fed by the Bible, and it very often happens with the Bible open, but not in every circumstance. It can happen in the car as we talk with our children, after church as we chat with someone about the content of the sermon, over the back fence as we talk with a neighbour about the gospel, in a one-to-one Bible reading meeting with a friend over coffee, in an article that we share and discuss on Facebook, in a small group Bible study as we thoughtfully explore and explain the Bible text with each other, and so on. The number and variety of possible 'word ministries' are almost limitless, but what they will all have in common is some facet or other of the biblical word about Jesus Christ.

- All the same, most Christians will find that by ability, training or opportunity, they gravitate to some forms of speech more than others. Some will be expert encouragers by letter; others will have a gift for striking up conversations with strangers; some will have the patience and kindness to sit with a troubled soul for hours and offer wise and sensitive words of comfort; others will have the skill to lead groups of people in Bible reading and prayer. This is not a matter of inward examination to discover our 'gift' so much as what we learn about ourselves over time as we respond to the opportunities and needs that God puts in front of us.

---

30 Titus 1:10-11 and 3:9-11 offer two of many such warnings.

31 In this connection, our summary word 'proclamation' has its limitations. It connotes in English a formal prepared speech or announcement in some kind of public setting. Some of the immensely variegated speaking of the word that Christians will engage in will be like this, but by no means all or even most.

- This is how the diversity of gifts and the unity of proclamation fit together (or how 1 Corinthians 12 and 1 Corinthians 14 fit together). The motivation is the same, the source is the same, the means are the same, and the end goal is the same. What varies is the particular manner and occasion in which we speak or exemplify the word of God.
- The home is a particularly important sphere in which 'every Christian word ministry' can and should flourish—between husbands and wives, between parents (and grandparents!) and children, between siblings. Titus 2:1-10 paints a delightful picture of the gospel-shaped household, in which the sound doctrine of the gospel is being lived out and exemplified and taught between the older men and women and the younger.[32]
- Thought of in these ways, there may well be more prayerful speaking of God's word happening in and around your congregational life than you first thought. This is worth identifying and building on! (And we'll talk in more detail about how this can be done in Phase 4.) The first step may well be a clear, persuasive teaching of the sorts of disciple-making convictions we've been exploring in Phase 1 so that what is already happening, even embryonically, can be named, framed, understood, promoted and expanded.

Overcoming inhibitions

There may be more 'every member word ministry' happening in nooks and crannies around our congregations than we think, and we rejoice when we hear about it. However, it's also fair to say the majority of people in our churches don't see it as a normal part of their Christian lives to be prayerfully speaking the word to someone else for their growth. It's just not part of their expectation,

---

32 See the addendum at the end of Conviction 5 for more on the home as a sphere for ministry.

or 'personal culture'—and so it is not part of our church culture. When there is a 'silent majority' (so to speak) in a congregation, it is difficult to change 'the way we do things around here' to include a wide-ranging, varied speaking of the word. People can see by looking around them that there is no expectation that this should happen, and no example that they can notice and follow.

As we've talked with many pastors about this, and indeed trained many lay people in speaking the word, the problem is rarely theoretical. Not many people push back against the convictions that we've been outlining. Very few want to deny that everyday Christians have a role in speaking the word, and given the biblical evidence this is not surprising.

The two biggest barriers are simply a personal reluctance or embarrassment to speak, and feelings of inadequacy and lack of confidence in knowing where to start. Let's look briefly at how to address both of these.

a. Addressing motivation

Although speaking the word of God is a unique and spiritual activity, it is like other human speech in the sense that when something is really important to us, we can't help but speak about it to the people we love.

This is essentially why we don't speak the word of God more to the people around us. We don't value the word enough, and we don't love people enough. It's a heart problem—our hearts are not sufficiently fired by the wonder of God's mercies and the majesty of Jesus Christ; and our hearts are not sufficiently full of love and compassion for those around us.[33]

---

33 Dietrich Bonhoeffer puts it like this: "It is inconceivable that the things that are of utmost importance to each individual should not be spoken by one to another. It is unchristian consciously to deprive another of the one decisive service we can render to him. If we cannot bring ourselves to utter it, we shall have to ask ourselves whether we are not still seeing our brother garbed in his human dignity which we are afraid to touch, and thus forgetting the most important thing, that he, too, no matter how old or highly placed or distinguished he may be, is still a man like us, a sinner in crying need of God's grace. He has the same great necessities that we have, and needs help, encouragement, and forgiveness as we do" (*Life Together*, trans. John W Doberstein [1954], SCM, London, 2015, pp. 80-85).

So here's a question, which (by now, if not before) you should quickly be able to answer: *How can a loveless human heart be transformed?*

Answer: by the power of the word and Spirit of God, ministered in prayerful persevering proclamation by his people! We need to teach and pray that the eyes of our people's hearts will be enlightened to grasp the hope to which he has called us, and the riches of his glorious inheritance in the saints, and the immeasurable greatness of his power toward us who believe.[34] And we need to teach and pray that the Lord would cause our people to "increase and abound in love for another and for all".[35]

In other words, learning to treasure the glories of God's grace and to love those around us is simply part of growing as a 'learner of Christ', and takes place as all Christ-learning does: through prayerful teaching that happens in a variety of ways, of which the Sunday sermon is the centre and flagship.

In practice, this might mean preaching a series (say) on 1 Peter and explaining the classic Reformation doctrine of 'the priesthood of all believers' from 2:1-10. In Christ we are all members of a "holy priesthood", which means not only that we *all* have access to God through Christ, but that we *all* offer spiritual sacrifices to God in him (as priests do).[36] And one of these priestly services is proclamation—to "proclaim the excellencies of him who called you out of darkness into his marvellous light".[37]

Or we might expound 1 Peter 4:7-11 and teach that love for one another should drive us to mutual service of all kinds, including speaking to others as if speaking the "oracles of God".[38]

However, diagnosing and treating the heart needs to happen

---

34 Eph 1:18-19

35 1 Thess 3:12

36 1 Pet 2:4-5

37 1 Pet 2:9

38 1 Pet 4:11. Sometimes we use the doctrine of gifts to disable rather than enable. So we read this passage as a justification for *not* speaking, by concluding (perhaps with relief) that "I have the gift of service, not speaking". But the logic of the passage is that love will drive us to service of all kinds, including speaking, and that we will do so "by the strength that God supplies—in order that in everything God may be glorified through Jesus Christ".

personally and individually as well as corporately. Within the various smaller ministry 'trellises' of church life (in groups and one-to-one meetings and the like) we will also need to teach and pray to this end.

b. Addressing lack of confidence

The other significant inhibition to address is the sense of inadequacy or lack of confidence that many Christians feel in speaking to others. We can do two main things to address this:

- The first is to lower people's sights from the scary things they might *think* you mean by 'word ministry' (e.g. walking up to strangers and evangelizing them, or leading a Bible study group, or preaching a sermon) to where they might need to start with word ministry in helping someone close to them take one step to the right (e.g. a husband and wife reading the Bible together for 15 minutes once a week). We need to keep teaching and exemplifying the fact that 'speaking the word of God' happens in a multitude of forms and contexts, and that each of us will have particular strengths and opportunities for doing so.

- The second step is to build people's confidence in simple and varied ministries through teaching, example, encouragement and training (e.g. by utilizing some simple training courses or frameworks).[39] Persuading, teaching and equipping everyday Christians to prayerfully speak the word of God looks like any other area of Christian living and godliness in which we 'learn Christ', such as learning to pray or learning patience or learning to be content. People will be at different points and will have different challenges. Some will be a long way back or have given up; some will

---

39 To give two simple examples: a) You could make it a goal to teach as many couples as possible how to read the Bible with one another, using *One-to-One Bible Reading*; b) You could make it a goal to teach as many members as possible the basic elements of the 'ministry of the pew' on Sunday, using a resource like *Six Steps to Loving Your Church* (Matthias Media, Sydney, 2013).

have made a start; some will be well on their way. Like everything else, it is a matter of helping each person take one step to the right from where they are, through patient teaching, instruction and prayer.

We will give more practical suggestions about making progress in these areas in both Phase 2 and Phase 4. But before we conclude, we need to explore the relationship between the few and the many.

The expository pulpit and the expository church

In his fine book on the Bible's theology of the 'word' and its relationship to preaching, Peter Adam comments that:

> ...while preaching... is one form of the ministry of the Word, many other forms are reflected in the Bible and in contemporary Christian church life. It is important to grasp this point clearly, or we shall try and make preaching carry a load which it cannot bear; that is, the burden of doing all that the Bible expects of every form of ministry of the Word.[40]

If we acknowledge there are varying forms of the ministry of the word, how are we to understand the relationship between them—and especially between the formal, regular, authoritative, recognized form of that ministry (the preaching and teaching undertaken by the pastor of a congregation), and the informal, often temporary, frequently unrecognized and less globally

---

40 Peter Adam, *Speaking God's Words*, p. 59. In his recent book on preaching, Timothy Keller agrees with Adam's analysis and classifies the variegated word ministries into three levels—with the sermon as 'level 1', informal personal encouragement and counselling as 'level 3', and an intermediate semi-formal form of speaking ministry (like leading a Bible study) as 'level 2'. This is an interesting and potentially useful taxonomy, so long as we recognize the blurred boundaries that will exist particularly between levels 2 and 3. See Timothy Keller, *Preaching: Communicating Faith in an Age of Skepticism*, Hachette, London, 2015.

authoritative forms of word ministry that congregation members will undertake?

The first thing to say is that this not a zero-sum game. Simply by saying that 'every member word ministry' is important, we do not automatically devalue or diminish the importance of pastoral preaching, as if there is only so much value to go around. Conversely, if we uphold the centrality and irreplaceability of the expository sermon (as we do, alongside both Adam and Keller), we do not thereby consign the word ministry of all Christians to the outer darkness (far from it).

In our view, the word ministry of pastoral leadership (especially in expository preaching) takes on an even greater importance when it is seen in relation to a flourishing 'every member word ministry'. For the sermon is not just one word ministry among many; it is the foundational word ministry that feeds and regulates and builds all the others. In a church where the four Ps are being widely practised by many believers across the congregation, the sermon is an occasion not just where one man speaks, but where he teaches a multitude to speak. In his preaching, a pastor sounds the tuning fork so that the whole orchestra knows in what key to play. He teaches and guards the sound deposit of the gospel so that all may know it clearly and thoroughly (for how else will they speak it?). He shows them not only what the Bible says, but how they can read and speak that truth for themselves. He constantly teaches the sound doctrinal framework that shapes the Bible reading and speaking of the whole congregation.

Pastors are 'learners-in-chief', who serve as examples, guides, shepherds, teachers and equippers of the other learners over whom they have oversight. The Sunday sermon is the weekly flagship event that encapsulates that service. It is of course not the only thing the pastor does, but its importance is fundamental.

We are saying that an expository pulpit is hugely important, because it anchors and builds an expository church—that is, a church in which every aspect of the congregational life is centred on the speaking of the Bible's message concerning Jesus Christ. We could represent it like this:

THE EXPOSITORY CHURCH

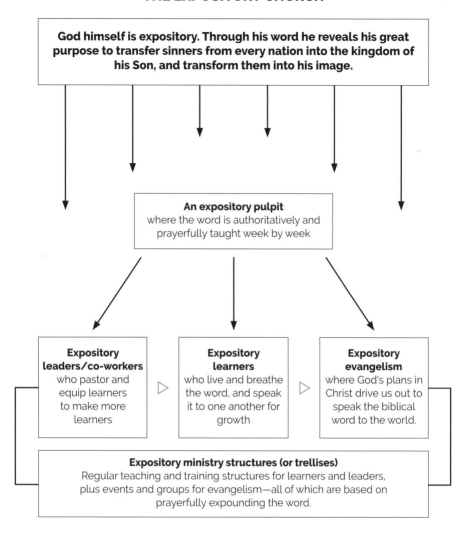

God himself is expository. Through his word he reveals his great purpose to transfer sinners from every nation into the kingdom of his Son, and transform them into his image.

An expository pulpit
where the word is authoritatively and prayerfully taught week by week

Expository leaders/co-workers
who pastor and equip learners to make more learners

Expository learners
who live and breathe the word, and speak it to one another for growth

Expository evangelism
where God's plans in Christ drive us out to speak the biblical word to the world.

Expository ministry structures (or trellises)
Regular teaching and training structures for learners and leaders, plus events and groups for evangelism—all of which are based on prayerfully expounding the word.

In other words, we could answer the question 'Who makes disciples?' as follows: *By their preaching, training and example, pastors equip every Christian to be a Christ-learner who helps others to learn Christ.*

There is more to be said about the practical issues raised by this conviction, and there will be time for that in due course (especially in Phases 3 and 4).

For now, however, let us finish with these words from New Testament scholar Claire Smith. In the conclusion to her rigorous study of Paul's churches as learning communities, she proposes that:

> ...the model of education that emerged was a 'community' model rather than a 'schooling' model. The goal of the latter in the modern era, is standardized outcomes of attainment, where students do their own work, and there is a clear distinction between teachers and students. The goal of the former is a 'common life', where each member is involved in teaching and learning, the less experienced use the more experienced as resources and guides, and the community is formed as the members learn shared beliefs and values, and these individuals form the community.[41]

This is the kind of transformational learning community that we have been seeking to describe from Scripture, and which *The Vine Project* aims to help you build.

DISCUSSION

1. Look closely at the 'Expository Church' diagram:
   a. What do you appreciate about it?
   b. Where do you think it could be improved or modified?
   c. Do you think it currently describes your church? Why/ why not?

2. What are the main reasons (do you think) that many people in our churches are not engaged in speaking the word to others in the church, home or community?

---

41 Claire Smith, *Pauline Communities as 'Scholastic Communities': A Study of the Vocabulary of 'Teaching' in 1 Corinthians, 1 and 2 Timothy and Titus*, WUNT 2.335, Mohr Siebeck, Tübingen, 2012, p. 386.

3. Look at a selection of the following texts (some of which are mentioned above):

1 Thessalonians 5:11-14   Titus 1:7-9, 2:1-10
Hebrews 13:7-15   Ephesians 4:11-29
1 Peter 2:9-12   Colossians 3:12-17
1 Peter 4:7-11

   a. What do you learn in each one about the nature of speaking the word, and the different forms it takes?
   b. What various reasons or motivations are given for all learners of Christ to be speaking the word to others?

Conviction 5: Where to make disciples

Of our five convictions about discipleship and disciple-making, this final one may seem a little strange, or even unnecessary. The other four convictions answer obviously important questions: why we should make disciples, what a disciple actually is, how we go about it, and who does the work.

However, this final conviction concerns the *field* in which disciple-making takes place—the *where* of recruiting and teaching 'learners' of Christ.

This is more important than we might think. In our experience, one of the barriers to a thoroughgoing disciple-making culture in many churches is a misunderstanding of where disciple-making should happen. For many churches, making disciples has two main locations.

Firstly, the default understanding in many churches is that discipleship takes place in a private location. Discipling is usually seen as personal, intimate work. It happens in one-to-one meetings, in coffee shops, in long walks where we talk about our Christian lives, or perhaps in small groups that meet in people's homes. For many people, 'discipling' is often particularly associated with spending time with new believers to ground them in the basics of the faith. Accordingly, if we wanted to improve 'discipleship' or 'discipling' in our church, we would mainly be thinking about places or contexts *outside* of our regular Sunday church gathering. Again, there's an unstated assumption at work here—one that needs to be examined and interrogated—about *where* (that is, in what contexts, locations, events and activities) discipling or disciple-making should take place.

Secondly, when it comes to the challenge of 'making disciples of all nations' it's very common for this to be viewed mainly as a missionary enterprise that should be taking place 'in the nations'— that is, in an overseas location somewhere. For many churches, a Great Commission commitment means having a missions budget, supporting overseas mission agencies, praying for missionaries, and so on. The often unstated assumption here is that the 'nations' (that is, the people over there in other countries) need to hear the gospel and become disciples of Jesus, but that somehow our own location—our street or suburb or community—is less of a concern.

So where should disciple-making happen?

Even though the answer to this question is in many ways implicit in what we have already looked at in the previous convictions, it's worth taking some time to clarify and sharpen our understanding.

The learning church

Put simply, 'learning Christ' happens wherever the word and Spirit of God are at work over time through people—because that is how 'learning' Christ takes place (as we saw in Conviction 3). It happens at the very beginning of our Christian lives as we are delivered from darkness into light, and as we learn the foundations of the faith; and it continues to happen as we grow and are transformed towards maturity in Christ.

This means that 'discipling' can and should happen in any and every sphere of our lives:

- when we preach the gospel and the word of God to ourselves—which is really what we're doing when we prayerfully read and mull over the Scriptures on our own
- when we meet with one or two other people (formally or informally) and prayerfully speak the word of God to each other—when we read the Bible together with our spouse or our child, or we share a Bible word (or hear one) from a workmate or neighbour, or we chat with someone over coffee after church and talk about the word of God we have heard
- when we gather in a small group to read and study and speak the word of the Bible with each other and to pray
- when we gather in a larger group to hear the word of God taught and explained, and to respond to it together in repentance and faith (i.e. when we go to church).

To put it another way: if a disciple is someone undergoing 'transformative learning' in Christ, then a church is a transformative learning community in Jesus Christ—a gathering that God has called together in order that we might learn his Son. Everything we do and promote and facilitate as a church community—personally, in pairs, in groups or all together on Sunday—should teach and model Christ, so that all may learn Christ.

This is a much larger and richer vision than the tendency, so common in modern churches, to departmentalize 'discipleship' into a specialty area mainly focused on personal disciplines or small group life. God's massive plan is to make learners of Christ from every nation through the four Ps (Proclamation, Prayer, People, Perseverance), and it is as part of the fulfilment of this plan that he gathers us together in communities—in churches (or assemblies).

God in his wisdom has drawn us together as a church and given us each other—not only because our destiny is precisely this (to be gathered together around Jesus Christ in redeemed wonder and joy and celebration), but because we need each other. God gives us each other as the means by which we hear the word of Christ and learn Christ.

Dietrich Bonhoeffer is one of those theologians that everyone seems to want to quote and claim for their own. We have no such pretensions, nor do we wish to imply that what we are saying here is any more or less likely to be true because we're quoting him. But this passage from *Life Together* insightfully expresses what we're trying to say about the church being a community whose operational principle is the mutual speaking and hearing of the word:

> Christianity means community through Jesus Christ and in Jesus Christ. No Christian community is more or less than this...
>
> What does this mean?...
>
> First, the Christian is the man who no longer seeks his salvation, his deliverance, his justification in himself, but in Jesus Christ alone... The death and the life of the Christian is not determined by his own resources; rather he finds both only in the Word that comes to him from the outside, in God's Word to him... The Christian lives wholly by the truth of God's Word in Jesus Christ. If somebody asks him, Where is your salvation, your righteousness? he can never point to himself. He points to the Word of God in Jesus Christ, which assures him salvation and righteousness. He is as alert as possible to this Word. Because he daily hungers and thirsts for righteousness, he daily desires the redeeming Word. And it can come only from the outside...
>
> But God has put this Word into the mouth of men in order that it may be communicated to other men. When one person is struck by the Word, he speaks it to others. God has willed that we should seek him and find his living Word in the witness of a brother, in the mouth of a man. Therefore, a Christian needs another Christian who speaks God's Word to him. He needs him again and again when he becomes uncertain and discouraged, for by himself he cannot help himself without belying the truth. He needs his brother man as a bearer and proclaimer of the divine word of salvation. He needs

his brother solely because of Jesus Christ. The Christ in his own heart is weaker than the Christ in the word of his brother; his own heart is uncertain, his brother's is sure.

And that also clarifies the goal of all Christian community: they meet one another as bringers of the message of salvation. As such, God permits them to meet together and gives them community. Their fellowship is founded solely upon Jesus Christ and this 'alien righteousness'. All we can say, therefore, is: the community of Christians springs solely from the biblical and Reformation message of the justification of man through grace alone; this alone is the basis of the longing of Christians for one another.[1]

No doubt different readers will come to this book with different ecclesiologies and different traditions, not only with respect to polity and governance but also with respect to how the Sunday church gathering takes place (what it is called, how it proceeds, what the music is like, and so on). We do not think it likely that we can canvass all these issues, let alone come to an agreement on them.

However, whatever our differences in ecclesiology, tradition or church style, there is one fundamental point on which we should all agree: the church, in all aspects of its life, is a community for transformative learning in Christ.

If this is true, then our Sunday gathering should be the prime, central, flagship occasion in which 'learning Christ' takes place, and from which all the other learning in the community draws its direction and impetus. If transformative learning is at the heart of our life together as God's people, then it must be at the heart of our regular Sunday gatherings.

In saying this, we are by no means suggesting that Sunday church should take on the style and ambience of a school room! This is not the kind of 'learning' that's involved (as we hope we

---

1   Bonhoeffer, *Life Together*, pp. 11-12.

made clear in Conviction 2). Whenever true learning in Christ takes place, God himself is at work—speaking his word, and inclining our hearts to respond in obedience and faith and thanksgiving and love and praise. There's nothing dispassionate or merely intellectual about this kind of learning, whether it be happening in our bedroom as we read the Scriptures, or in a small group or in our Sunday gatherings. It's a living, relational, transformational encounter with God by his word and Spirit, as we hear his voice and gladly respond to him.

Sunday is not only the prime occasion on which we learn Christ with each other—it's also one of the most powerful drivers of our entire church culture. If 'the whole way we do things' on Sunday does not communicate, exemplify, express, promote and otherwise champion 'learning Christ', then there is very little chance that our church culture will change in any significant way.

As we've talked to pastors over the past six years, this has been a significant issue—and so this conviction is particularly important. Do you believe that Sunday is a theatre for disciple-making? Do you see one of its key purposes as helping all those present to take a 'step to the right' through the prayerful proclamation and speaking of the word of God? And what would it look like, in your own context, for this to be the case? We have already touched on this in Conviction 4, in talking about how an 'expository pulpit' helps to generate an 'expository church', and we will come back to this subject in Phases 3 and 4.

But first we need to think about the other key location in which disciples are made.

The nations dwelling in darkness

That disciples should be made *everywhere* is a direct consequence of the universal lordship of the risen Jesus Christ (which we considered in Conviction 1). Because "all authority in heaven and on earth" has been granted to him as Lord and King of God's eternal kingdom, then his learners are to recruit and make other learners from all nations.[2]

Now it is easy for us to think of 'the nations' as overseas countries, but that is not really what Jesus was referring to—as if the task of the disciples was to evangelize their way through a list of ancient nation states.

He was talking about the peoples of the world—all the massive variety of nations and tribes and tongues and races, out of which Israel was called to be God's own special people, his holy nation. This non-Jewish 'rest of the world' is routinely called the 'nations' or 'Gentiles' in the New Testament (the one Greek word *ethnē* is commonly translated as either 'nations' or 'Gentiles' in most English translations).

Perhaps we can start to feel what a radical and shocking statement this might have been for the eleven disciples there on the mountain with Jesus. The Jewish Messiah had risen from the grave to save his people and be the ruler of all. But his commission to them was not to make disciples of Israel, but of the *nations*—them out there, the pagans, the people who were considered so unclean and defiled that a Jew was not even allowed to eat with them. It was a commission to make disciples of the enemy, of the despised heathens who had defeated and oppressed Israel for centuries.

Of course, this might not have been shocking to the disciples if they had been listening to Jesus' teaching during the previous three years, and had known their Old Testaments.[3] God's grand plan had always included the nations. From the time of the great scattering at the tower of Babel, when God confused the languages

---

2 Matt 28:18-19

3 Perhaps we might sympathize with the disciples' slowness to understand, because at some stages of his ministry in Matthew's Gospel, Jesus sends the disciples exclusively to "the lost sheep of the house of Israel" (10:6). But these lost sheep continually reject their Messiah and suffer judgement (12:39f.), and in their place the nations are invited to participate in the kingdom (e.g. 15:21-28). In many places, Matthew anticipates that the people of other nations are to be included in the kingdom (4:15-16, 8:5-13, 10:18, 13:38, 24:14). This movement—of the disciples being sent to Israel, of rejection by Israel, and of the inclusion of all the nations—is itself a picture in miniature of the sweep of salvation history.

of the people and dispersed them all over the earth, God's purpose was always to gather them together again; to bless the nations through the one man (Abraham) and the one nation (Israel) that God had chosen.[4]

In many ways, the story of the Old Testament is the story of Israel being called out from among the nations as God's special holy treasured possession, in order that they might be a blessing to the nations, a kingdom of priests to represent God to the world.[5] The ultimate vocation of Israel was to be the vehicle of salvation and light and blessing to the whole earth.

Sadly, Israel repeatedly fails in this vocation, and ends up being more like a curse than a blessing to the nations. The prophets arise and declare judgement on the people of Israel for their rebelliousness and faithlessness, and declare that they themselves will be exiled and scattered among the nations because of their sin. But at the same time, the prophets look forward to a time when God would send his Servant, through whom Israel would finally and truly be "a light for the nations, that my salvation may reach to the end of the earth".[6]

Matthew's Gospel opens with pagan astrologers (the Magi) being guided to Bethlehem, the city of David, where they fall down and worship the newborn Christ. The message is unmistakable: through this child, the blessing to the nations will finally come. A few chapters later, Matthew quotes Isaiah to say that this Jesus truly is the one in whose name the nations will hope.[7]

One of the key storylines in all the Gospels is the rejection of Jesus by his own people. It's almost as if the constant rebelliousness and faithlessness of Israel throughout her long history comes to a climax at this point—the very point at which God himself comes to her as Saviour and Messiah. Jesus knew very

---

4   Gen 12:1-3, 17:1-8, 22:15-18

5   Exodus 19:1-6 makes it clear that the reason God had redeemed Israel out of Egypt to be his own treasured possession was in order for them to be a "kingdom of priests" (i.e. to mediate God to the nations).

6   Isa 49:6

7   Matt 12:20-21

well that this was where his mission was heading; that the leaders of his own people would reject him and hand him over to the 'nations' (or Gentiles) to be crucified.[8] The Jews and the nations may have been divided by a high wall of culture and religion, and by centuries of war and hostility, but they were united in this—in a sinful conspiracy to kill the author of life. "This Jesus", says Peter to the assembled Jews at Pentecost, "delivered up according to the definite plan and foreknowledge of God, you crucified and killed by the hands of lawless men".[9]

In doing so, they fulfilled the age-long plan of God. In uniting to crucify Jesus, the Jews and the nations starkly demonstrated the fundamental problem that they share—that they both are citizens of "this present darkness".[10] And in God's astounding wisdom, this ultimate act of rebellion and sin was in fact the very act that also united them in salvation—for through the death of Jesus, the barrier between the Jews and the nations is broken down, and both are reconciled to God "in one body through the cross".[11]

Thus, when Jesus calls on the disciples to go and "make disciples of all nations", it is a climactic moment in salvation history. The Messiah has come and died and risen to be the Saviour and King not only of Israel, but of all the nations—of every tribe and clan and culture in all the earth. He is sending out his 'learners' (those who have turned back to him, and have been forgiven, and have devoted themselves entirely to learning his ways) to make other learners who do the same.

In other words, the 'community of learners' that Jesus is building now functions as the royal priesthood that Israel was always meant to be. We are called out in order that we might speak out: "But you are a chosen race, a royal priesthood, a holy nation, a people for his own possession, that you may proclaim the excellencies of him who called you out of darkness into his marvellous light".[12]

---

8   Matt 20:18-19
9   Acts 2:23
10 Eph 6:12; see the extended section in Conviction 1 on this.
11 Eph 2:14-18
12 1 Pet 2:9

The *where* of making learners of Christ must therefore be not only within the community of his people, but in every corner of the darkness in which people are trapped in rebellion against the risen Lord Christ—every street, every neighbourhood, every community, every people group, every subculture, every nation. The where of making disciples is everywhere from the family dinner table to the proverbial mission fields of deepest, darkest Africa (a place, incidentally, where one is more likely these days to find a 'learner' of Jesus than in the middle-class suburbs of the 'Christian' West).

There's an irony in all of this, for the many churches and Christians in the West who see 'making disciples' or 'mission' as something that takes place somewhere else, overseas, among 'the nations'. The irony is of course that *we are the nations*. We non-Jewish pagan Westerners are the very people the first disciples were sent out to disciple. We are the "far off" people, who according to Paul in Ephesians are "strangers to the covenants of promise, having no hope and without God in the world".[13] And the nice couple next door, who wave over the back fence and collect our mail when we're away—they are every bit as much a part of 'the nations dwelling in darkness' as we once were, and every bit in need of hearing the gospel of Christ and being incorporated into the massive, worldwide gathering of learners that God is assembling in Christ.

Our ghetto mentality

Most churches struggle to look out beyond their doors, and the boundaries of their fellowship, to the neighbours and peoples and subcultures and communities that are all around them in need of Christ. We tend to default to an inward sort of clubbishness, to a comfortable satisfaction with ourselves and our own

13 Eph 2:12-13

friends and community. And we find it hard to change and put ourselves out for the sake of reaching people who are different from us, who aren't part of our ethnic or cultural family, whom we might dislike or feel we have nothing in common with.

This is nothing new. In fact, the apostles and other early disciples struggled mightily with the implications of Jesus' universal mission to make disciples of the nations. Their mission may have been the culmination of God's historic plans; and it may have been the inescapable consequence of the worldwide reign of Jesus the Messiah; but this doesn't mean that the Jewish ethnocentrism of the apostles dissolved overnight. The first half of the book of Acts chronicles their growing understanding that taking the gospel to the nations meant taking it to people they had to this point regarded as beyond the pale—as pagans and heathens whose houses they would not even enter.

Peter's visit to the house of Cornelius in Acts 10 shows us the revolution that had to take place in Peter's thinking and attitudes towards the nations. This is the same Peter who had stood with Jesus on the mountain and heard the Great Commission, who had been with him in the upper room and been told that "repentance and forgiveness of sins should be proclaimed in his name to all nations",[14] who had been given the Holy Spirit so as to be a witness of Jesus to the ends of the earth.[15] And yet Peter still needs a thrice-repeated vision and a special word from God to persuade him to do something he had (in all likelihood) never done before in his entire life—"to associate with or to visit anyone of another nation".[16]

But having been shown by God "that I should not call any person common or unclean", Peter preaches the gospel to the gathered nations in Cornelius' house, and the Holy Spirit falls visibly upon them as a further proof to him (and them) that God's offer of forgiveness and new life is for all.

---

14 Luke 24:47
15 Acts 1:8
16 Acts 10:28

The following chapters in Acts show this extraordinary realization dawning on the early Jewish-dominated Christian community—that "to the Gentiles [nations] also God has granted repentance that leads to life".[17] We see Paul initiating the mission to the nations, and the Jerusalem church struggling to come to terms with the implications of gospel fellowship between Jews and Gentiles.

As Gentiles (which is most of us), we might be tempted to scoff at how hard the first Jewish believers found it to admit that God "made no distinction between us and them, having cleansed their hearts by faith".[18] Surely they should have been able to see, we say to ourselves, that their food laws and other traditions needed to flex and not stand in the way of the spread of the gospel. Surely they should have grasped more quickly what the apostle Paul saw so clearly—that food and drink and other cultural trappings were matters of freedom in Christ, and that for the sake of the gospel we should become all things to all people so that by all possible means we might save some.[19]

But of course, we should not be so quick to judge. Most churches today have precisely the same struggle. We find it hard to *go out* to people who are different from us, and reach them where they live. There are 'households of Cornelius' all around us that we would never dream of visiting or associating with, perhaps because we think it 'unlawful', or perhaps because it simply threatens us and makes us feel uncomfortable.

We also find it hard to *welcome in* people who are different from us, that they might learn Christ in our midst. Like the Corinthian church, we will (and should) have guests and outsiders in our church gatherings, and yet most of us resist being flexible in traditions and practices and cultural trappings for the sake of our guests. We like things the way they are—or if not, we want things to change so that church is *more* to our liking (whether in

17 Acts 11:18
18 Acts 15:9
19 1 Cor 9:22-23

music, language, style, size, architecture, or whatever).[20]

This conviction—about the where of disciple-making being all nations—challenges not only our willingness to move out to peoples and cultures who are different from us, but also our willingness to transform our homes and churches into places that are welcoming to people and cultures who are different from us.

It challenges us to lift our eyes to the vision we saw back in Conviction 1, from Revelation 7: of a numberless multitude, from every nation and people group and language imaginable, all standing before the throne of God and before the crucified and risen Christ, with their robes whitened by the blood of the Lamb, and crying out in celebration: "Salvation belongs to our God who sits on the throne, and to the Lamb!"[21]

Where, then, does learning Christ take place? *It happens in every facet and activity of the transformative learning communities we call churches; and through our churches, it also happens in every corner of this present darkness.*

---

20 There is a substantial issue lurking here that we can only touch on—namely the debate between those who say that the church should go out in mission to the cultures and communities around us (the 'missional' approach); and those who try to craft church meetings that are attractive to outsiders ('attractional' church). We don't think these should be alternatives to choose between! Churches should always be finding ways to go out to their surrounding communities with the gospel (rather than waiting for them to come to us); but we should also conduct our church gatherings in such a way that if and when outsiders do join us, they find the experience a welcoming, accessible and intelligible one that points them to Christ and the gospel. To put it another way: even though church is the gathering of the saved, because it is a gospel-shaped community it will always have a heart for the lost, both in going out into the world and in welcoming enquirers and outsiders into our meetings. We will say considerably more about all this in Phase 4.

21 Rev 7:10

DISCUSSION

1. The Bible's most extended discussion of the dynamics and purposes of church is found in 1 Corinthians 12-14. This has become a controversial passage over the past 50 years or so, because of debates over the nature of speaking in tongues and prophecy. Without spending too much time on these controversial details, read through these three chapters and make note of the following:

   a. What are the key metaphors or pictures of church life?

   b. What are the chief traits that should characterize what we do when we gather?

   c. In what ways are we all different?

   d. In what ways are we all seeking the same thing?

   e. How do you think chapter 13 is related to chapters 12 and 14? See if you can give a one-sentence summary of each chapter that explains the basic argument of the whole section.

2. What does a 'learning community' look like in practice, do you think? See how many different ways you can imagine—formally and informally—for people to help others take a 'step to the right' as part of your church community.

3. How did Paul deal with ethnocentric, tribal, inward-looking thinking and behaviour in himself and the churches? Read and reflect on 1 Corinthians 8-10 and Galatians 2.

4. Think of as many subcultures or communities that you are in contact with (individually or as a church):

   a. How successfully are you reaching out to make 'learners' of Christ in these communities?

   b. If people from some of these communities came to your church, what would they find helpful or unhelpful about your current church meetings?

5. See if you can track down some statistics on the ethnic, religious and socio-economic make-up of your local area.

   a. How closely does the profile of your church membership match your local community profile?
   b. Which subcultures or types of people do you think your church members find it hard to associate and engage with? Why is it difficult for them?
   c. Think of some church members who could have a special role in reaching subgroups in your community—not just ethnic and religious groups but peoples associated by age, job, disability, loneliness, financial need, sporting or cultural interest, and so on. (Don't feel the need to do anything with this information just yet—we'll come back to all this in Phases 3 and 4.)

Addendum: The home as a context for making disciples

If disciples are made in the life of the church, and in the nations, where does the home fit?

For many churches with a Reformation heritage, the Sunday gathering has long been understood as the gathering of Christian households that have 'churched' throughout the week. Family worship or devotions were embedded in the normal rhythm of godly family life. Indeed, what better context could there be for 'learning Christ' than in the day-to-day relationships of the home, where the Bible is read, prayers are offered and the gracious lifestyle of the gospel is on show (or not) through all the ups and downs of family life?

As we have talked with many pastors about this, there is general agreement that this pattern of household discipling has all but disappeared.

This is a disaster not only for families, but also for the church and for its mission in the world.

The New Testament household

In Scripture the connection between church and household is very close.

The home was a common location for believers to gather —such as in the houses belonging to Aquila and Prisca in Ephesus,[22] Prisca and Aquila in Rome,[23] and Nympha in Laodicea.[24] The early chapters of Acts present a picture of the local church in Jerusalem expressing its life through public meetings in the temple and smaller meetings in houses. Both aspects were essential to the life of the church.[25]

For nearly 300 years, until Constantine began building the first basilicas throughout the Roman Empire, Christians gathered in private houses—not in church buildings designed for public worship. The household was both a fellowship and a place of meeting.

At one level the reasons were pragmatic and reflected contemporary socio-economic conditions. The first Christians needed a space in which to gather and the ancient household provided a distinctive 'home' for the early Christian fellowships.

But the significance of this goes beyond mere pragmatics. The ancient household (Greek: *oikos*) was closely related to the church (Greek: *ekklēsia*). It's not that they were equivalent —unbelievers were still members of the *oikos*—but the church was embedded in the society through its households. When you came to church in these early centuries you came into the fellowship of the extended household—but one that

22 1 Cor 16:19
23 Rom 16:3-5
24 Col 4:15
25 Acts 2:46, 5:42, 8:3, 20:20

had been transformed through the gospel.

The gospel transforms the created order, including marriage, family and all social relationships, as part of God's new creation in Christ. The Christian household is renewed by the word of God so that it reflects the love and peace of Christ in its interpersonal relationships.

Paul speaks of what this renewal looks like in practice in what have become known as the 'household codes'.[26] In these household codes, we see what it means for everything to be done "in the name of the Lord Jesus".[27] How are wives and husbands to relate in Christ? How are parents to discipline and instruct children in the Lord? And what of the relationships that might now exist with servants or slaves who worked in the household?

In the gospel, where there is neither Jew nor Greek, male nor female, slave nor free,[28] these household relationships are not destroyed or abolished, but they are radically transformed. The old ways of conflict, anger, bitterness, domineering, harshness, cruelty, selfishness and malice are to be put to death, like all the other fleshly characteristics of our former life; and instead we are to put on respect, submission, discipline, honour, service, kindness, justice, forgiveness, self-sacrifice, and over all of them love, which binds them together in perfect unity.

The household was the basic everyday sphere in which disciples learned to obey all the commandments of Christ, especially his new commandment to love another.

And this new gospel-driven behaviour and sacrificial love in households could not help but be seen. In Titus 2, the godly behaviour of the younger women and of the slaves both

---

26 The two main passages are Colossians 3:18-4:1 and Ephesians 5:22-6:9, but also see Titus 2:1-10 and 1 Peter 2:13-3:7.

27 Col 3:17

28 Gal 3:28

testified to the gospel.[29] In the renewed Christian household, the extreme sociological and ethno-religious divisions of the ancient world—between Jew and Gentile, free and slave, man and woman, upper and lower classes—were overturned. The Christian household was not only the nucleus of the church, but provided a compelling witness to the surrounding community of the transformative learning of Christ.

The household was also the laboratory in which Christian leadership was practised and seen. A man's pastoral leadership in the Christian household was a pointer towards his qualifications for leading the household of God (the church). After all, when you came to church in those early centuries, you entered the home of your pastor/elder and could see firsthand if he was fond of too much alcohol or heavy-handed with his family, or whether his children were out of control.

The very fact that overseers, elders and deacons were to be appointed on the basis of their example, leadership and teaching in family life is a strong indication that each household was to be led toward Christlike transformation by the grace of the gospel.[30] When fathers (in particular) are exhorted not to embitter their children but rather to train them in the knowledge of the Lord, they are not only following the pattern in Israel of teaching children the word of God,[31] but also reinforcing the basic pattern of disciple-making in the church—of patient and loving instruction in the word of God.

Conclusion

How do we make disciples in the home? By way of the same four Ps as in the church and the world. If we think of our

---

29 In the one case by the word of God not being "reviled" (v. 5); in the other by adorning the "doctrine of God our Saviour" (v. 10).
30 1 Tim 3:1-13; Titus 1:1-9
31 Eph 6:1-4; cf. Deut 6:1-9

homes as 'little churches' and lead them accordingly, we won't go too far wrong.

The Puritan Richard Baxter is renowned for his mission to catechize families, and to enlist the leaders of households as co-workers in the ministry:

> We must have a special eye upon families, to see that they are well ordered, and the duties of each relation performed... If we suffer the neglect of this, we shall undo all. What are we like to do ourselves to the reforming of a congregation, if all the work be cast on us alone; and masters of families neglect that necessary duty of their own, by which they are bound to help us? If any good be begun by the ministry in any soul, a careless, prayerless, worldly family is like to stifle it, or very much hinder it; whereas, if you could but get the rulers of families to do their duty, to take up the work where you left it, and help it on, what abundance of good might be done! I beseech you, therefore, if you desire the reformation and welfare of your people, do all you can to promote family religion... Get information how each family is ordered, that you may know how to proceed in your endeavours for their further good.
>
> ...
>
> You are not like to see any general reformation, till you procure family reformation. Some little religion there may be, here and there; but while it is confined to single persons, and is not promoted in families, it will not prosper, nor promise much future increase.[32]

In practical terms, this means that in thinking about how we are going to teach, motivate, support and equip all our

---

32 Baxter, *The Reformed Pastor*, pp. 100-102.

people to be Christ-learners who help others to learn Christ, we must not exclude the home as a key location for that to take place. We mustn't limit our thinking to church activities and youth groups on one hand, and evangelistic activities on the other. The home is like a nexus where the church and the world meet. It is both a location where much fruitful '4P ministry' can take place—between husbands and wives, and parents and children, and extended family—and a little pocket of Christ's kingdom, bearing witness in streets and neighbourhoods to the transforming effect of the gospel.

Of course, like any aspect of our lives and churches, our homes are far from perfect. In fact, for some of us, it feels like a forlorn hope to see our family reformed by the gospel. Our deepest sadness is that some of our family members are lost in darkness without Christ. "How do you know, wife, whether you will save your husband? Or how do you know, husband, whether you will save your wife"?[33] That is it exactly —we don't know, even when we have built our family life on the gospel. For many of us the gospel has divided our families just as Jesus knew would happen.[34] We suffer this greatly, and blame ourselves for 'getting it wrong' somehow, and beg for God's mercy on our fractious household.

But the truth remains: if we want a church culture of transformative learning, our households need to reflect this vision, and our families need to be taught and encouraged and equipped to embrace it. The connection between home-based and church-based disciple-making is very close. The one will nurture the other.

33 1 Cor 7:16
34 Matt 10:34-39

DISCUSSION

1. What ambitions for our children are sometimes at odds with the goal of discipleship?

2. What will our homes look like if they are transformative learning communities around the gospel?

3. How does this compare to what they look like now?

4. How can our church programs increase home-based learning rather than replace it?

5. How do you think the Bible's teaching about households applies to the increasingly common phenomenon of single people sharing a house together?

6. Why do we often find ourselves more involved in disciple-making outside the home than within?

7. How could our church equip parents to grow their home as a discipling community? What are the roadblocks to achieving this?

8. What regular habits of Bible reading, prayer and fellowship do you need to recommit to?

Summary

Before we start to apply our newly sharpened convictions to our own lives and to the whole culture of our church, we need to briefly pause to consolidate and summarize.

Let's recall the key points from the five convictions, and summarize them diagrammatically as we go.

Conviction 1: Why make disciples?

The reason we want to make more and more disciples of Jesus Christ is this: *because God's goal for the whole world and the whole of human history is to glorify his beloved Son in the midst of the people he has rescued and transformed.*

God is now putting this plan into effect, by rescuing people out of "this present darkness" into the kingdom of his Son by his death and resurrection—people who are being transformed to be like Jesus, and who now have a sure and certain place around Christ's throne in a new creation where evil and death are no more.

This is the zoomed-out picture that explains why making more disciples is so important and so urgent a task.

We could represent it like this:

Rescued and transformed

Domain of darkness

Kingdom of the Son

A redeemed people gathered around the risen Christ

Conviction 2: What is a disciple?

We then clarified exactly what a disciple is: *a forgiven sinner who is learning Christ in repentance and faith.*

We saw in the Gospels that a 'learner' (or 'disciple') of Christ is someone who has recognized the dark and lost state they were living in under God's judgement, and who has turned to Christ in repentance and faith as Master, Saviour and Teacher to commit themselves totally to obeying him, to learning to keep all his commandments, and to living out that repentance and faith daily for the rest of their lives. This kind of 'transformational learning' is really another way of describing the totality of the Christian life.

We saw how this same framework of thinking carries into the rest of the New Testament, where 'learning Christ' means hearing the word of the gospel (of Christ's saving rule), responding to that word in faith, and thereby passing from death to life in Christ—with a resulting urgency to kill off the sinful worldly behaviour that remains from their former life, and to put on instead the new clothes of Christ.

To become a 'Christ-learner', then, is both a decisive and gigantic step of repentance in accepting the salvation that God has won *for* us through Christ (symbolized by baptism), *and* an ongoing daily commitment to living out the implications and consequences of this massive salvation that God has won for us (symbolized by the yoke).

We could add one small detail to our diagram to represent this—namely an 'L' (learner) sign above the person who has been transferred out of darkness and into the kingdom of the Son, and who now continues that transformational learning in every sphere of life, especially in the 'transformational learning community' that we call 'church'.

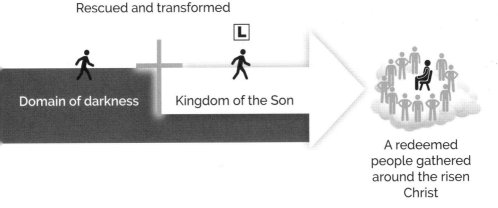

Rescued and transformed

Domain of darkness   Kingdom of the Son

A redeemed people gathered around the risen Christ

Conviction 3: How are disciples made?

How does this rescue and redemption happen? The making of disciples is *God's work*, achieved as his word and Spirit work through the activity of Christian disciples and in the hearts of those they speak to. We summarized that activity as *the persevering proclamation of the word of God by the people of God in prayerful dependence on the Spirit of God*, otherwise known as the four Ps:

1. **P**roclamation of the word in multiple ways
2. **P**rayerful dependence on the Spirit
3. **P**eople are God's fellow workers
4. **P**erseverance, step by step

We suggested that the goal of every form of Christian ministry could therefore be summarized simply as seeking to help each person, wherever they happen to be, to take 'one step to the right' through these four Ps—that is, to hear the gospel and be transferred out of the domain of darkness into the kingdom, and then to press forward towards maturity in Christ in every aspect of life, by the constant, persevering, prayerful proclamation of God's word by people in multiple ways.

Our diagram would now look like this:

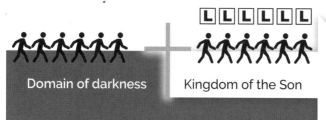

Rescued and transformed

Domain of darkness

Kingdom of the Son

A redeemed people gathered around the risen Christ

Help those around you take a step to the right through the four Ps

Here's an additional thought that we didn't cover in Conviction 3, but which will help you to take these ideas forward into the phases that follow.

To think more clearly about the different 'places' people occupy on this spectrum of moving to the right, we could usefully identify four broad stages that people pass through on their road 'to the right':

- Some people are very 'far away' from Christ and his kingdom; they may not have ever met or spoken with a Christian person. Very often the first thing they need in order to take a step to the right is to meet and *engage* with a Christian.
- Others have met and engaged with Christians or Christianity in some way. The next step for them is to hear the gospel; that is, to be *evangelized.*
- For those who have responded to the gospel in faith and repentance, their next step is to be *established* as a Christian, to send down roots, and to begin to grow in godliness and Christlikeness (a 'walk' that will continue for the rest of their lives).

- As Christians are established, and grow in love and knowledge, they will become increasingly concerned not only to step to the right themselves, but to help others do so in whatever way they can. They will benefit from being *equipped* to do so through teaching, encouragement, coaching and prayer.

Feel free to come up with your own way of summarizing this road that most people travel, but we like to use these four Es as handy signposts for different stages of the journey: *Engage, Evangelize, Establish* and *Equip*.[1]

We could add them to our diagram like this:

Rescued and transformed

Domain of darkness
engage » evangelize »

Kingdom of the Son
» establish » equip

Help those around you take a step to the right
through the four Ps

A redeemed
people gathered
around the risen
Christ

Conviction 4: Who makes disciples?

In this conviction, we dug deeper into the idea that it is the joy and privilege of *all* God's people to be involved in the four Ps. We looked at the biblical teaching of how God by his Spirit opens the mouths of all disciples to speak the one word of Christ, in a richly varied way. We concluded that speaking the word of God to others

---

1   We'll utilize these four broad categories or stages later in Phases 3 and 4, both to evaluate our current church culture and to plan for change. We think you will find these Es (or some other version of them you might want to devise yourself) to be a useful mental framework for thinking about the different aspects of your church culture. But we want to emphasize at this point that they are just that—a useful framework for thinking, not a Scriptural designation or a set of hard-and-fast labels.

for their salvation and encouragement is an expected and necessary component of the normal Christian life. And correspondingly, a healthy church culture is one in which a wide variety of word ministries are exercised by a constantly growing proportion of the membership.

We then looked at various practical examples of what this might look like, and at some of the questions, barriers and inhibitions that arise.

We concluded by suggesting that expository preaching is vitally connected to this kind of 'every member word ministry'. An expository pulpit is the foundational word ministry that feeds and regulates and equips and builds an 'expository church', in which the word of the Bible is being ministered at multiple levels in a rich variety of ways by the congregation.

In other words, we could answer the question 'Who makes disciples?' as follows: *By their preaching, training and example, pastors equip every Christian to be a Christ-learner who helps others to learn Christ.*

Or to use our language of 'moving to the right', we could change the summary statement at the bottom of our diagram to reflect this integrated picture of the expository church:

Rescued and transformed

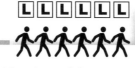

Domain of darkness
engage » evangelize »

Kingdom of the Son
» establish » equip

A redeemed people gathered around the risen Christ

By their preaching, training and example, pastors equip every Christian to help those around them take a step to the right through the four Ps

Conviction 5: Where to make disciples

Our final conviction clarified that making and growing 'Christ-learners' is not just something that happens with new Christians, or in small groups, or in one-to-one counselling. It is the basic activity that should be at the centre of everything we do as a church—that is, as a transformational learning community—including and especially our Sunday gatherings. One way of describing Sunday church is as a 'theatre for disciple-making', in which we seek to help everyone present take a 'step to the right' through the prayerful proclamation and speaking of the word of God.

We also clarified that the missional or evangelistic side of making Christ-learners is not something that only happens overseas in traditional 'mission work'. The *where* of making more learners of Christ is all around us—in our families and streets and communities, in every corner of this present darkness in which people are so desperately in need of the saving gospel of Christ.

Where, then, does learning Christ take place? *It happens in every facet and activity of the transformative learning communities we call churches; and through our churches, it also happens in every corner of this present darkness.*

PROJECT

Now it's over to you. It's time for you to draw together all that you have learned through sharpening your convictions, by coming up with your own way of expressing them.

Exercise 1: Write a manifesto

From your work on the five convictions, write your own short summary of what you believe about discipleship and making disciples. You might like to use our five headings or come up with some of your own. You might like to use (or modify) our diagram to illustrate your summary, or devise your own.

What you are trying to express is your theological DNA, or vision for Christian ministry. Don't have too many headings or sub-points—the idea is to write a short readable document (of, say, no more than 1000 words) that can function as a sharp summary of what you believe and what drives you.

We suggest that one person on your Vine Project Team be given the job of coming up with a first draft that the rest can tweak and debate and improve.[2]

Exercise 2: Boil it down

Having finalized your manifesto, try to boil it down into one simple, compelling summary statement that would cut through and make sense to your people. This is not necessarily the church motto that would go on the sign out the front, or that you would advertise to outsiders in the local paper—this is an internal mission or purpose statement that reminds your members what you're on about as a church.

Keep it to one sentence if possible. Avoid waffly or vague ideas. Don't try to make it catchy or clever until you're absolutely sure of what you want to say.

Exercise 3: Prepare a hypothetical vision session for your members

As a further way of clarifying your convictions and how you'd communicate them, build on Exercises 1 and 2 by putting together the draft of a 'vision session' with your whole church—the content of a special one-off meeting where you laid out before the whole congregation the key convictions that were going to be the basis of moving forward together.

---

2   We'd also suggest that it might be best if the person who does this draft is *not* the senior pastor of the church—unless your team is sufficiently comfortable with one another to critique the draft even if it is written by the pastor.

a. What would you include in such a presentation?
b. Which Bible passages would you read or explain or discuss?
c. What key illustrations or examples would you use?
d. How would you persuade your congregation of the need for change, given these convictions?
e. What questions would you anticipate?
f. What might you give them to take home and read, for further discussion?

We'll revisit this exercise in Phase 4, but the draft you come up with now will be very helpful not only in crystallizing your convictions, but in beginning to think about how you are going to communicate them to the congregation as a whole.

PHASE 2 //
REFORM YOUR PERSONAL CULTURE

Reform your personal culture

Most strategic review or planning processes, including those that churches undertake, skip straight past the step we're about to outline.

They start where we have started—by identifying and clarifying core beliefs or convictions or values or purposes (or whatever you want to call them). They then move on to how to bring the organizational culture more into line with those values or purposes. Where are the problems or obstacles? What do we need to address, and in what order? Where exactly do we want to head, and how can we get there? And what are the action steps?

All these questions are important, and we will come to our own version of them in due course.

But first we want to urge you to spend some time on a part of the process that many people leave out, and which you also (we suspect) will be tempted to skip.

We want you to take some time to *reform your own personal culture*. Is 'the whole way *you* do things' influenced and shaped by the convictions we've been clarifying? Does your own personal culture reflect the convictions that you have just clarified and endorsed?

We will expand on what this might mean in practice below, but first we should understand why this step is so vital.

It is for two reasons.

The *first* flows out of the nature of the convictions themselves (as we explored and expounded and refined them in Phase 1). To 'learn Christ' is to learn not just concepts and content, but a way of being and living in the world. It is never less than concepts and content, but it is necessarily more. The goal for learners (or 'disciples') is not just to know and remember the commandments of Christ, but to *keep* or obey the commandments of Christ, to live for Christ and to seek to be like Christ in every word and deed.[1]

This makes 'learning Christ' more like learning to play golf than learning times tables. It is the kind of knowledge that must be lived and practiced, or else it has not really been learned at all.

This is one of the reasons Paul insists to Titus that any elders he appoints must be people not only of good doctrine, but good character and lifestyle—because if an elder is not like this, he has not grasped the meaning and significance of the "trustworthy word" that has been entrusted to him.[2] He would be like a golf pro who had read countless instruction books and watched endless YouTube videos, who looked the part and could talk the lingo, but who was actually lousy at golf. Until he plays, and plays well, it is nonsense to say that he has 'learned golf', let alone that he is competent to teach anyone else.

This is what the knowledge of the truth in Christ is like. It "accords with godliness" as Paul says to Titus.[3] It has a corresponding mode of action and behaviour and life and character. It must be lived if it is to be learned at all. And so an elder or overseer—someone who is seeking to help others 'learn Christ'—must himself demonstrate by his life that he has 'learned Christ' himself.

The very nature of our convictions is such that clarifying what they are is only the first step in believing and embracing and owning them. We must *live* them if we are to truly learn them.

---

1   See Col 3:17
2   Titus 1:5-9
3   Titus 1:1

We must also live them if we are to teach them to others, and this is the *second* reason for pausing to make sure that we are living our convictions. We cannot 'make learners' of Christ unless we show by our lives what learning Christ means.

Christian 'learnership' is the full package. It is a transformed mind and heart being worked out and lived out daily in every sphere of life. Teaching this package means not only causing people to learn gospel ideas and knowledge and truth, but also causing them to learn a way of life. This necessarily involves modelling and imitation.

This is a constant theme in Paul's writings. He wants Christians to learn his ways and imitate his life:

> What you have learned and received and heard and seen in me—practise these things, and the God of peace will be with you. (Phil 4:9)

> Give no offence to Jews or to Greeks or to the church of God, just as I try to please everyone in everything I do, not seeking my own advantage, but that of many, that they may be saved.
> Be imitators of me, as I am of Christ. (1 Cor 10:32-11:1)

He wants his ministry protégés Timothy and Titus likewise to learn from him, and in turn to be examples to their people:

> You, however, have followed my teaching, my conduct, my aim in life, my faith, my patience, my love, my steadfastness, my persecutions and sufferings that happened to me at Antioch, at Iconium, and at Lystra— which persecutions I endured; yet from them all the Lord rescued me. (2 Tim 3:10-11)

> Let no one despise you for your youth, but set the believers an example in speech, in conduct, in love, in faith, in purity. (1 Tim 4:12)

> Show yourself in all respects to be a model of good works, and in your teaching show integrity, dignity, and sound speech that cannot be condemned, so that an

opponent may be put to shame, having nothing evil to say about us. (Titus 2:7-8)

And he wants the chain of example and imitation to continue, as those who follow the godly model of life that Paul has taught them, in turn serve as examples for others:

> Brothers, join in imitating me, and keep your eyes on those who walk according to the example you have in us. (Phil 3:17)

> Older women likewise are to be reverent in behaviour, not slanderers or slaves to much wine. They are to teach what is good, and so train the young women to love their husbands and children, to be self-controlled, pure, working at home, kind, and submissive to their own husbands, that the word of God may not be reviled. (Titus 2:3-5)

> And you became imitators of us and of the Lord, for you received the word in much affliction, with the joy of the Holy Spirit, so that you became an example to all the believers in Macedonia and in Achaia. (1 Thess 1:6-7)

This connects with what we saw in Phase 1 (Conviction 3) about *how* learners learn. It happens through God's word, prayerfully spoken over time in dependence on the Spirit—through and to God's distinctive people, his saints. The ones who do the prayerful speaking are those whose lives have been set apart by God to be different (i.e. all Christian saints). And those distinctive lives are part of the teaching package. Our lives demonstrate to other learners what 'keeping the commandments of Jesus' looks like.

This of course makes most of us feel uncomfortable and inadequate. We are painfully aware of our sins and failures, and how far short we fall in keeping Jesus' commandments. We feel that our lives are a constant cycle of failure and forgiveness; of striving for holiness and repenting when we fail to reach it. How can we ever be good enough to function as a model for others?

And yet this is precisely the example we are to set to those around us—not of someone who keeps all the commandments of Jesus, for no-one does this or ever will do this (not this side of glory). The example we give is of someone who is *learning* to keep all the commandments of Jesus, who is seeking to grow and make progress and be transformed and bring forth the fruit of the Spirit. In other words, the example we set is someone who by God's word and Spirit is moving to the right one step at a time— not someone who has already arrived at the heavenly fulfilment of Christian maturity.

This is critical to the whole process of culture change.

If we want to see real change in the culture of our church, we need to start with seeing real change in the culture of our own Christian lives—not only in the way we think and the convictions we hold, but also in how those convictions are expressed and embodied in everything we do: in the structure and norms of our life, in our habits and speech and behaviour and relationships and activities and priorities, in all the bits and pieces that go together to make up 'the way we do things'.

The culture of a church will not change unless a critical mass of 'Christ-learners' has caught the vision of moving themselves and others to the right, one step at a time. If you are one of a small group of change agents who want to initiate and lead that process of change (i.e. if you are the kind of person this book is aimed at), then now is the time for some sober self-examination. You cannot initiate and lead a culture-change process if your own personal culture is not up for change as well.

This is because the change you are proposing and leading is not a change of program or structure or model. It is fundamentally a transformation of lives by God through his word and Spirit. Our purpose is not to bring a new idea or a new angle or a new organizational technique to our churches; we are bringing the word of God, along with its call to repent and lead a new life in Christ. And we cannot bring this word to others without responding to it ourselves; that is, without decisively unlearning the false knowledge and life we once lived, and committing ourselves to 'learn Christ'.

To put it another way, what you are doing together as a Vine Project Team (in the whole process we are engaged in) is really a *prototype* of the culture transformation that you eventually want to see take place throughout your congregation. You yourselves (as a team) need to be a 'transformational learning community'.

All this is just as true, of course, for those of you who are involved in planting a new church (as opposed to renovating an existing one). There is almost nothing more valuable for a new church-planting team than to 'own' and personally live out the culture that you want to be the basis of your new fellowship.

The point is clear enough, and perhaps does not need to be laboured further. But what does it look like in practice? How can we be living, breathing advertisements for the convictions that we want our whole church or fellowship to embrace?

Before we look at some practical examples, suggestions and exercises, a word of warning is necessary. Whenever one Christian (in this case, us) tells another Christian (in this case, you) what obedience or Christian maturity might look like, or how it should be lived out, or what practical steps ought to be taken to show that you are in fact living out your convictions, one of the dread enemies of Christianity pricks up his ears, licks his lips, and starts sniffing about for an opening.

That enemy is Legalism—the idea that Christian living can be codified into a set of practices or rules, the performance of which constitutes 'obedience'. If practising our convictions can be defined in terms of a certain class of things we ought to do, then the Legalist that lurks inside all of us will rise up and say, "So if I simply do these things in a way that other people recognize as acceptable, then I'm fine. I've demonstrated my obedience, and I can feel pretty good about myself—before others and before God."

So the warning is this: as we look at some practical suggestions for living out our convictions, treat them as just that—suggestions and guides and ideas that you can draw on as you work out under God what it means for you to live your convictions.

As a handy way of grouping and outlining these suggestions, we're going to use our illustration of moving ourselves and others 'to the right'. If we are going to examine ourselves, and repent, and make plain to everyone that we ourselves are seeking to make progress as learners of Christ, in what areas and in what ways could we do so?

1. Moving to the right ourselves

It starts us with us, and our own personal growth in learning Christ.

We are firstly a 'learning community of one' before we are a learning community with others. We each stand before our God as one who has been singled out for his kingdom and purposes, with the privilege of responding to this grace by walking according to our calling.

If you are reading this book and have read this far, there is a reasonable likelihood that you already know quite a bit about walking the Christian walk. You may be a church pastor or ministry worker, or part of a team that is seeking to lead change in your church or fellowship group. Whatever your role or stage of life, chances are that you would be regarded as a solidly mature believer.

How should mature Christian believers approach their own growth in Christ?

Perhaps counter-intuitively, we need to answer *"with urgency"*, for this is the example that Paul sets us and that we should set for others. This extraordinary passage from Philippians is worth mulling over at length:

> Indeed, I count everything as loss because of the surpassing worth of knowing Christ Jesus my Lord. For his sake I have suffered the loss of all things and count them as rubbish, in order that I may gain Christ and be found in him, not having a righteousness of my own that comes from the law, but that which comes through faith in Christ, the righteousness from God that depends

on faith—that I may know him and the power of his resurrection, and may share his sufferings, becoming like him in his death, that by any means possible I may attain the resurrection from the dead.

Not that I have already obtained this or am already perfect, but I press on to make it my own, because Christ Jesus has made me his own. Brothers, I do not consider that I have made it my own. But one thing I do: forgetting what lies behind and straining forward to what lies ahead, I press on toward the goal for the prize of the upward call of God in Christ Jesus. Let those of us who are mature think this way, and if in anything you think otherwise, God will reveal that also to you. Only let us hold true to what we have attained.

Brothers, join in imitating me, and keep your eyes on those who walk according to the example you have in us. (Phil 3:8-17)

Paul highlights one of the glorious paradoxes of the Christian life. The further along the road we are, the more we long to pick up our pace. The more mature we are, the more urgently we see the need to leave behind our old life, to count as loss all that we previously regarded as gain, and to strain forward to what lies ahead—because the more mature we are in Christ, the more starkly we perceive the contrast between the darkness that still lingers in our lives and the light-filled kingdom of his Son into which he has transferred us.

But how exactly do we press on, and strain forward, and keep putting to death the remnants of our old lives?

Our convictions tell us that the 'how' is through the word of God, applied regularly and vigorously to our hearts by the Spirit of God, producing a transformed mind and life, step by step, over time.

And because you are a mature Christian who has been around the block several times, you know precisely what is coming next: an exhortation to read your Bible more—and who could argue with that?

This time around, however, we'd like to suggest a variation on that familiar theme. We'd like to suggest not that you read your Bible more but that you *inwardly digest* your Bible more. This phrase comes from one of the most beautiful and profound prayers of the Anglican *Book of Common Prayer*. It reads:

> Blessed Lord, who caused all holy Scriptures to be written for our learning: Grant us so to hear them, read, mark, learn, and inwardly digest them, that we may embrace and ever hold fast the blessed hope of ever-lasting life, which you have given us in our Saviour Jesus Christ; who lives and reigns with you and the Holy Spirit, one God, for ever and ever. Amen.

This prayer articulates what we have already been learning about learning—that it is not just a matter of hearing or reading the words that God has caused to be written, but of marking, learning and inwardly digesting them.

This prayer asks that God would grant us a growing intensity of engagement with the word that he has caused to be written "for our learning"—that we would not just *hear* it, but *read* it for ourselves; that we would not just read it, but *mark* it (i.e. take heed of it, pay careful attention to it—as in the expression 'Mark my words!'); that this careful attention would lead us to *learn* the Scriptures, to know them thoroughly and intimately, so that we can readily recall and remember their teaching; and that this learning would penetrate to our souls and become part of us, that we would *inwardly digest* the nourishment of his word.

If your Christian life is anything like ours, there is no shortage of opportunity to hear and read the word of God. In church we hear the Bible read and a sermon preached. Most of us would attend at least one other group in the week where the Bible is opened and read and discussed. Many of us would be regularly studying it at some depth in preparation for leading a Bible study or preaching. We may be reading a Christian book that expounds and explains God's word. And there is our own personal Bible reading that we will be seeking to maintain (usually with some difficulty).

For most of us, the deficiency is not in hearing or reading, but in marking, learning and inwardly digesting. We hear and read lots of Bible, but we spend too little time prayerfully mulling it over, allowing it to sink in, doggedly re-reading and rethinking those parts we don't understand until God gives us understanding, pondering how this word opposes or displaces the worldly thinking we currently default to, thinking about how this particular word speaks to our sins and our character, reflecting on the hope this word holds out to us, writing down or committing to memory key verses or insights we want to remember, and above all praying earnestly that God might mould and shape and transform our lives in light of this word.

Hearing, reading, marking, learning and inwardly digesting need not be a solitary endeavour. Any and all parts of the process can be very usefully practised in fellowship with others; that is after all why God has given us each other—to help us hear, read, mark, learn and inwardly digest.

But even with the help and fellowship of others, there is a point at which we stand alone before God, with our own sins and struggles and victories and failures. Someone can lead us to food, cook it for us, and even cut it up into small pieces and feed it to us, but in the end we have to chew and digest it for ourselves for it to have any nutritional value for us.

Some of the Puritans called this practice of allowing the word of Scripture to penetrate deeply into our hearts 'divine meditation'. For them, it was a vital part of the spiritual life. As Thomas White put it: "It is better to hear one sermon only and meditate on that, than to hear two sermons and meditate on neither".[4]

If there is one practical suggestion we would make in moving to the right in our own personal learning of Christ it would be this: for every hour you spend hearing and reading God's word, spend an hour prayerfully marking, learning and inwardly digesting it.

---

4   Thomas White, *A Method and Instructions for the Art of Divine Meditation*, Thomas Parkhurst, London, 1672, p. 17; cited in Allan Chapple, *True Devotion: In Search of Authentic Spirituality*, The Latimer Trust, London, 2014, loc. 4151.

For example, on Monday, don't read a fresh passage of Scripture. Take out your notes from the sermon the day before (whether you were a listener or the preacher!). Read over the passage a few more times; dwell on the key words and sentences; mull over the most important truths and challenges; give thanks for all those blessings and gifts that the passage reminds you of; pray over all that it prompts you to request for your own life and for those around you; and so on.

Over time this practice of prayerful 'inward digestion' will bear rich fruit. Indeed, it may be something that you would like to see become part of the culture of your church. But of course, for that ever to happen, it must start with you. If we wish everyone in our congregation to be feeding on and digesting and praying over the word of God, then we cannot ignore the importance of doing so ourselves.

We started by quoting a Reformed Anglican prayer, and we should conclude by returning to prayer. We pray for God to "grant us" this kind of listening ear and mind and heart, knowing that in turn it will lead to more prayer. The more we absorb and digest the truth of God's word, and the more our trust and dependence upon it is nourished and strengthened, the more we will be moved to cry out to God in intercession for our families, our neighbours, our friends, and for the whole community of Christ-learners that we are blessed to belong to. We have said this already, and will do so again in what follows, but it can hardly be repeated too often: there is no transformation without prayer. Prayer comes before trans-formation, as we beg for God to change us by his Spirit; and prayer follows transformation, as we verbalize and express our growing trust in Christ. All the thinking and evaluating and planning and strategizing that we're undertaking in our Vine Project must be underpinned by constant prayer for God to do what we cannot plan or strategize for—the transformation of hearts.

2. Moving others to the right

Our convictions tell us that the normal Christian life is transformative learning in Christ—a learning in which all of us seek to move ourselves and everyone around us to the right through the prayerful, patient, Spirit-imbued speaking of the word of God.

If we are to live out this conviction and set an example in doing so, the way forward is simple to express, if not always easy to do. We need to think about the different spheres and contexts of our lives, and ask ourselves two questions:

- Whom do we want to move one step to the right?
- How are we going to do that?

Let's look briefly at the main contexts and spheres of our lives, and throw out some ideas to get you thinking about how you would answer those two questions.

At one level, this will be overwhelming. You will no doubt start to think about all that could be done—and all that you're currently *not* doing—to move people in your own life to the right. But don't despair or give up. You can't do everything, nor does God expect you to. But look for where you could bring reformation and change to your own personal culture, and make a start.

Four major contexts

As a simple way of thinking about the totality of our personal lives, let's look at four common spheres of relationship most of us find ourselves in:

- **Our households:** How are we seeking to move our spouse, or children, or family members to the right through the word and prayer? Have we even thought of our families in this way—as those who, like us, need to learn Christ? What could you do to insert regular Bible reading, discussion and prayer into the rhythm of your household life? Thinking about it another way: what does each individual person in your household need in order to take a 'step to the right'?

- **The world:** Think about your workplace, the school your kids go to, your neighbours, your friends and acquaintances—who in that sphere of life do you have regular contact and relationship with? Where are these people up to in their journey to the right? What could you do to move them a step or two further along, through the word and prayer?
- **Small group ministries:** Many of us are involved in small groups of different kinds—Bible study groups or home groups, or ministries to particular groups of people (like youth ministries, or children's ministries). Think about your involve- ment in these groups. How are you going with moving people to the right in these contexts? What could you do to make some progress? For example, is there someone you could meet with to read the Bible one-to-one for a period of time?[5]
- **Church on Sunday:** What could you do to treat Sunday more as a theatre for 'learning Christ'—whether in your attitude, your conversation with people before and after, your welcome of newcomers, and so on?

In most of these contexts or spheres of action, you don't have to operate as a lone wolf. In thinking and talking this through as a Vine Project Team, you may come up with some ideas and suggested actions that you can do together. For example, you could decide to:

- do some training together in evangelism, and then go doorknocking or street evangelizing together
- run a gospel course together to which you could invite your friends[6]
- work together on welcoming newcomers at church, and following them up in the weeks after their visit.

5   David Helm's excellent little book *One-to-One Bible Reading* provides all the information and guidance you need to get started in one-to-one Bible reading, if you haven't done so before.

6   Like *Christianity Explored* (3rd edn, Good Book Company, New Malden, 2011) or Dominic Steele's *Introducing God* (3rd edn, Media Bible Fellowship, Annandale, 2013).

Whatever it ends up being, commit yourselves together to personal transformative learning—to becoming more like Jesus in your own lives by loving others enough to want to move them to the right.

Timing of this phase

The next phase in our culture-change process (Phase 3) involves looking honestly at the culture of our church or fellowship, and evaluating how that culture lines up with our convictions.

There is a natural tendency to want to get cracking on that next part of the process, and to begin to make some progress—but be careful. This second phase, of evaluating our own lives and lining them up with our convictions, is a vital step in the process. The more thoughtfully and thoroughly we look at ourselves and seek to change the culture of our own lives, the better equipped we will be to look at church life as a whole and do likewise.

Rather than quickly condemning people or programs or activities that don't measure up to our convictions, the experience of examining our own lives might give us pause. It may help us to understand where, how and why our convictions are hard to live up to and put into practice. It may help us perceive more clearly what obstacles we'll need to overcome in order to change our church's culture.

In other words, by seeking to bring change to our own lives, we will come to the church culture-change process not as armchair experts, but as active participants who have confronted all the difficulties and challenges personally. We will be ready not only to lead by example, but also better equipped to understand the nature of the change that we will be calling upon others to undertake.

All of which is to say—don't rush too quickly to Phase 3. Allow time for the challenges of Phase 2 to bite. Give yourself time to get your hands dirty, to experience what it's like to change the attitudes and expectations and practices of your own life, and to make some personal progress.

Of course, neither can you wait till you've finished Phase 2 before you begin Phase 3, because Phase 2 is never finished. It's not a stage we embark upon and then pass through. It's simply putting into practice the vision of the Christian life that we say we hold, and continuing to do so. Like Paul, we will always be in the process of forgetting the darkness that is behind us and straining forward to the prize that lies ahead.

As a rough guide, before moving on to Phase 3 we'd suggest giving yourself at least as much time in Phase 2 as in Phase 1—that is, spend at least as much time in reforming your own personal culture as you spent in clarifying your convictions.

> As you engage in reforming your personal culture, we encourage you to make the most of the support available at **thevineproject.com**.

DISCUSSION AND PERSONAL COMMITMENTS

1. Moving to the right yourself (or learning Christ)
Think about these questions to evaluate your progress as a learner of Christ, and make some fresh plans and commitments.

a. How much time do I spend each day doing things like reading blogs, the newspaper and magazines, using Facebook and other social media, and watching TV?

b. How much time do I spend each day reading and mulling over God's word and praying for myself and for others?

c. What fresh commitments will I make to daily engage with God in his word and pray to him?

d. What can I do to learn more from sermons in both understanding and practice?

2. Moving others to the right (or helping others to learn Christ)

Talk through the different spheres of life mentioned above:

- household
- world
- group
- church

What would it mean for you to live and breathe your convictions in each of these contexts? Work out *one action* you wish to take in each sphere to move others to the right, and prayerfully commit yourself to do so over the next few months. Here are some thoughts and examples to spark your thinking in each area.

Household

a. What is one new habit you could form or resurrect to grow your household as a 'learning Christ' community?

b. Think about the rhythm of your day and week as a family. When are the regular times you could utilize for discussion, Bible reading and prayer? If there are no regular times (if it is all total chaos), are there some changes you need to make to carve out some time?

c. Think and pray about each member of your family. Can you think of one issue or truth or struggle that each one needs help with? What could you do to help them 'move to the right' in that area?

World

a. Think of three unbelieving friends you'd like to pray for and try to engage with about Christ. What is an achievable next step for each one of them?

b. Think and pray towards reading the Bible personally with someone who wants to know Christ. Read Colossians or Mark's Gospel using the Swedish or COMA method, or try something like *You, Me and the Bible*.[7]

c. Brainstorm some ideas in your Vine Project Team for how you could work together in engaging with your friends and sharing the gospel (e.g. everyone invites a friend to a group BBQ; as a group you run an evangelistic course like *Introducing God*; etc.).

Small group or class

If we are serious about infusing disciple-making into our whole church, our small groups will need to be incubators of this culture. And there's no better place to start than in a group or class that you're currently part of. What would it mean to start shifting the culture of your group in the direction we've been discussing? You could, for example:

- Meet one-to-one with one of the younger or less mature Christians in the group to establish them in the faith, and to equip them to bring the gospel to their family and networks.
- Start sharpening and clarifying the convictions of the group about disciple-making (e.g. by working through *The Course of Your Life* or by reading *The Thing Is*).[8]
- Equip the group with some basic ministry skills and experience, using resources such as these:[9]
   - *Six Steps to Loving Your Church*
   - *Two Ways to Live: Know and Share the Gospel*[10]
   - *One-to-One Bible Reading*

7 Tony Payne's *You, Me and the Bible: A Reading Guide to the Six Central Ideas of the Bible*, (Matthias Media, Sydney, 2014) is a six-part guide (with optional video resources) to help you read the Bible with an unbelieving friend. Visit matthiasmedia.com for details.

8 Tony Payne, *The Course of Your Life*, Matthias Media, Sydney, 2011; Tony Payne, *The Thing Is*, Matthias Media, Sydney, 2013. For more details about *The Course of Your Life*, visit matthiasmedia.com/coyl.

9 These three resources are all available at matthiasmedia.com.

10 Phillip D Jensen and Tony Payne, *Two Ways to Live: Know and Share the Gospel*, rev. edn, Matthias Media, Sydney, 2003.

The value of working on these sorts of skills in small groups is that you can practise together and continue to review what you've learned. You can urge each other to actually use what you've learned, and you can share stories of success and struggles. Leaders can also model how they use these disciple-making skills and tools. We will think further about building the disciple-making culture into our small group and class ministries in Phase 4.

Church

What would it look like if your whole Vine Project Team demonstrated what it means to come to church to help others learn Christ—that is, if you began to put into practice your sharpened convictions about Sunday church being a theatre for disciple-making? For some practical ideas on how to get started, read and discuss *How to Walk Into Church*.[11]

3. Team prayer

As you keep meeting together during this phase of the Vine Project, share and pray about your successes and failures, and encourage each other to keep going.

You might even choose to write some team prayers, based on the five convictions in Phase 1 and the actions you have committed to above. These prayers might include confession and repentance about where you have not lived out your convictions, and of course thankfulness and praise for God's mercy and for his grace in not only teaching us Christ but also using us to teach that same grace to others.

---

11 Tony Payne, *How to Walk Into Church*, Matthias Media, Sydney, 2015; or work through the small group resource *Six Steps to Loving Your Church*, which works through the same material. Both are available at matthiasmedia.com.

PHASE 3 //
LOVING, HONEST EVALUATION

Loving, honest evaluation

A re you satisfied with how things are going at church?

This is one of those loaded questions that deserves an emphatic yes-and-no answer—if such a thing is possible.

On the one hand, it's really quite wicked *not* to be satisfied with our church. How can we not be profoundly contented and joyful at all that God has done to rescue and deliver us, and call us into the gathering of his people, and grow and edify and encourage us through our fellowship? What sort of ungrateful clods would we be to occupy a default state of grumpy dissatisfaction with church? Surely we should look around us at the stumbling, bumbling bunch of nobodies (including us) whom God has rescued to be his people, and rejoice, and rejoice, and rejoice again.

And yet rejoicing at church doesn't exclude a godly dissatisfaction with church—any more than our personal thankfulness to God for forgiveness excludes dissatisfaction with the sin that remains in our lives. Our churches are just so 'this present evil age'. They're messy and incompetent, because they are comprised of messy and incompetent people. If Christians are, in Luther's words, *simul justus et peccator* ('at the same time justified and sinful'), then our churches are much the same: *simul fantastic et frustrating*.

In this sense, our attitude to the current state of our churches should be much the same as towards our Christian lives—deeply satisfied, but always dissatisfied. As we saw in Phase 2 (and in Philippians 3 in particular), the Christian life is a story not only of holding true to what we have attained in Christ, but of straining forward to what lies ahead. We yearn for growth and change, pray for it, and make every effort to work for it through the means God has provided. And yet at the same time we should be vastly contented, and rejoice—not only that God has rescued and redeemed us and that everything is already done in Christ, but that he himself is working through us with all his powerful energy. The double nature of the Christian life is also the double nature of Christian ministry and church life.

This sense of godly dissatisfaction is a good place to start as we come to a vital stage in the Vine Project—the phase where, as we Australians like to put it, we go into the room of mirrors and take a good hard look at ourselves.

We won't spend too long seeking to justify the importance of this phase. It should be uncontroversial—if we're going to make any significant progress in bringing real and lasting change and improvement to our church or ministry, we need to arrive at a clear, honest picture of where we're starting from. We need to understand where our convictions are being lived, practised and expressed, and where they are not. We need to understand where the real problems are, as well as where the real potential is. Without honestly and openly confronting the facts of our situation, any plans or desires about changing the culture or making progress in disciple-making are just wishful thinking.

This honest evaluation has an important side benefit. It helps to build a sense of urgency; it makes it painfully clear to us that things cannot stay as they are. It's like the diagnosis the doctor gives us (that we're pre-diabetic or at serious risk of heart failure) that finally provides the motivation to do what we know we should have been doing anyway (improve our diet and get more exercise). An honest, accurate diagnosis of the threats we face can concentrate the mind wonderfully.

This may seem obvious, but that doesn't make it easy. In fact, because this phase is challenging and often confronting, many of us are tempted to slide quickly past it.

We have seen this quite often as we've talked to pastors about *The Trellis and the Vine* over the past six years. Many pastors have been excited about refocusing on disciple-making or 'vine work', and have done what they normally do in such circumstances—just started something new. It may have been a new emphasis on one-to-one Bible reading, or a training course on personal ministry, or a sermon series on the subject, or any number of other activities or ideas. There's some initial enthusiasm, and even some scattered positive outcomes, but soon (usually within 12 months), the attempt at making a difference has been absorbed by the existing culture and structures and general busyness of the congregation, and the pastor wonders whether anything will ever really change.

It's worth saying that this is not because churches are more resistant to change than other human organizations or groups. This is just part of how most groups of people function, especially when they've been doing something together for a while. A culture develops—a 'way of doing things around here'—that has its own contours and geography; its own historical foundations and framework; its own habits, rituals, traditions, language, and all the rest.

Churches are not immune from this very human phenomenon. In fact, most church cultures share with other human organizations a high level of discomfort with any sort of honest open questioning of the way things are. This is a touch ironic, because of all people Christians ought to be the ones who embrace honest constructive re-evaluation. After all, Christians believe in the inevitable effects of sin and imperfection in all activities and groups (including churches); we believe in the possibility and desirability of growth and change by the power of God; and we believe that honesty and truthfulness are godly virtues.

But of course the very presence of sin in our midst is itself the chief obstacle to open, loving, honest self-evaluation and constructive criticism. We may believe in theory in the value of honest and open evaluation, but it can go wrong in multiple directions depending on the particular sins we're most susceptible to.

We can become defensive and self-protective because our

worth is tied up in what we do rather than in the grace God has shown us in Christ; or we can get snarky and over-critical because when we put someone else down it in some way lifts us up; or we might find reasons for things to stay the way they are because we like them that way, and our own comfort and satisfaction is more important to us than the salvation and growth of other people.

But perhaps the most devastating sin that gets in the way of loving, honest evaluation is flattery. We want people to feel good about themselves (and us), and so we avoid criticism and say only nice things. We exaggerate the positives and politely gloss over the negatives.

Proverbs has some timely words on this subject:

> Better is open rebuke
> than hidden love. (Prov 27:5)

> Faithful are the wounds of a friend;
> profuse are the kisses of an enemy. (Prov 27:6)

> Whoever rebukes a man will afterward find more favour
> than he who flatters with his tongue. (Prov 28:23)

Of course, it also warns about the opposite danger:

> There is one whose rash words are like sword thrusts,
> but the tongue of the wise brings healing. (Prov 12:18)

> A soft answer turns away wrath,
> but a harsh word stirs up anger. (Prov 15:1)

As we come to talk about different aspects of church life—and in this phase we will be talking about this a lot and in detail—we need to do so with a commitment to loving, godly honesty. In fact, before you get into the meat of the evaluation exercises and activities, make sure you spend some time on Evaluation Exercise 1, which looks at some Bible passages about love, honesty, trust, how to speak with one another, and so on.

Talk openly together about the challenges of this kind of evaluation, and prayerfully make a commitment together that you will proceed in a spirit of mutual trust, love and honesty.

About Phase 3

This phase follows on from the previous two:

- In Phase 1, you took the time to clarify your convictions about 'learnership' and making learners. You came to a common mind about the purposes and truths and values that all ministry should reflect.
- In Phase 2, you deepened and embraced your understanding of these convictions by living and modelling them; by reforming your personal culture around them. You started (or continued) to experience what these convictions looked like in practice.

Now, in Phase 3, you are going to bring these convictions to bear on the current state of play in your group or fellowship or church. And to be effective, this evaluation will need to look at church life from multiple angles.

For example, we will need to talk about *people*. If our convictions say that Christian ministry is about moving every person 'one step to the right', then in order to get some sense of where we are, we'll need to think about where all our people are on the journey. We'll need to think about whether the vision of 'making learners of all nations' is grasped by our people (or by many of them). We'll need to consider how every person in our fellowship could move to the right—what do they need to 'learn' next in becoming like Jesus?

We will also need to evaluate all the different ministry *activities* that take place from week to week—or to put it another way, the various 'trellises' that we have in place that are meant to facilitate and optimize the 'vine work' of moving each person to the right through the word and prayer.

This will include evaluating all aspects of our main *Sunday gatherings*, because (as we noted in Phase 1, Conviction 4) Sunday is the prime time for disciple-making. It is the key flagship time for making learners of Christ through the prayerful speaking of God's word. It sets the tone and teaches and reinforces our convictions. More than any other single activity, the regular Sunday gathering forms and shapes the culture of your entire congregational life. It's the heartbeat. If Sunday is not 'aligned' with your convictions—if it is not teaching and exemplifying and reinforcing what you essentially believe about ministry—then there is little chance of meaningful culture change ever happening.

The goal is to have a clear and realistic picture of your activities, structures, events and programs:

- Which ones are working well (i.e. are well aligned with your convictions), and should be championed and built upon?
- Which ones have real potential, with some work?
- Which ones do not currently embody your convictions and don't seem to have much potential for change?
- Where are the gaps: those areas where you're not doing much, and where new programs or structures or activities might be needed?

The goal of this phase is discovery, understanding and clarity. It's not to generate new ideas or solutions (that's our next job, in Phase 4). It's very easy in the midst of evaluation to jump straight to what we should do about it. Try to resist this temptation! You might find it useful to have an ideas file or 'parking lot' for suggestions and new ideas that arise during the evaluation phase—somewhere to note down the idea or suggested solution, so that you can come back to it in Phase 4.

As with most aspects of the Vine Project, the suggested evaluation exercises below are more of a menu to choose from than a curriculum you must follow. Please feel free to modify them to better fit your circumstances and the time you have available. Having said that, we would strongly urge you to do some version of exercises 1-4 as a bare minimum before summarizing your findings and moving on to Phase 4.

Two further tips before you get started:

- Make an audio or video recording of your entire Sunday church service/meeting. You will make use of this in one of the evaluations below. Get it organized now so that you can get on to that evaluation when you're ready.

- If you are in the process of church planting, then you won't need to spend as much time in this phase (since you are trying to establish a new culture rather than shift an existing one). However, we would suggest that you at least do Exercise 2 and Exercise 4.

As you engage in loving, honest, evaluation, we encourage you to make the most of the support available at **thevineproject.com**.

Evaluation Exercise 1: Getting your hearts ready for evaluation

Before we get started on the nitty-gritty of evaluation, we need to get our hearts and minds in the right place, and talk openly about the pitfalls of this kind of exercise.

1. Start by looking at the following passages together and jotting down anything you learn about:

   a. Our heart attitudes and motivations as we talk together (both the right motivations and those we should avoid)

   b. How we should actually speak to each other—that is, the content of what we should say and the way in which we should say it (again, both what we should do and what we should not)

   c. The consequences of the various kinds of speech

   Ephesians 4:25-5:2   Proverbs 15:4
   Colossians 3:12-17   Proverbs 27:5-6
   Proverbs 15:1-2

2. With these biblical ideas in mind, which of the following 'sins of evaluation' do you think you personally might be most susceptible to? Talk about the one (or two) that you think you are most in danger of, as well as any thoughts you have as to how to avoid this trap:

a. Being overly pessimistic or negative about particular ministries or people
b. Being unrealistically optimistic or positive about particular ministries or people
c. Scoring points or settling scores (e.g. "I always said that Ministry X would never work, but no-one listened to me")
d. Getting some personal satisfaction from pointing out the shortcomings or failures of others
e. Becoming defensive or resentful about any perceived criticism of ministries and activities you are involved in
f. Wanting to avoid tension and conflict at all costs, and so not being willing to express a negative or a criticism
g. Getting bogged down in detail (e.g. on all the administrative reasons why the Christmas event last year was such a debacle)
h. Talking only in generalities and being unwilling to discuss concrete examples and specifics
i. Other: _____

3. See if you can come up with a summary sentence—like a motto—that will be your guide as you speak together about how things are going at church. Perhaps something along these lines:

As we do this evaluation, in all our discussion together we will seek to be motivated by _____ rather than _____, to speak in a _____ manner and avoid _____, and to pray that the result will be _____.

Evaluation Exercise 2: Where are your people up to in learning Christ?

The very first step in evaluating the current state of play is to think about your people—every single precious one of them that God has drawn into your church or fellowship, or in some cases to the fringes of your fellowship.

At one level, this is simply because ministry *is* people. Making learners means recognizing that each individual person is at a different stage of 'learnership'; it means thinking about what each person needs next in order to 'learn Christ', and indeed what each person can contribute to helping others to learn Christ.

But another reason it's very important to think carefully about your people is that this will be a determinative factor in the plans you make (in Phase 4). There's no point coming up with some grand scheme for growth and change in disciple-making if it doesn't start with the often messy reality of who people really are, and if it doesn't draw on the goodwill and hard work of the people you actually have.

This evaluation exercise, then, involves thinking about every single person in your congregation—whether members, occasional attenders, fringe people or newcomers—and doing your best to say where you think they are up to in 'learning Christ'.

For the sake of the exercise we'll use the four broad stages we described in our Phase 1 summary (Engage, Evangelize, Establish, Equip), but we'll add a few subcategories:

- **Don't know:** someone whom no-one on your Vine Project Team knows well enough to be able to say where they are up to.
- **Engaged:** non-Christian people who have come into contact with your church in the past 12 months, either through a church event or through personal relationship with one of your members; they may be an occasional or even regular attender, or someone you know about but who does not come to church.

- **Evangelized:** non-Christian people who in the past 12 months have heard the gospel clearly explained, along with a call to repentance and faith.
- **Established—new:** someone who has become a Christian in the past 12 months, and is being established in the faith.
- **Established—stuck or struggling:** someone who has been a Christian for some time (not a new convert) but who seems to be stagnating spiritually or really struggling in their faith; who does not show any obvious signs of growth in understanding or godliness (e.g. shows no willingness to serve others).
- **Established—growing:** someone who has been a Christian for some time, and shows signs of ongoing growth in understanding and godliness, including a willingness to serve others in some way (e.g. they might be involved in various rosters at church, or helping out in different areas).
- **Equipped—ad hoc:** someone who shows evidence of helping other 'learners' in the Engaged, Evangelized or Established stages move to the right through the word and prayer (whether in a formal ministry structure or informally), but who has not received any particular training or help in doing so.
- **Equipped—trained:** someone who has received or is receiving training to help other 'learners' move to the right through the word and prayer (whether in a formal ministry structure, such as a small group, or informally).

1. Print out a list of everyone in your congregation or group, and then do your best to locate everyone in one of these stages of 'learnership'.

    You could do it by having some large sheets of paper (one for each stage/category), and just writing the names on the sheets. Or you could use a spreadsheet with the stages/categories as columns (i.e. running along the top) and people's names as rows (i.e. running down the left-hand side).

    You'll find that some people can be placed in more than one stage—for example, nearly all the people whom you might put in one of the 'Equipped' categories will also be in one of the 'Established' categories. For the sake of this exercise, place people in the farthest category to the right that you think they belong in (i.e. where the categories run from left to right starting with 'Don't know' and finishing with 'Equipped—trained').

Before you begin, here are some important things to note:

- This is necessarily an imprecise exercise, not only because the categories we're using are reasonably broad but also because there is overlap, and because sometimes it's just hard to say where someone is up to. That's fine.
- In talking together about where other people are up to spiritually—even in a general way—we must make an absolute commitment to avoid gossip. Nothing that is said or discussed must go beyond your discussion, and if you find yourselves digging to an inappropriate degree into the details of someone's life, cut the conversation short and move on.
- Keep it general. This is an exercise in taking the spiritual temperature of the congregation, not in sharing juicy tidbits or confidences about people's lives.
- Keep it prayerful. Ask God to be with you by his Spirit as you reflect on where each congregation member is at in their Christian lives. If you have time, pray briefly for each person as you work through the list.

2. After you've finished working through every name you have, use some of the following discussion questions to reflect on what you've learned about the congregation:

   a. Add up all the people in the different categories or stages, counting each person once. What do these numbers tell you about your congregation? Where are you strongest? Where are you weakest? Where are the gaps?

   b. Go through the list again and get a rough estimate of how many people have moved at least one stage to the right in the past 12 months (e.g. from 'Evangelized' to 'Established—new', or from 'Established—growing' to 'Equipped')?

c. Think about those people who have moved to the right. How did this happen? What means or methods or activities helped them do this?

d. Where do you think the most significant barriers or obstacles are in moving to the right—in other words, which category do you think (in your context) is hardest for people to move out of?

e. Looking at those you thought were 'Established—stuck or struggling', what does it look like in your context for someone to be in this category? What are the signs of someone being spiritually 'stuck'? What are the areas in which people are really struggling?

f. What percentage of people is in the 'Don't know' category? What are your reflections on this?

g. Are there people in any of the 'Equipped' categories that you also think are currently 'Established—stuck or struggling'? What issues or problems might arise here?

h. Thinking back over this whole exercise, what are the three most important lessons you've learned about the make-up of your congregation?

Evaluation Exercise 3: How effective are your regular programs and activities in moving people to the right?

This exercise is similar to the last one, except that you're going to evaluate all the activities and programs you run, according to how effectively they move people to the right through the word and prayer over time.

1. List all your regular ministry programs (or 'trellises') down the left-hand side of a page or spreadsheet—all the different small groups, regular events, and ministries of various kinds. (Don't include your main Sunday church gathering at this point—

we'll think about that on its own below.) Across the top, list the following categories as column headings:

- **Engaging** (getting to know non-Christian people; beginning to open conversation about spiritual matters)
- **Evangelizing** (actually explaining the gospel clearly to non-Christian people)
- **Establishing—new** (helping new or young Christians to become firmly grounded in the faith)
- **Establishing—growing** (helping well-established Christians to keep growing in understanding and godliness)
- **Equipping** (teaching and training Christians to move others to the right in the other three categories—engaging, evangelizing, establishing)
- **Notes** (a column for jotting down any significant insights and questions that come up in your discussion about this ministry)

Now give each activity or program a rating from 1 (not effective at all) to 5 (very effective) in any of the categories for which they are relevant.

What does 'effective' mean? This is very important to be clear about. What we mean by it is this: *an activity or program is 'effective' to the extent that it facilitates the prayerful speaking of the word of God (in whatever way) over time with the result that people 'move to the right'*. In other words, you're looking for how much (or little) this ministry features what we've called above the four Ps—Proclamation, Prayer, People, Perseverance—and whether this has produced fruit (in people moving to the right).

Effectiveness isn't necessarily demonstrated by the numbers of people coming or by how positive people are about the activity. It's an assessment about the degree to which you think this particular ministry is actually achieving what your convictions say you want to achieve.

This is an exercise where you'll need to be particularly committed to honest, unfiltered but non-confrontational discussion. Many of the spiritual issues we mentioned in the introduction to this phase (above) will be particularly relevant in this discussion. It is almost certain that there will be some difference of opinion among you as to what 'score' each ministry or activity should receive. Recognize this up front, and do your best to come up with a consensus.

2. After you've finished talking through each ministry or activity, reflect on what you've learned, using these questions as a guide:

   a. Which are your most effective activities or programs in moving people to the right?
   b. Which activities/programs do you think have the most potential to be more effective with a bit of work or refocusing?
   c. Which ministries are least effective, and will be hardest to improve?
   d. If you had to choose some ministries or activities to scale down or close down in order to free up time and resources for more effective ministries, which would they be?
   e. Which stage or category is your strongest? Where are you weakest?
   f. Draw a graph with the five categories as the horizontal axis, and 'effort-time-resources' as the vertical axis. In which areas are most of the effort and resources being spent across the congregation? Where are the gaps? What does the shape of this graph tell you about your strengths and weaknesses in moving people to the right?
   g. What are your conclusions from this exercise?

Evaluation Exercise 4: How effective are your Sunday gatherings in moving Christ-learners to the right?

As we noted in Phase 1 (Conviction 4), our main Sunday church gathering is the flagship for all our convictions about making 'learners of Christ'. Rather than disciple-making being something that happens almost everywhere else *except* on Sundays, we need to regard our main church gathering as a key place (if not *the* key place) in which our people 'learn Christ'—where they are 'moved to the right' through the prayerful proclamation of God's word in the power of the Spirit, week by week.

How well does your Sunday gathering help people in each of the stages of Christian growth to 'move to the right'? How well does your Sunday gathering regularly communicate and exemplify the church's vision or convictions—for example that you are seeking to become a community of 'Christ-learners' all helping each other and everyone else to learn Christ?

As a way of getting this discussion going, listen back to the recording that you made of a random Sunday gathering at your church. Make notes as you go under the headings below. (Read through them all before you start, so that you know what to listen for.)

Engage/evangelize

1. Were there any examples of jargon or information or practices that would be confusing or alienating for non-Christian people who had been invited to church, but which could have been phrased or introduced in a way that made them more intelligible? (Imagine that your non-Christian neighbour was sitting next to you in church on that Sunday—were there times you would have wanted to lean over and whisper to them to explain something that was going on? Were there times you would have felt awkward or embarrassed for them?)

2. Was there any welcoming or introductory speech that made non-Christian people feel at home, or that explained what was going on?

3. Was anything said or done during the meeting that would help a non-Christian visitor know what they could do next in order to learn more about Christ?

4. Did anything (e.g. testimonies, news, prayers, interviews, sermon content etc.) demonstrate or communicate that your

church was actively committed to engaging and evangelizing non-Christians?

5. Can you think of anything that would have led visitors to feel that your church community lives in the real world of work, relationships, pain and disappointment (rather than in some kind of rosy paradise)?

Establish—new

1. If Christian people were visiting your church, was anything said or done during the meeting to make them feel welcomed and valued?

2. Were there any examples of rituals or traditions or practices that might be unintelligible or confusing to a new or young Christian, or to a visitor or newcomer?

3. Was anything said or done during the meeting that would help someone new to Christianity know what they could do next in order to become part of your community, or grow as a Christian (i.e. take a step to the right)?

Establish—growing

1. Were there any examples of 'transformational learning'—of the Bible being taught openly and clearly so hearts and lives could be changed by the work of God's Spirit?

2. How much time in total was spent in prayer?

3. Which aspects of the meeting gave an opportunity for people to respond to God's word—in prayer, in thanksgiving, in praise?

4. What time was given for people to reflect on their lives to confess sin, seek forgiveness and change their ways?

Equip

1. Did anything (e.g. testimonies, news, prayers, interviews etc.) showcase or communicate that it is the joy and privilege of all of us to be involved in 'moving people to the right'?

2. To what extent did the sermon/Bible teaching help the congregation learn how to read the Bible for themselves (i.e. to what extent did the preacher show how he had drawn his message from the text of the Bible)?

3. To what extent did the sermon stretch those present to think hard about biblical truth and how it applies to major issues in the church and the world?

Overall

Thinking back over the whole church meeting:

1. Would a visitor to the church that day have come away with the strong impression that prayerful reading and teaching of the Bible is your main game (i.e. that you trust in the Bible as the means God uses to 'move people to the right')? Why/why not?

2. Would you have been glad to have a non-Christian friend sitting next to you during that particular meeting? Why/why not?

3. Would you have been glad to have a Christian friend who was considering joining your church sitting next to you during that meeting? Why/why not?

Evaluation Exercise 5: What happened with your newcomers?

How your church treats its newcomers is often a good litmus test of how clearly focused you are on moving each individual person forward in Christ. Talk through together, as best you can, the pathway or process that a newcomer experiences as they arrive at your church.

1. How effectively are they initially welcomed when they first walk in?

2. Is anything done to try to obtain their contact details for follow-up?

3. What happens to newcomers directly after the church meeting? Do they tend to hang around for coffee? Do people talk to them? What's it like for them?

4. Is any information conveyed to newcomers about your church (a welcome pack, brochure, etc.)?

5. What follow-up happens in the week immediately after their visit? Do they get an email, a phone call, a personal visit?

6. What would a newcomer experience in the three months following their first visit (assuming they come back)? Would anyone particularly look out for them, or keep in touch with them? Is there a clear next step for them to learn more or to become part of things?

Evaluation Exercise 6: The numbers

Numbers can be a blunt instrument for evaluation. On their own, they don't tell the whole story. Good numbers can be a sign of spiritual health, or they can indicate that you are running a non-demanding, people-pleasing ministry that lots of people like!

All the same, reflecting on the numbers can stimulate good conversations about what we're doing or not doing well. If, for example, the number of non-Christian people being converted through our ministry is very small, this *may* be simply because God has not sovereignly blessed our widespread, thoughtful, enthusiastic efforts to share the gospel. Or it *may* be that we're not actually engaging or evangelizing very much at all (which tends to lead to not many people being converted!). The question is worth asking.

Weekly attendance

Draw up a table of weekly average church attendance over the past five years. If your church has multiple meetings or branches (e.g. a morning service and an evening service), look at the numbers for each of them, as well as the total. Reflect on the following:

1. What are the trends?

2. What progress can you give thanks for?

3. If there is a decline in numbers, what factors do you think have contributed to this?

4. Are some of your meetings/services doing significantly better than others? If so, what are your reflections on why that might be?

5. If the trends of the past five years continue, what will your numbers be in five years time?

Conversions

1. How many individuals can you name who have become Christians in the past 12 months?

2. Is this more or less than during the previous 12 months (as far as you can remember)?

3. What are your reflections about this?

4. Where and when is 'engaging' and 'evangelizing' taking place in your congregational life? What has been effective or is worth building on? What has been ineffective and why?

Equipping

1. As far as you know, how many people undertook some form of intentional development or training in the past 12 months that prepared them to move other people to the right, in the following areas?

a. Sharing the gospel with a non-Christian person

b. Reading the Bible one-to-one with someone else

c. Following up a new Christian to establish them in the faith

d. Leading family Bible and prayer times

e. Leading in children's or youth ministry

f. Leading a small Bible study group

g. Other: _____

2. What are your reflections on all of this? How would you rate your efforts in equipping Christians to minister to others?

Evaluation Exercise 7: Roadblocks

Any process of growth or change will face obstacles and road-blocks, and these vary from place to place. As much as possible, it's good to think in advance about what those roadblocks might be, and make plans to overcome them.

Look through the following list of common obstacles to change, and rate them from 1 (not currently or likely to be our problem) through to 5 (currently or likely to be a big problem for us):

a. Our members have a variety of ways of thinking about church and ministry. We're not united around a common set of convictions.

b. Many of our members are spectators or passengers rather than active participants.

c. Those of our members who are active and who get involved would mostly see their role as serving on a particular roster or in a logistical capacity—on committees, organizing events, helping out with programs etc. They don't see their role as being to move people to the right one step at a time through the word and prayer.

d. Many of our members don't have active friendships or engagement with non-Christian people.

e. Our members lack the loving sacrificial spirit that is needed to get alongside people and encourage them toward Christ. We're all a bit consumed with our own problems and challenges.

f. When we look at our church members, we see many who are anxious and broken and barely able to survive in life and faith day by day. How can we ask them to think about helping others to learn Christ when they are barely hanging on to Christ themselves?

g. Our members are too busy in life. There's a feeling that getting everyone involved in ministry (i.e. in moving others to the right) is something that might work for youth or young adults or empty-nesters, but not for busy people like us.

h. Because of our particular demographic, many of our people do not see themselves as initiators or leaders or contributors in any sphere, let alone as people who could help others know Christ.

i. Many of our members feel inadequate in knowledge and skills to minister to other people.

j. Our members have no expectation that God will use them in another person's life to see that person grow in Christ.

k. Our local communities are very complex and seem out of reach. There is a huge social and cultural gap between our church members and our neighbours. We're not sure where to start in connecting and engaging with our community.

l. There are some key strong personalities in our church who are very invested in things remaining the way they are. They are likely to oppose any efforts to change things.

m. Our keen members are already busy serving in various ministries and on rosters for various tasks. It's hard to see how they could find time for anything else (e.g. any new plans we come up with).

n. Our church program is very full. It's hard to see any 'space' (in time or in people's energy) for anything new or different.

Summary and conclusion

Think back over the various evaluation exercises you have done.

1. How would you characterize or summarize your church culture? See if you can come up with just one or two words that best capture the kind of church you are. It doesn't have to start with 'C' but here are some examples that do:

   - Confused church (we don't fight with each other, but we have no clear sense of who we are and what we're trying to do)
   - Conflicted church (there are competing ministry philosophies vying for prominence)
   - Comfortable church (we know who we are, we like it that way, and we're happy to tick along)
   - Cluttered church (lots of committed people doing lots of things, but not actually seeing many people converted or growing)
   - Cynical church (we're a bit jaded and sick of new programs and fads)
   - Consumer church (our culture is built around providing an enjoyable spiritual experience for those who come)
   - Caring church (there's a warm personal sense of care for one another, but not much 'moving to the right')

2. Look back over your evaluations and see if you can come up with your top three for each of the following:

   a. Which three areas or ministries within your church have the most potential (i.e. by investing in them, you would be most likely to bring change to the whole church culture)?
   b. If you had to scale down or close down three activities, ministries or programs, which would they be?
   c. What are the top three obstacles or potential roadblocks that are likely to stand in your way?
   d. What are the top three things you'd like to improve about your Sunday gatherings?

PHASE 4 //
INNOVATE AND IMPLEMENT

Introduction

Perhaps you have been impatient to get to this phase of the process—the one where you actually make some plans and implement them. We hope and trust that the vital groundwork you've done in the first three phases will now bear fruit in some concrete plans for change. So far, we have:

- clarified the core convictions that we want to see drive our whole church culture (Phase 1)
- sought to live and breathe those convictions in the 'personal culture' of our own lives (Phase 2)
- evaluated our current ministry culture, and sought to understand exactly where it does or does not align with our convictions (Phase 3).

Now we come to what we don't mind admitting is the most difficult and challenging phase of the process.

It has certainly been the most difficult for us to write. We've struggled with what to include and what to leave out—there is just so much we could say under each heading.[1] We've also had to work hard at making our suggestions and advice general enough

---

1 This is another reason to sign up for regular updates at **thevineproject.com**. We'll keep adding material to the website that didn't make it into the book.

to be widely usable and applicable in a range of different ministry contexts, and yet specific enough actually to be of use in helping you plan for significant change.

We hope that we've managed to strike the right balance, and beg your forgiveness (in advance) for those places where we haven't. Our goal throughout is to give you a picture of what a transformative learning community might look like in all its different facets—a taste or sense of the massively diverse possibilities that exist for changing the way your church thinks and speaks and acts, such that a new culture develops over time.

We also strongly suspect that this will be the toughest phase to work through for you as a Vine Project Team, for at least four reasons.

Firstly, this is the phase where you're inevitably going to upset some people, because this is the phase where you start actually changing things—where you initiate new things, tweak existing things, and stop doing other things. No matter how carefully, sensitively, lovingly and thoughtfully you manage this, some people will have negative feelings. It's an inescapable part of our fallen human nature. When you start a new something, some people will be suspicious, resistant or cynical. When you tweak or upgrade an existing something, some people will complain that they preferred it the way it was (which is how we've been doing it for ages). And when you stop doing something, some people who were particularly invested in that ministry will grieve its passing.

This, of course, is no reason to give up on the change process. After all, if you left things exactly as they were, a different bunch of people would complain that nothing ever changes and that we're getting nowhere! But it is a reason to plan carefully so as to minimize disruption and disappointment where possible, to work hard on bringing people with you as you make changes, and to pray hard that God would shed his love abroad in the hearts of his people to make them more concerned for others than for themselves. (By the way, it's worth making a special effort to bring some of your constructive critics inside the tent. It's not as pleasant as holding hands and singing 'Kumbaya', but loyal opposition is a great asset for sharp thinking, workable plans and, in time, broad buy-in.)

Secondly, this phase will be difficult because churches are complex. Planning how to get all the different parts of the church 'machine' working together in the direction of disciple-making is tricky—there just seem to be so many moving parts! And when we add to that the fact that each one of those parts is a complex, messy, unpredictable, fallen human being (including we who are doing the planning), then the process becomes even more challenging. It will require God-given quantities of persistence and thoughtfulness to think through a plan that makes sense of the complex entity that is your church. It will need God-given reserves of persistence, forbearance and kindness as you treat all the members of your community as precious people and not just pawns in your grand plans. And you will need to keep trusting firmly in God—that he uses the faltering and imperfect plans and efforts of people, even of sinful people like us, to work his amazing purposes out.

Thirdly, this phase will be complicated because your context and situation will significantly shape your plans. We are writing in a Western, First-World context, so our examples and stories tend to assume adequate church facilities in relatively peaceful societies with economic conditions that allow for pastors and teams to receive appropriate salaries and execute strategic plans. But we know from talking with readers of *The Trellis and the Vine* that some of you will be ministering in the jungles of the Amazon or in the townships of Cape Town or in the cities of Eastern Europe, and everywhere in between. We believe that the biblical convictions of Phase 1 and the preparation of Phases 2 and 3 are applicable everywhere, but this next phase of making and implementing plans will be shaped very much by your context.

The *fourth* reason this phase will be tough is because execution is always hard. A significant body of management literature has built up around this very common phenomenon in strategic planning. Most organizations (whether businesses or schools or churches) find it quite possible to put together a sensible and coherent strategic plan for making progress on their goals. But actually following through over time and putting the plan into effect? That's much harder.[2] It's why so many strategic planning documents sit gathering dust in bottom drawers all over the world.

This is something to be aware of up-front, and to factor into your planning. Don't come up with such huge, ambitious, blue-sky plans that you're setting yourself up for a quick failure in execution. Recognize that, as with all house renovations, actually turning plans into reality takes longer, costs more, and is fraught with more hiccups and obstacles than you thought possible. (This is why there's a Phase 5 in our suggested process—it's important to plan how you're going to deal with inevitable obstacles and failures, and keep the momentum going.)

Well, if you're still game to proceed, let's dive in.

If you're going to see significant culture change over time in your church or ministry, you will need to generate and implement significant plans in at least four key areas:

1. Your main gathering (in most churches this will be the Sunday church gathering)—so that it better functions as a 'flagship' for the culture you want to create.
2. The rest of your church life (all your programs, ministries, groups and activities, including the home life of each member)—so that they provide clear and effective path-ways for 'moving people to the right'.
3. Your long-term plans for growth—so that you're antici-pating and preparing for the growth that (God-willing) your plans will produce.
4. Your communication and common language—so that a new way of thinking and talking about disciple-making and ministry becomes normal in your fellowship.

In this phase of the Vine Project, you will devise a strategic plan for each of these four focus areas. After working through them,

---

2   For a good summary, see Lawrence G Hrebiniak, 'Execution is the Key' in *Making Strategy Work: Leading Effective Execution and Change*, Wharton School Publishing, Upper Saddle River, 2005, pp. 1-29, available online (viewed 2 March 2016): http://ftpress.com/articles/article.aspx?p=360437

you may decide that there are other key plans you need to make that aren't included in our process.[3] That's completely fine, but these four areas are the ones to start with.

It's also worth acknowledging that these four focus areas overlap and interconnect. For example, Sunday will serve as a rallying point, and a source of spiritual vitality and direction for all the ministries, groups, activities and programs throughout your church life. Communication and common language will be just as important in small group and other ministries as it is on Sunday. And plans for long-term growth relate to Sunday, and to other ministries, and to communication.

This means that it probably doesn't matter very much in which order you think through the four focus areas, because you will need to work through all four and then come back and go through them all again—to see where your various plans are interlocking or conflicting, to consider which focus areas and actions you want to prioritize, and so on. (But note: there is some obvious logic in thinking about language and communication *after* you've settled on your vision and plans and priorities in the other focus areas.)

In each of the four areas, we will put forward a range of ideas and suggestions that show how your convictions (from Phase 1) can be expressed and embodied and reinforced to create a new church culture. In each case, the process will then be for you to think about your current circumstances (from the evaluation in Phase 3), and draw up a simple strategic plan for bringing change to each area, including:

- a small set of clearly articulated strategies or priorities
- some simple, measurable, realistic goals for those priorities
- a set of actions to start heading towards those goals (including who's going to do them, by when, with what resources/cost).

Let's get cracking.

---

3   For example, we talk briefly about the home under Focus Area 2, but you may wish to make it a focus area all on its own.

Focus Area 1: Make Sunday a flagship

I f we are going to bring change to 'the whole way we do things around here', then we need to think about our main weekly gathering—for two obvious reasons.

The *first* is that our main church services or meetings are prime occasions for learning Christ. We've touched on this point already in Phase 1 (Conviction 4)—that our Sunday gatherings can't be excluded from the 'where' of making learners of Christ, as often seems to be the case in church life. In fact, far from being excluded, the occasions when the whole congregation gathers are the primary and essential times in which God's people are edified in their learning of Christ through the word and Spirit of God.[1] Whatever else happens on Sunday, or whatever else we hope to achieve or do on Sunday, if we are not seeing 'transformative learning' taking place through the prayerful speaking and teaching of the Bible, then something has gone wrong somewhere.

The *second* reason we have to think carefully about Sunday is that it sets the tone and direction for everything we do as a church

---

1 For convenience, we will keep referring to these gatherings or meetings of the whole congregation simply as 'Sunday' or 'Sunday church', since that's the day on which nearly all of us have these gatherings.

community. Sunday is the rallying point, the flagship, the heartland—or whatever other metaphor you'd like to use to describe that regular event which constitutes and defines and glues together a community of people. Sunday is where we are most 'us' as a church—where our character and purposes and 'culture' as a congregation are most clearly expressed. It's where we communicate most often and most clearly what we're on about. If we want our whole church culture to change in the ways we've been discussing, then Sunday also has to change. The 'whole way we do things' on Sunday has to teach and express and reinforce and embody the convictions we have about making disciples.

This may sound harsh, but if our Sunday gatherings do not embody our convictions (if they express a different culture that is based on different underlying convictions), and if we do nothing to address this (perhaps because it feels too hard), then realistically we can forget about making any meaningful progress on culture change in our congregation. Introducing a new emphasis on 'transformative learning in Christ' or 'taking a step to the right', but doing nothing to express and teach and model this on Sunday, will end up being like the thought experiment we did early on in 'Changing the culture'—of trying to insert evangelical theology into an Anglo-Catholic culture without changing anything in the way the Sunday service was conducted. It is almost certain to fail.

If we are going to make real progress, our Sunday gatherings must be places where 'transformative learning' takes place through the word of God and prayer, and where the whole culture that we want to foster is modelled, expressed, championed and propagated. We want our Sunday gatherings to be places where people experience our convictions in the way that everything is said and done, and in the way that the members live and breathe them. We want a thoughtful visitor to come to church for a few weeks and be able to say, "I can see exactly what these people are on about"—with their perceptions matching our convictions.

Now here is one of the points in this book where the existing traditions and cultures of our readers will be most diverse. As we've talked 'trellis and vine' with many pastors over the past six years, we have found widespread agreement on our evangelical convictions about ministry and disciple-making among Reformed Baptists and Not-At-All-Reformed Baptists, among folk from Congregational churches, traditional Presbyterian churches, independent Bible churches, Anglican or Episcopalian churches, Reformed Charismatic churches, and more besides.

But interestingly, despite a high level of convictional agreement among these many and various churches, when it comes to the way we 'do' Sunday, there is a massive array of practices and styles. We each have a language, an order in which we do things, a set of rituals and traditions, a musical style, a dress code, a vibe. In some cases, that Sunday culture has only been established in the past 10 or 15 years; in other cases, it goes back centuries. But in nearly every case, it will feel for most of us, and for the congregation, that it has been ever thus.

We'd like to suggest that whether your Sunday culture has a more formal feel and comes by way of the classic liturgical forms of the Reformation, or whether it has a more informal modern-evangelical vibe, there is a great deal you can do to move your Sunday meeting culture to the right—to make it a flagship for transformative learning. As we outline a range of suggestions and ideas for doing so (below), we're confident that you'll be able to do the 'cultural translation' to apply them to your own situation.

We also trust that you'll treat the ideas we've assembled as wisdom rather than law. We want to stimulate your thinking, and give you the benefit of our 60+ years of combined thinking and learning and experience in trying to build disciple-making cultures. But we are very aware of how much we still have to learn from others, how limited is our finite human understanding of the complexities of life and ministry, and how wonderfully God has gifted other people (including those in your Vine Project Team).

The plan for this first focus area is to look at each broad stage of people moving to the right as a Christ-learner (Engage, Evangelize,

Establish, Equip),[2] and to think about how Sundays could facilitate this movement and model the whole process to the congregation. We'll look at:

1. Engaging unbelievers on Sunday
2. Evangelizing on Sunday
3. Establishing on Sunday
4. Equipping on Sunday
5. Equipping *for* Sunday
6. Stories about Sunday

Then we'll spend some time planning to make Sunday a flagship.

1. Engaging unbelievers on Sunday

What's it like for a complete outsider to come to your Sunday gatherings? We're talking about a non-Christian person who has been invited by one of your members, or who has just wandered in—someone on the far left-hand side of our 'move to the right' spectrum, who knows very little about Christ or church or Christianity.

Does your Sunday service engage them? Is it comprehensible and accessible to them? Do they feel welcomed and appreciated?

It is quite possible to 'do' church in a manner that is open and welcoming and accessible to the outsider, without changing the basic purposes and activities of our church gathering, or dumbing down the level of content, or reducing the number of important spiritual activities that outsiders might be unfamiliar with (like prayer).

In saying this, we don't intend to venture into the world of 'seeker-sensitive church'—that is, a Sunday meeting such as was very popular in the 1980s and 90s, where the whole service is built around appealing to the non-churched visitor, with a warm attractive ambience, a Bible-lite practical message, and an invitation to

---

2   These are the four broad categories we introduced in the convictions summary at the end of Phase 1.

find out more.[3] We're simply suggesting that we can 'do' church in a way that is not incomprehensible and embarrassing for the outsider.

It's like taking in a guest at your house for Christmas dinner. This often happens in our part of the world. If there's someone at church who doesn't have any family to share Christmas with, then you invite them to join your family for Christmas lunch. Now in doing so, you don't change who you are or what your family does in any significant way at all. But you make very sure that your guest is looked after. You warmly welcome them, and introduce them around. You explain what is going on at different points— why Uncle Fred always has to sit in that chair, what the background is to your funny family games or rituals, how to play, and so on. You put yourself out to make your guest feel at home and part of the family, even though it's not their home or their family.

Likewise in church—outsiders are not part of our church family. We don't stop being who we are, or pursuing God's purposes, just because we have guests present. But we do welcome our guests, who, like the 'outsiders' in 1 Corinthians 14, turn up and (God-willing) come to know and worship the living God in our midst.[4]

As we've already noted,[5] there are not two words of God, one for unbelievers and one for believers. The gospel of Christ that saves is the same gospel of Christ that matures and transforms us. So another way of asking the question is this: Is the word of Christ prayerfully proclaimed in church on Sunday in a way that is accessible and understandable for both believers and unbelievers?

There are a multitude of little things we can do to make an outsider feel engaged and welcome, rather than confused or uneasy:

---

3   In the seeker-sensitive model as pioneered by Bill Hybels at Willow Creek Community Church, Sunday was really an evangelistic rally to gather in outsiders—the 'real' church gathering, with deeper Bible teaching and the rest, took place on a week night.
4   1 Cor 14:16-17, 23-25
5   In Phase 1 (Conviction 3).

- Mention them during the meeting—for example, "If you're new with us today, and especially if you're new to church or to Christianity, we're really glad to have you with us. We always have visitors here at church, including people who are at all different stages in their relationship with God— it's great to have you with us." Of course, the way you do this will vary according to the size of your church and the norms of your surrounding culture.

- Provide little explanations that serve to orient an outsider to what's happening—for example, "We're going to read the Bible together now, because that's where God speaks to us. The passage we'll be reading is from John chapter 1. You'll find that on page 756 of the church Bibles."[6]

- Be aware that visitors often listen very carefully to our notices or announcements. What we announce and how we announce it can have a big impact on what an outsider thinks we're on about, and how welcome they feel in our midst. Our announcements advertise not only the particular events but what sort of community we are, what we think is important, and so on.

- Preach as if outsiders are present. When introducing a topic or applying a biblical truth, assume that some listeners aren't Christians, and engage them appropriately. Pause to explain jargon as you go along. (We will say more below about preaching to believers and unbelievers in the same sermon.)

- Avoid in-jokes and embarrassing activities—that is, ones that Christians might be accustomed to or tolerate, but which an outsider would be embarrassed by. (An example from our part of the world: don't sing a children's song and require all the adults to stand up and do silly actions.)

- Provide a next step for the outsider—ways to find out more, opportunities to read the Bible with someone, a gathering or event especially for new people, and so on.

---

6   As with all things, this should be done judiciously. You don't want your gathering to die the death of a thousand explanations.

If you want to gauge how friendly or engaging your church is for outsiders, one simple way is to invite a friend to come to church with you—and then see what it feels like as the service proceeds. You will suddenly notice all those things, small and large, that are awkward or embarrassing or alienating for your friend, because he or she is sitting right there beside you. (Of course you should ask your friend what they noticed too.)

Another interesting exercise is to visit an unfamiliar cultural context and see how it feels. We are not necessarily recommending this, but someone we know once took a group of leaders from his church down to the local TAB (that's Australian for 'betting shop'), for them to experience what it was like to be a total outsider. This was a place that none of these men had ever been before, and it was an instructive experience. They were dressed very differently from everyone else. They didn't know where to stand or where to look. They tried to work out what to do by following the signs and imitating the guys standing around, but found it difficult. And when they finally went to place bets, they felt embarrassed and totally out of place.

This is what church feels like for many outsiders.

If we make church a place that is friendly and welcoming and engaging for a non-Christian outsider—that is, if we conduct our church meetings expecting non-Christian outsiders to be there—then we send a powerful message to everyone present. We communicate to the visitor that they are very welcome, but *we also constantly communicate to our members that church is a good place to invite their non-Christian neighbours and friends to.*

Like everything in this section, this also relates to equipping. If we want our members to invite outsiders along to church, and to be warm and welcoming to them when they are there, we will need to think about how we are going to help them learn to do this. Part of 'moving to the right' on Sunday is moving the congregation itself forward, so that they understand and are equipped for engaging with newcomers. (We'll come back to this below under 'Equipping for Sunday'.)

Having said all this about making church as welcoming and

accessible as possible for the outsider, our goal is *not* to remove the 'weirdness factor' from church for unbelievers. Unbelieving visitors will still find aspects of our meetings strange. Some will be completely surprised by the communal singing; some will never have sat for 30 minutes and listened to anything like a sermon before in their lives; others will find it weird that we would all bow our heads and close our eyes and pray. But we will still do those things, because they are part of learning Christ. Our goal is not to remove everything that might be unusual or foreign or outside the unbelieving visitor's experience—otherwise, there wouldn't be much point in them turning up!

In other words, we won't ever stop being distinctively Christian, and doing what we do. It's just that we'll try to make it as easy as possible for an outsider to be there, to 'look in' at what is happening, and to be intrigued and affected (by God's grace) enough to want to come back.

DISCUSSION

1. What do you think is the attitude of your members towards inviting a non-Christian friend or family member along to church?

2. What elements of your current church meeting would you class as:

   a. confusing or incomprehensible for an outsider?
   b. embarrassing for an outsider?
   c. welcoming and friendly to an outsider?
   d. engaging and relevant for an outsider?

3. If you were going to make just three changes to your church meeting to make it more engaging for an outsider, what would they be?

4. If an unbeliever came to your church on any given Sunday, what would they conclude about what it means to be a 'Christ-learner' from the things you do together? Apart from the content of the sermon, what would the different aspects of the gathering communicate to them about what you believe?

2. Evangelizing on Sunday

Is your Sunday church service a place where non-Christian visitors hear the gospel?

In one sense, it follows on naturally enough from thinking about engaging outsiders to considering whether or how we might evangelize outsiders who come to our Sunday gatherings. And we might say that of course Sunday should be a gospel event, and that the death and resurrection of Jesus would surely be proclaimed.

But then again, some of us may feel a little uneasy about this. Isn't Sunday church primarily a time for corporate worship, or for the edification and the strengthening of the saints? If Sunday is for evangelism, when do the saints get fed solid food?

Historically, some churches have reflected their view of the relationship between Sunday church and evangelism by having two services on Sunday: the morning 'worship' service and the evening 'gospel' service.[7]

In our view, this separates things that God has not separated—namely, the powerful word of the gospel and the edification of the church. The church is certainly the gathering of God's redeemed people around their Lord, in order to listen to his word and to respond to him in repentance and faith and thanksgiving and

---

7 This was really a precursor to Willow Creek's seeker-sensitive approach, which had the 'outreach' service as the main event on Sunday mornings, and the 'worship' or 'teaching' meeting on Wednesday nights.

praise. But if the word we hear and respond to in church is not constantly holding up Christ, and turning our eyes to him as Saviour and Lord, then it is not the Bible that is being preached— because the gospel of Christ is the central message and key to the whole of Scripture. He is the one to whom the whole Old Testament looks forward, and about which the whole New Testament is obsessed.

Christianity does not have two messages, one for the outsider and one for the insider. The gospel word that builds someone into the church is the same word that builds them up in the church.[8] And the more that this word builds and sanctifies and matures a congregation of believers, the more evangelistically minded they will be. Phillip Jensen puts it like this:

> An edified Church will be holy, sanctified and different to the world, having members who are Christlike in character and life. Such members will all be committed to the salvation of mankind, for this was the very mission of the Christ (1 Timothy 1:15). A holy huddle of people, uncommitted to world evangelism, is not holy for its members are not like Christ.[9]

Perhaps we might say that although the primary purpose or focus of Sunday church is not 'evangelism' (i.e. the addressing of the gospel to non-Christian people), Sunday church should still have an evangelistic dimension or mindset. It will commend Christ to believer and unbeliever alike.

Several consequences flow from a lack of evangelistic mindset on Sunday:

---

8 Interestingly, the word 'edify' (Greek: *oikodomeō*) means simply 'to build'. Most of our English translations add the word 'up' (to 'build up'), implying that the building is of someone who is already part of the church. But when Christ said "I will build (*oikodomeō*) my church" (Matt 16:18), he was talking about the whole process—of preaching the gospel and seeing people enter the fellowship of the church and grow to maturity. The church is built by the gospel (cf. Acts 20:32; Rom 15:20-21; 1 Cor 3:9-11; 2 Cor 10:8, 13:10; Eph 2:19-22). We might say that people are 'built in' to the church just as they are 'built up' in the church, and in both cases it is by the powerful word of Christ by his Spirit.

9 Phillip Jensen, 'Evangelism and church', *PhillipJensen.com*, 9 April 2011 (viewed 6 January 2016): http://phillipjensen.com/articles/evangelism-and-church/

- You will struggle to create an evangelistic 'culture' in the congregation if there is no evangelistic awareness or edge to your Sunday meetings. Evangelism will become a bolt-on addition to your program, rather than something that is intrinsic to your fellowship. Sunday sets the tone. If the tone has an evangelistic edge to it, you will be constantly communicating the truths of Conviction 5 to the congregation—that everyone in this world is trapped in "this present darkness" and desperately needs to hear the truth of the gospel.
- As with 'engaging' (above), if there is not an evangelistic dimension to church (and especially to the preaching), then the congregation members will not bring their non-Christian friends to church to hear the word of God. Conversely, whenever you preach as if non-Christians are present, you send the very clear message that church is somewhere you can invite your friends to.
- Obviously, if there is no evangelistic content to your church meetings then those non-Christians who do wander in, and those nominal or unconverted attenders who are in every church, will not hear the gospel and be saved.

What does it mean, in practical terms, for Sunday church to have an evangelistic edge? It means at least four things.

a. Preaching with an evangelistic mindset

Preaching evangelistically doesn't mean inserting a gospel outline like *Two Ways to Live* into every message, or finishing every sermon with an altar call. In simple terms it means preaching the gospel by teaching the Bible—because the Bible is an evangelistic book. It constantly points to the person and work of Christ, and calls on us to repent and put our faith in him. Phillip Jensen, one of the great modern exponents of this sort of preaching, suggests that evangelistically minded preaching will have the following elements. It will:

- show the listener that what is being said comes out of the Bible, which is being read like any other text is read
- explain the meaning of biblical words and concepts in ordinary language
- explain the foundational doctrines of the gospel as they come out of the passage (or serve as necessary background to the passage): creation, sin, judgement, atonement, resurrection, glory
- locate the message of the passage in the story of the gospel as it unfolds throughout the Bible, climaxing with Jesus Christ—that is, it will preach the aspect of the gospel that comes out in this passage (biblical theology)
- show how the truth of the passage makes sense of the world
- humbly and graciously challenge current alternative assumptions or worldviews that fail to explain reality, with the expectation that people holding these views are very likely in the room (in other words, avoid talking about 'us' and 'them' —this will make any of 'them' who happen to be present feel decidedly unwelcome)
- apply the gospel to the real-life circumstances of people's lives (this will commend the gospel to believers and unbelievers, showing that the gospel, applied in this particular area, is good news)
- call for a response to the gospel of obedience, repentance and faith (i.e. preach for transformation)
- clearly and unequivocally declare the gospel-centred truth of God that comes out of the passage, and address the ways in which our hearts resist this message.[10]

This is a recipe for making every sermon something that commends the gospel to believer and unbeliever alike.

To put it another way, we want unbelievers to come away from church thinking, "These people face the same questions and

---

10 See especially chapter 5 in Jensen and Grimmond, *The Archer and the Arrow*. Also see Colin Marshall, 'Preaching with an evangelistic mindset', in Peter G Bolt (ed.), *Let the Word do the Work*, pp. 75-84.

troubles as I do, and they engage with the Bible in a way that is real and honest. It doesn't feel like a religious façade. I'm not sure what's true yet, but I'd like to keep learning what they're on about. I don't feel patronized or like an outsider from Mars."

Of course, some Bible passages and seasons of the year will lend themselves to being more specifically or pointedly evangelistic than others. Take advantage of those times—for example, let the congregation know in advance that the sermons over the next two weeks will be particularly good for bringing along a non-Christian guest. But the more the congregation expects every Sunday to be a time when non-Christian people are welcomed and addressed and will hear the gospel, the more likely they are to take up these special opportunities.

b. Telling stories that show the gospel at work

Most churches manage to find some way that is appropriate for their context in which congregation members can testify to the power of the word and Spirit of God in their lives. This may be in the form of the classic 'testimony' or in a short interview. It may relate to a particular incident or theme; it may be a report of how the gospel has been at work in a particular ministry or activity that the church runs.

In whatever form they take, regular stories about the everyday power of the gospel convey powerful messages and encouragement—to believers and unbelievers alike.

c. The personal witness of congregation members

Of course, not everything that happens at church happens formally or up the front. Conversations that happen before, and especially after, the meeting have great potential for evangelism. A non-Christian visitor or a nominal/non-Christian regular attender is perhaps not likely to seek out the preacher afterwards to talk further about the implications of his message. But they are sitting next to someone with whom that conversation could easily happen—if that congregation member is ready, willing and able to have the conversation.

This again comes down to 'equipping', and we will deal with it below under that heading. One of the chief ways we can bring an evangelistic edge or mindset to our Sunday gatherings is to teach and train and equip our members to have that mindset, and to know how to put it into practice in simple and achievable ways.

d. The shape of what you do

We've talked above about how 'the whole way we do things' communicates something, to believers and unbelievers alike. This includes how we structure the different elements of our gathering—what has traditionally been called the 'liturgy'. Without wanting to commend any particular form or order of church service, or get into debates about formality and informality, we would nevertheless recommend pausing to consider what the shape or 'trajectory' of your church meeting communicates— because it will communicate something, even if that 'something' is that not very much thought has gone into it.

The order in which you do things, and how you link these different elements together, can communicate gospel truths very powerfully—all the more so because it happens at a meta level, week by week. For example, in some classic Reformation orders of service, there is a movement from an acknowledgement or confession of sin, to assurance of salvation, to a response of praise and thanksgiving, to the hearing of the word (in reading and sermon), which leads again to a response of prayer and repentance. This is just one example of a shape to what is happening that in itself commends the gospel to believer and unbeliever alike.

DISCUSSION

1. What aspects of your current Sunday meeting or culture have an evangelistic edge to them? Which of these do you think have the potential to be built upon or improved? How?

2. Brainstorm some new ideas for making your Sunday gatherings more evangelistic in their tone.

3. In addressing the area of preaching with an evangelistic mindset, you'll need to discuss the quality of the preaching at your church or fellowship. Talking about this in your Vine Project Team might be a sensitive or awkward subject—assuming that the pastor is probably part of the team. Perhaps we could all agree that no matter how well your pastor preaches (and no doubt he is excellent!), there is always room for feedback and improvement.

   With that said, work out a program or method for working collegially as a team to improve this aspect of the preaching. For example: for a month, you could take turns to be the designated 'non-Christian visitor' for a Sunday, and to listen to the sermon specifically with non-Christian ears, making a note of:

   a. concepts or illustrations that connected with you and made sense as an 'outsider', as well as elements that didn't (e.g. jargon, unexplained concepts)
   b. areas or aspects where (as a 'non-Christian') you found that the message applied to your life or your view of the world
   c. aspects of the message that you found intriguing or appealing as a non-Christian, as well aspects that you might have found needlessly offensive or off-putting
   d. aspects of the message that you found challenged your views or called on you to repent as a non-Christian.

   Pass this feedback on to the pastor, who will collate it and report back to the group on some things he'd like to improve in his preaching. (And then pray together for the pastor, and work out how to provide some ongoing feedback in a useful way.)

4. Would the content of what is prayed for in your Sunday meetings convince someone that you were a group of people who longed to see the lost come to know Christ? How could you improve in this area?

3. Establishing on Sunday

One way of describing what is happening when we meet all together on Sunday is that Jesus is building his church—that he is present with us to speak his nourishing, life-giving word, and to move our hearts to respond to him by his Spirit. To put it another way, one of God's purposes for Sunday is transformational learning.[11] We meet together in the presence of God to be taught and edified so that we might grow to maturity in Christ (this is the 'establish' part of the growth spectrum).

In our observation, most churches have plenty of room for improvement in making 'transformative learning' an intrinsic part of their Sunday culture. Let's work through some examples of how we can create this kind of 'Christ-learning' culture on Sunday.

a. Preaching for transformative learning

'Sermonettes create Christianettes', the old saying goes. If we want our people to keep taking steps to the right, the sermons need to stretch them and urge them forward. Transformative preaching digs into the word, unfolds and explains its message clearly and compellingly, and applies the gospel challenge of each passage to the hearts and minds and lives of the hearers.

This doesn't at all mean that the preaching has to be academic, impenetrable, and loaded with quotes from commentaries on the

---

11 See the discussion in Phase 1, Conviction 5, about church being a theatre for disciple-making.

meaning of the Greek. That usually doesn't foster learning! But it does mean that we unapologetically approach the sermon as a high point of the meeting; as a time of serious, important engagement with the word of God; as the time when we all sit under God's word together, seeking to hear, read, mark, learn and inwardly digest it.

Preaching is far too big a subject to deal with adequately here.[12] To make just five brief points and suggestions:

- Think about each sermon as an exercise in helping people take a 'step to the right', to make progress in their understanding and obedience. As people hear you (the preacher) expound the main idea of the Bible passage, where are they starting from (i.e. what is the issue or dilemma or question or problem or sin that the passage addresses, and that probably forms your introduction)? Where do you want to take them (i.e. what is the new understanding or truth that leads to a new way of living that the passage teaches)? And how are you going to get them there (using the main points of the passage itself to move from the introduction to the conclusion)?

- Use whatever pedagogical techniques you can lay your hands on to help your listeners learn and understand (illustration, repetition, diagrams, outlines, variation in tempo, and so on).[13] Remember: the outcome you're after is not just to present the Bible's message; it's to cause your hearers to learn a truth that will change their lives.

- As a preacher, keep modelling your own determination to grow and press forward in Christ. Without making the sermon all about you (!), share from time to time how the passage has challenged your life, how it has changed your mind or taught you something new about God and his ways.

---

12 A refreshing and very practical approach to preaching as a learning experience can be found in Gary Millar and Phil Campbell, *Saving Eutychus: How to Preach God's Word and Keep People Awake*, Matthias Media, Sydney, 2013.

13 Again, you'll find some excellent ideas in Millar and Campbell's *Saving Eutychus*.

- Think of the sermon as part of a learning process rather than a one-off event. Publicize the passage to be preached on in advance; provide opportunities for people to read and think about the passage before Sunday (e.g. a few questions for personal reflection; or a Bible study that small groups can do in advance). Create the expectation that we're all coming together to learn from this part of God's word. Likewise think about ways to follow through after the sermon; provide some challenges or reflection questions for people to mull and pray over on Monday morning, or in their small groups during the following week.
- Consider how to have a question time after the sermon. Some churches do this directly after the sermon, with an opportunity for the congregation to ask questions, make comments and so on. Other churches do this sort of question time with the pastor after the main meeting has concluded. Either way, it can be enormously useful in enabling the preacher to clarify or reinforce points he has made, and clear up misunderstandings. However, it also changes the tone and expectation of what is happening: we're here together in church to learn from the word of God, to keep thinking and asking and clarifying until we understand and learn. The preacher has unfolded and explained the word, but it's the word that is truly authoritative and powerful—and the preacher sits under it as well. Question times can bring a small but helpful change in the 'learning culture' of Sunday.

b. Active prayerful listening

Learning is obviously a two-way experience. We can encourage and help Sunday to be a time of learning by encouraging and helping the congregation to be active listeners and learners. For example:

- As noted above, if the passage is known in advance, and there is an expectation of reading and thinking about it in advance, congregation members will come to the sermon more thoughtful and expectant about what they might learn.

- It can be useful to distribute printed outlines of the sermon so that listeners can see the direction of where the exposition is going, and can jot down notes and challenges and applications—not only to aid learning and memory, but to serve as material for subsequent 'inward digestion' and prayer. A culture of note-taking can be useful in promoting active listening and learning.
- Listening is a spiritual activity—"Take care how you listen", said Jesus.[14] The right sort of listening is something that can be learned, and that we should teach and encourage. We mean listening that is repentant and open-hearted, that is thoughtful and discerning, that is prayerful and humble, and that engages with the speaker (in eye contact if nothing else). Christopher Ash's little booklet *Listen Up!* is an excellent resource for equipping the congregation to be better listeners.[15]

c. Mutual teaching and encouragement

If we want to create a culture in which all of us are Christ-learners who seek to help other learners learn, then Sunday has to be a time when we practise and model this conviction. If the only person who has any ministry of the word on Sunday is the pastor, we send entirely the wrong message.

There are two main ways we can foster and model a widespread mutual ministry of the word on Sundays:

- Firstly, we can find ways within the structure of the meeting for members of the congregation to testify and encourage the congregation. In one church we were involved in, this was called '14:26 time'—after 1 Corinthians 14:26—and varied from week to week. It can be a short prepared testimony about a lesson someone has learned from the

---

14 Luke 8:18 (HCSB)
15 Christopher Ash, *Listen Up! A Practical Guide to Listening to Sermons*, The Good Book Company, London, 2009.

word, or about how the gospel has enabled someone to deal with suffering and difficulty, or about how someone became a Christian. It can be a brief interview about some word ministry that a congregation member is involved in, or a story about how God has answered your congregational prayers. It can be a brief reflection by a mature godly member of the congregation after the sermon on how the message challenged or taught him or her. All this needs to be done thoughtfully and in an orderly way,[16] and usually with some preparation. However, the more that this kind of edifying contribution from congregation members becomes part of your normal culture, the more spontaneous it can be. (In the church that Col goes to, even the men are now starting to pipe up and say something!)

- Secondly, we can encourage and equip our members to see Sunday as a place for mutual conversation and encouragement around the word of God. Once again, we'll say more about this below (under 'Equipping for Sunday'), but we should aim to get to a point where members come on Sunday with a prayerful expectation that God will use them to have encouraging, word-based conversations—whether with visitors and newcomers, or with regular members. The prime time for this is usually over coffee after the 'formal' church time—whether in chatting together about the key lessons or issues from the sermon, or about what is happening in our lives and families, or about what we've been reading in the Bible during this past week. These can be short jolts of encouragement or longer conversations that spill over into further discussion and prayer during the week. The key factor is our expectation that God would use us to help each other in this way, and our prayers that he would open our mouths to speak and to take opportunities as they come.

---

16   1 Cor 14:33, 40

d. Responsive repentant prayer

In many contemporary evangelical churches that we have visited, substantial corporate prayer has all but disappeared. There will be a 30-minute singing time, a 30-minute message, various announcements, promotions and interviews, musical items, and of course the taking of the offertory—but it seems that the only time we can afford to devote to prayer is a short, perfunctory request as the meeting opens, or as the sermon concludes. This is quite astonishing when you think about it, and says a great deal about what we think we are doing when we gather as God's people.

Prayer is basic to the Christian life and to church life, because it is the language of faith. Prayer is verbalized dependence on God.[17] Moreover, our convictions tell us that transformative learning only happens when God's Spirit sovereignly applies God's word to human hearts. We should therefore be depending constantly on God in prayer that he would do this by his Spirit in our Sunday gatherings. These convictions should shape our congregational prayers. For example:

- The tradition in some churches of praying set prayers of confession of sin, if done well, can be very helpful. It frames our hearing of the word with an attitude of repentance and longing—that we know how far short we fall, that we are unspeakably grateful for the grace of the gospel, and that we want to learn and grow and be transformed by the word of God we are about to hear.

- Likewise, it's good to have a time of prayer after the sermon, where we respond as a congregation to the message, and beg God's aid in softening and transforming our stubborn hearts. Work at integrating the content of the prayers and thanksgivings with the topic or theme that the meeting is built around.

- Just as the time outside the formal meeting on Sunday is useful for mutual encouragement and conversation and

---

17 For an expansion of this point, see Phillip Jensen and Tony Payne, *Prayer and the Voice of God*, Matthias Media, Sydney, 2006, pp. 60-64.

teaching, so also it is an excellent opportunity to pray for and with each other. When you're talking with someone about some issue or event in their life, or sharing some encouragement or conversation about the sermon, why not conclude with a brief prayer together. In fact, this is also an excellent way to start a fruitful conversation—ask the person you're chatting with if there's anything they'd like you to pray for them. In our experience, this instantly gets the conversation past the weather and the football and on to things that really matter, and often opens up opportunities for significant mutual encouragement.

e. Singing that teaches

Martin Luther, as usual, captured the wonder of God's gift of music more memorably than anyone else:

> A person who gives this some thought and yet does not regard music as a marvellous creation of God, must be a clodhopper indeed and does not deserve to be called a human being; he should be permitted to hear nothing but the braying of asses and the grunting of hogs.[18]

All the same, the subject of music in church is also a Pandora's box of worms (to squeeze as much as possible from two metaphors). We're reluctant to open it too far, but let us make just a few comments about how singing can be part of the learning culture of your congregation.

Singing is a form of emotionally super-charged speech. It consists of words that—in a way we don't fully understand—pack more punch than words that are just spoken. This makes speech-that-is-singing a particularly powerful way of building a transformative learning culture in our Sunday meetings, in at least three ways:

---

18 M Luther, 'Preface to Georg Rhau's *Symphoniae iucundae*', trans. US Leupold, 1538, in J Pelikan and HT Lehmann (eds), *Luther's Works*, vol. 53, *Liturgy and Hymns*, ed. US Leupold, Fortress, Philadelphia, 1965, p. 324.

- Some aspects of our singing are addressed to one another. Singing is a simple and powerful way for the whole congregation to teach and encourage each other. When we sing together, we stand and declare to one another God's wonderful works and character. This is what 'praise' really is—declaring (usually with joy and celebration) what God has done, how marvellous God's character is, how great and good and magnificent is the Lord Jesus Christ and his gospel.[19] This means of course that we should carefully choose songs that actually do this—where the words are full of theologically and biblically rich teaching about what God has done in Jesus Christ. As has often been noted, many pastors carefully prepare and guard the 25 minutes of teaching that happens from the pulpit, while taking no notice of the 25 minutes of teaching that happens through the songs we sing.

- It's not just the truthful content of the songs that is encouraging and transformative—it's the fact that I can see you standing there enthusiastically and joyfully showing how much you believe it. Singing is a form of testimony. It's a chance for all of us to say, "Yes, here I stand! And this is what I believe." This is encouraging, in the way that all life-example is encouraging. It helps me to know that you believe these truths too, because when you open your lungs and sing with all your heart, you tell me that you do. This is why singing heartily is such an edifying thing to do in church—whether or not we have a good voice, and whether or not this particular song is to our musical taste.

- Singing is also a powerful way to respond to God, and to what he has spoken to us through the word. In song, we can rejoice and give thanks and pray and say to God how worthy and powerful and wonderful he is (again, this is 'praise'—the declaration of God's excellencies). Singing

---

19 For more on the nature of praise as 'declaring or advertising how great someone is', see Tony Payne, 'Confessions of a teenage praise junkie', *The Briefing*, no. 173, 20 February 1996, pp. 2-5, available online (viewed 6 January 2016): http://matthiasmedia.com/briefing/1996/02/confessions-of-a-teenage-praise-junkie/

gives us the opportunity to give expression to the affections that the word of God stirs up in us.[20]

f. Declaring historic creeds and confessions

Rather like singing, reciting creeds and historic confessional statements together in church is both declaration and response. We are speaking the great truths of the faith to one another, and at the same time testifying to one another of our belief in these truths. As a regular feature of our meetings, this can be a powerful 'learning' experience (especially if we explain their meaning and the context in which they were written). It connects the little outpost of God's kingdom that is our church with the historic faith that Christians from the very beginning and in all places have believed. It says to our people (and to outsiders) that we are not just a little tribe of weirdos, sticking out like a scarecrow in a cornfield. We are in fact one branch of a massive and ancient living tree whose roots go back deep.

DISCUSSION

There's a lot to cover and think about under this section. Talk through each of the areas we've looked at, and jot down one aspect you're already doing pretty well, one existing thing that could be improved and built upon, and one new idea for making progress:

a. Preaching for transformative learning
b. Active prayerful listening
c. Mutual teaching and encouragement
d. Responsive repentant prayer
e. Singing that teaches
f. Declaring historic creeds and confessions

20 For an excellent recent discussion of all these issues related to congregational singing, see Philip Percival, *Then Sings My Soul: Rediscovering God's Purposes for Singing in Church*, Matthias Media, Sydney, 2015.

4. Equipping on Sunday

The culture we're wanting to build is one in which all the saints see it as their privilege and joy to be involved in transformative learning together—so that all God's People, each in their own way, Persevere in Proclaiming the word, in Prayerful dependence on the Spirit, to help others take a step to the right (the four Ps).[21]

We can equip our people for this prayerful proclamation in many ways and contexts, but Sunday itself is one important place where this equipping can take place. Here are three ways this can happen:

- We can preach in a way that equips. There is a way of presenting a sermon such that the hearer thinks afterwards, "Wow, that was so encouraging. But I don't know how he managed to draw that message from the passage. I could never read the Bible like that." And there's another way of presenting a sermon where the listener thinks, "Wow, that was so encouraging. And what's more I could see how his message came straight out of the content of the Bible. I think I could read the Bible like that." If as preachers we present enough of the exegetical basis for our message— enough to show how it comes out of the passage but not so much that we bore our audience with a detailed commentary on every verse—then over time we do an enormous service to the Bible reading of our people. We teach them how to read the Bible for themselves by showing them every Sunday how we are reading our sermons out of the Bible.

- Our preaching can also equip the congregation to minister the word to each other by being sharable—that is, by each sermon having as part of its application how we might share this word with someone else. Through our preaching we can set the expectation and norm that the word doesn't terminate with us—that it's for sharing and passing on. You could even have a box on your outline/bulletin with

---

21 See Conviction 3 in Phase 1 for our discussion of the four Ps.

'What I learned from the sermon today'—and encourage everyone to jot something down in that space, and talk about it together over coffee afterwards.

- We can schedule regular short 'equipping' times during our Sunday gathering—for example, have one of the congregation give a brief report about how they're reading the Bible one-to-one with someone else, and what encouraging lessons and consequences have resulted. Draw out during the interview/testimony some simple lessons about how we can all read the Bible with one another. This will be short and can only achieve so much, but the regular repetition of this sort of testimony shows the congregation how we can all be involved in helping each other learn Christ through the word.

Everything we do on Sunday shapes how our people engage in ministry—including group leaders, Sunday School teachers, and so on. It shapes how they read and teach the Bible, their understanding of Christian truth, what they pray for, how they respond to God's word—the direction of all the little boats in your fleet is set by the flagship, and that flagship is your main Sunday gathering.

5. Equipping *for* Sunday

Many of the suggestions and possibilities we've raised in this first focus area involve a change in the mindset, expectations and (in some cases) skills of our congregation. We've suggested (among other things) that it would be wonderful if all our members would:

- think and pray and invite their non-Christian friends and family to church
- be welcoming and helpful to outsiders, visitors and newcomers

- be ready to share the gospel personally with non-Christian people they meet at church
- read the sermon passage in advance, and come prayerfully ready to learn and grow
- be primed to listen actively to the sermon with open, responsive hearts
- be enthusiastic about singing
- be ready and able to speak the word conversationally to others at any point during Sunday, particularly in the coffee time after church
- be ready to pray with other people if the opportunity arises.

Imagine a congregation filled with people like that! Imagine how different the entire experience of Sunday would be, not only for the whole congregation but also for anyone who was new or visiting.

None of this will happen magically or purely by osmosis. For most of our congregation members, learning to think and pray and act in these sorts of ways will involve taking a few steps to the right. And that's how it happens—by purposefully and intentionally equipping and training and encouraging our congregation members to grow in their understanding and way of life in these areas.

This kind of equipping usually happens best in a personal or small group setting, where you can:

- work through content and ideas and information together
- practise putting it into effect, then report back to each other
- pray together about your efforts
- encourage each other to keep going when you grow weary.

There are numerous good resources available to help with this. For example:

- You could get your small groups to read through Christopher Ash's little booklet *Listen Up!* together (on how to be a better sermon listener), talking through the content, praying about it, and encouraging each other to put it into practice.

- You could take a group (or several groups) through *Six Steps to Loving Your Church*, a six-session course that works through what every Christian could do before, during and after church to be a loving encouragement to those around them (i.e. by doing the kinds of things we've been discussing in this whole section).

Whatever resources or programs or books you use to equip people in this way, it's important to remember that changing people's mindset and expectations and actions in any given area takes time and encouragement and persistence. You could, for example, give someone *How to Walk Into Church* to read, and no doubt that would help them along the way in learning to think differently about Sunday. But unless there is some kind of ongoing process of learning—of talking about it, asking questions, seeing it in action, having a go at putting it into practice, talking again, and so on—then it's not likely that a whole new way of thinking and acting will be 'learned'. Equipping someone in this way takes time and personal interaction. As we'll suggest in Focus Area 2 (about designing pathways), we need opportunities and frameworks within our congregational life where this kind of equipping can happen regularly.

DISCUSSION

1. What are some of the ways that your current Sunday meeting communicates the 'equipping' message—that all of us can be equipped to be involved in moving others to the right? What could you change or add?

2. Thinking about your current congregation members:

   a. Who among them best exemplifies the kind of mind-set, and practices what we've been discussing in this section? Who actively seeks to help others 'learn Christ' on Sunday in multiple ways?

b. How might you encourage and help them to do even better?

c. How could they help you equip others to think and act in this same way?

6. Stories about Sunday

To help illustrate what the various suggestions and principles might look like in practice, throughout Phases 4 and 5 we'll be sharing some real-life stories of churches that are working hard to effect the kind of culture change that the Vine Project aims to help you achieve.

A few things to note with each of these stories:

- We've chosen a variety of different church leaders to interview for these stories—from small and large churches, from rural and urban and suburban churches, and from different denominations and traditions.

- These are by no means perfect churches, and many still have quite some way to go in seeing a disciple-making culture take hold. Nor do these churches all agree with each other or with us on everything.

- In each case, the names and details have been fictionalized, but otherwise the interview has not been enhanced or massaged to fit in with the message of this book. The stories are real.

- What we've included here is just a short excerpt from a longer interview. In each case, you can find the whole interview at **thevineproject.com**.

Gary's story

Gary leads an evangelical Anglican church in a multicultural community with a rapidly growing population.

What helps your members invite people to church?

A warm and friendly church is key. You can't underestimate a smile. You only get one chance for first impressions. However, I still do hear of new people at morning tea standing on their own surrounded by Christians who are not intentional enough to invite them into their conversations. That's exasperating!

Children's ministry has to be done very well and *appear* to be done well. People entrust their little darlings to you, and so often it can be the kids who get the parents to come to church.

We've also found it important to have consistently good preaching that is clear, engaging, faithful and Jesus-focused, and that is mindful of the non-Christians, who are addressed with gentleness and respect. We take it that the church is first for the believer but we must always have the eye on the outsider so that hopefully their questions are being addressed. We want to be an inclusive church, but on God's terms.

What are some other ways you've built that culture of the nations coming in and people inviting others, so that when they bring their friends and neighbours it's a positive, challenging engagement, and not 'cringey'?

Nowadays music has to be good. I think you can't get around that, for whatever reason. I can't work out if it's because Hillsong[22] has raised the bar or because everyone is getting more specialized in their own experiences of music.

We try to make sure that our facilities are clean and presentable. Especially with certain ethnic groups, if you have a messy place it's a real put-off.

I have this idea that I want my people to feel comfortable in their own skin, and at the same time I want them to sit tight with Jesus and loose with culture so that they can be "all things to all people".[23] So we try to celebrate their diversity as

---

22   A large Pentecostal church in Sydney, famous for its music ministry.
23   1 Cor 9:22

well. We have a little quota system so that there is a minimum level of ethnic and gender diversity up the front. We also have three translation booths so that at least the sermon is in their mother tongue. We have one plain English translator as well because I'm not very good for people with English as a second language—I talk too fast, I'm too Aussie, my idioms don't work for them.

Clarity is of high value for us, and so if someone isn't clear, they know they will get a strong reaction from me because we have enough people who have had a bad experience in formal education and who feel dumb. So we constantly say, "If you don't understand, it's our fault". We take the blame off them, and then we make it clear. With preaching, I don't care if you're funny; I care that you're faithful and clear—that's what matters to me.

The full interview with Gary at **thevineproject. com** includes more on how he approaches:

- **everyone being an evangelist**
- **one-to-one Bible reading**
- **avoiding the consumer culture where everything is packaged and programmed**
- **leadership training.**

~

Richard's story

Richard was appointed as the minister of a mainstream denominational church in a large regional city a few years ago.

When you came, what was on your heart to work on?

Everything, really. Essentially we wanted people to stop being passengers and start being participants. There was a sense that if you came to church, it was enough. People were nice and churchy but there wasn't that edge of "What am I doing through the week, and how can I be growing as a Christian?" I wanted people to actually engage with the sermon and to be challenged and changed by that. People didn't talk about the sermon over morning tea. On the bulletin, the space for taking notes from the sermon was only about one third of the page.

What were some of the first things you worked on?

I preached through Ephesians, because I wanted to give people a sense of the mission of God and the bigness of that. I love the theology in the first three chapters and the way it lands in 'every person ministry' in chapter 4 and onwards. I wanted to raise the bar on preaching and have a level of depth (I don't like the word 'excellence'). That's not what they were used to. And I wanted them to think hard and find that Sunday was worth coming to because we are all going to be challenged and changed by God through his word.

What else did you work on to make Sunday like that?

We just brought our instincts and did things we assumed were normal; we didn't realize till later how different they were. All the things we just took for granted—like including people in the Sunday services; expecting that service leaders would prepare and see it as a teaching role; just wanting things to be done well and thought out. One of the comments people were making—not unkindly—was, "You have a reason for everything you do".

I worked hard on saying not just what we're doing but *why* we're doing it—giving a gospel reason (e.g. "Let's have more space on the outline for taking notes in the sermon because we're gathering around God's word and that matters"). We talked about how we chose songs. I introduced ministry spots on Sunday (a 5-10 minute slot) on why we do things like singing, praying, leading, inviting. We talked about morning tea (refreshments) as a ministry opportunity. We came up with the idea of having a space in the bulletin where you could write down one thing you could talk about with others at morning tea, to drive that culture of 'one another' ministry.

I wanted to be overt and intentional about everything and help people think through why we do what we do.

The full interview with Richard at **thevineproject.com** includes his thoughts on:

- **using critical moments for change**
- **helping members to invite others to church**
- **shaping the culture through key leaders.**

~

David's story

David is the pastor of an independent (non-denominational) church plant in the centre of a large regional city.

How do you run church on Sundays to both engage non-Christians and stretch members in maturity?

Those two things are actually not that far apart. It's not like people who aren't Christians are dummies; I don't have to dumb down anything. I just need to be better at explaining what we are doing along the way. Every week our MC will get up and say something like:

> "Welcome to our church. It might be that Christian stuff is new to you and you've been dragged along and you've got questions. This is the place to be. You don't have to believe the things we believe to be here tonight, but we think the Bible has the answers to your questions and so we'd love you to stick around and keep asking questions with us. Tonight, we are going to sing, we are going to pray, we are going to read the Bible and have it taught."

We say this every week so our people know that there are non-Christians here every week.

Along the way we'll explain why we say "Amen" at the end of every prayer—"It's like saying 'mmm, hmm' at the end"—and people laugh. When we read the Bible, we always say, "The chapter is the big number and the verse is the small number". We also say, "It's normal for people not to own a Bible, so we have some up the back, and you can take that home". That sort of thing.

See the full interview with David at **thevineproject.com** for more thoughts on embedding disciple-making into the culture and structures of a church plant.

We aren't dumbing it down—I hope the messages are challenging and stretching. I'm shooting for a tertiary-educated audience, even though not everyone in our church is tertiary educated. Because of our location and long-term vision to be a base for church planting, ultimately I want to grow church planters.

PROJECT: PLANNING TO MAKE SUNDAY A FLAGSHIP

Look back over the discussions you've had under each segment in this first focus area ('Make Sunday a flagship').

1. Choose a few key strategies or priorities that you want to focus on over the next 12 months. Don't try to do everything! Start with four or five key things.

2. For each one of these strategies or priorities, set a simple, measurable goal. The purpose of this is threefold:

   • it keeps clear in your mind the kind of outcome you're hoping to achieve
   • it can sometimes give you a little push of motivation to keep going when your feet start to drag
   • it enables you to ask some questions at the end of the year about why you did or didn't reach your goal.

3. For each of the priorities and goals, write down the what, who, when and how much (what actions, by whom, by when, and with what resources or at what cost).

(Hint: after you've finished the practical step 3 of working out actually who is going to make all these things happen, you might end up deciding that you've taken on too many priorities!)

A worked example

Priority 1: We're going to work hard over the next 12 months at making our Sunday meeting as engaging for outsiders as possible, and at encouraging the congregation to invite people along.

Goal: Under God, we hope to see 50 different non-Christian outsiders visit our congregation in the next 12 months.

Actions:

What	Who	By when	Resources needed/ cost	Notes
Do 4-week audit of current Sunday service to identify issues potentially alienating to outsiders	Bill (with three others doing audit)	Bring summary report to Vine Project Team by March 1	Time: 3 hrs	
Train all service leaders in 'outsider-friendly' language, etc.	Fred to co-ordinate/ lead	Two separate meetings with service leaders by April 10	Time: 6 hrs	Need to provide ongoing feedback and encourage-ment to service leaders
etc.				

Focus Area 2: Design pathways that move to the right

I n the second evaluation exercise of Phase 3, you did your best to take a snapshot of all the people in your congregation or fellowship—of where they are up to in their 'learnership' of Christ. Most groups we have done this exercise with find it a somewhat overwhelming experience. So many people. So many ministry needs. So few leaders or people equipped to help in the task.

How on earth are we going to move all these people to the right, each with their own particular needs and situation in life? Given that the basic method is the four Ps of ministry (Proclamation Prayer, People, Perseverance),[1] then practically speaking how is this '4P ministry' going to happen in a way that helps everyone take steps forward from all the different places they occupy on the spectrum? (And this is not even thinking about the even bigger challenge—all those people in our neighbourhoods and communities that we haven't yet engaged with or evangelized.)

Part of the answer of course is the focus area we've just looked at. Our main Sunday gathering should function to move people to the right from wherever they are. But some things are hard (or almost impossible) to do in a large group meeting like church. How

---

1   See Conviction 3 in Phase 1 for our discussion of the four Ps.

are we going to use every other aspect of church life to move people to the right—that is, all the different meetings and interactions, whether one-to-one, in small groups or medium-sized groups, whether in one-off events or regular structures?

Now if you happened to be in a house church of 24 people, the answer to these questions might be relatively simple: "There are three of us who provide some leadership here. We'll take seven people each, and work with them personally and individually to help each one move forward. Simple."

But of course few of us are in situations that uncomplicated (mind you, small house churches have all sorts of complications of their own!).

Your group doesn't have to get very much bigger before some kind of system or framework becomes necessary to organize and facilitate and support the growth of each person. Without what we are calling in this chapter 'pathways', 4P ministry is very hard to sustain and grow beyond the people you can influence and relate to personally. The larger your group, or the larger is your vision for how much you want to grow, the more thought and care and hard work you will have to put into building, maintaining and constantly tinkering with the 'relational architecture' that connects people with each other in 4P ministry.

In one sense, being thoughtful and proactive about how our ministry structures promote gospel growth is just good practical wisdom, and we don't need to construct an elaborate theological underpinning for our particular way of doing it. However, doing this work does accord theologically with our vision of churches as 'learning communities'. God has put us together because we're better together. We need each other. Love will drive us to work out how we can enable and facilitate as many 4P ministry relationships as possible—and that is what we're doing when we design and implement structures or pathways or systems (or whatever you want to call them).

To put all this in the familiar terms of our well-worn metaphor, if 4P ministry is the 'vine work' that drives spiritual growth in people's lives at all levels, then designing structures or pathways is the vital 'trellis work' that enables the vine work to happen broadly and deeply across the congregation and beyond.

Four final caveats before we press on:

- *Firstly*, we've settled on the language of *pathways* for talking about the structures or systems you set up to try to help as many people as possible to move to the right. No language or metaphor is perfect. 'Pathways' isn't bad, because it evokes people walking in a certain direction, making progress, moving from one milestone to the next, and so on. But feel free to come up with your own language and description.

- *Secondly*, try to avoid the two extremes of scorched-earth reinvention and fiddling-while-Rome-burns. At one extreme is the approach that treats everything about the current culture and ministry structures as incurably sick, and wants to scrap everything and start again. As much as this might be tempting at times, it's almost always a mistake to make the current culture your enemy—and that's what you'll do if you try to destroy everything and build from scratch. On the other hand, it's a waste of everyone's time just to do a bit of timid tinkering on the edges, when the culture is in need of deep and lasting change. In most cases, the key is to find those aspects of your current culture that reflect your convictions and have potential for growth—and you identified these in Phase 3—and build upon them. Tweak them, re-energize them, pour resources into them—put whatever strengths the current culture has to work for you in driving change.

- *Thirdly*, it's worth saying (even if it's obvious) that there is overlap between the four categories or stages on our spectrum (Engaging, Evangelizing, Establishing, Equipping). Where does engaging with someone stop and evangelizing them begin? Sometimes it's clear; at other times it's harder to say. In particular, where's the line between establishing and equipping? These two will always be overlapping, because establishing is a lifelong process that never finishes, and equipping is an aspect and consequence of becoming more mature and established in Christ.

- *Finally*, always remember that no system or structure will be perfect, or will encompass all that God is doing in your midst through his people. Ministry will be messy, both because people are messy and because we are finite, imperfect people ourselves. Despite all our best and most careful efforts, some of our plans won't work. Don't be too tied to them, or invest them with too much importance. A trellis is not alive—it's a construct that can be dismantled and reassembled. A trellis is also meant to support the vine, not determine precisely where all vine growth will happen. Some really fruitful 4P ministry will constantly happen informally alongside and outside your structures. Sometimes a ministry or person will rise up and flourish quite apart from all the careful organization we've done. Be ready to go with it, and to build on it, even if it sits oddly with your structure. The important thing is that people keep growing as learners of Christ, not that we have nice neat pathways.

Enough, then, of the introductory words and caveats. Let's look at each of our four main stages in moving to the right, and think about how we can design pathways that help people move forward through them.

The key questions we'll need to ask under each of the following headings are:

- What existing ministry structures or groups can we improve or what new things do we need to launch in order to more effectively conduct 4P ministry in this area?
- What's the next step for people who have been ministered to in each phase? (E.g. How does someone move from being engaged to being evangelized? Or from being evangelized to being followed up and established in the faith?)
- Who is going to lead these new or improved ministries or groups? What sort of equipping or training is going to be needed? This will become increasingly urgent or apparent

as you work through 'Engaging', 'Evangelizing' and 'Establishing' below. You'll almost certainly find that the ideas you have for making progress in each area are not matched by the people you have available to lead them or run them. That's what the 'Equipping' stage is about!

- As important as the structures and leadership are, *content* is just as vital. What is actually being proclaimed and taught in our different groups and ministries? Is it the biblical word of Christ, or something else?
- Is it a single pathway we're talking about or pathways (plural)? We'll mostly refer to pathways (plural) in the material below in recognition that you will usually create multiple paths or options for people to keep moving forward. However, in another sense you could usefully think of it as one big integrated highway on which your ministry helps people travel from 'engaging' through to 'equipping', with a number of different 'lanes' on the road that are suitable for different people and circumstances.

We'll work through each of the four stages, offering some ideas and suggestions for you to mull over and discuss, and telling some stories about how churches we know are working on this. Then, at the end, you'll need to design your own draft pathways that integrate the four stages together.

Pathway stage 1: Engaging

As we've talked over many years with pastors around the world about ministry and evangelism, one theme has been distressingly common: most evangelical churches in the Western world have little or no engagement with their local communities.

A generation ago, this was different in many places. The church was seen as part of the community life. Churchgoing was a normal thing to do, even if many of those who came were only nominally Christian. Church was where you had your babies christened, where you got married, and where you may even have turned up at Easter and Christmas. The pastor was a respected local figure, and someone to go to in times of grief and trouble. People knew about church, and knew many of the people involved there. The relational platform existed, in other words, on which a gospel conversation might take place.

Those days have gone, or are rapidly going, for most Western churches. Our local communities feel increasingly strange and complex and out of reach to us. The cultural gap between the 'world community' and the 'church community' is becoming a chasm. For many in the 'world community', church is either a non-existent irrelevance or (increasingly) a harmful fringe group with bigoted attitudes.[2]

Churches are struggling to deal with this changing environment. Perhaps because we have a tradition or cultural memory of being naturally and easily connected with the local community, many churches don't know how to reach out actively or engage with their local communities. They've never had to in the past, and now they're not sure where to start. When this is combined with how busy most congregations are just trying to survive and cope with their own issues, it's not surprising that the picture is disappointing. When we have talked with pastors about their church's level of activity and success in reaching out beyond the walls of the church, just to engage with and get to know and form good friendly relationships with their local communities, the reports back have been bleak.

How can we help people onto this first step of our pathway? We need to think about this, because it is very hard to evangelize the thousands of people living all around us in "this present darkness" if we don't know them or have any contact with them!

This sort of engagement can happen in a number of contexts.

---

2 The increasing secularization of modern Western culture is a massive and complex topic, and beyond our scope to discuss here. For example, although there are common themes there are also significant differences between the versions of secularism operating in the UK, France, the USA and Australia.

a. Personal relationship

As the church's institutional prominence and respectability declines in Western culture, it will be increasingly important for church members to be the front-line of community engagement, as they go about their daily work and relate to their neighbours and friends.

Put simply: we need to encourage and help our members to get to know non-Christian people, to mix with them, to form friendships, and to become engaged with the subculture or community in which they live and work. If our members aren't inviting people into their homes and lives, it's no use urging them to invite people to church events and activities.

We can facilitate this sort of engagement in two main ways:

- by not filling the week with so many church activities and programs that there is no time for our people to engage with their neighbours
- by equipping and training our people to think this way about themselves and their neighbours.

This second point will be a common theme in much of what follows. One of the key steps in designing 'pathways' is teaching and equipping your people to walk on these pathways, as people whose joy and privilege it is to help as many others as possible move to the right. One significant reason that many of our members do not engage with their local neighbourhoods and friends is that they haven't grasped the vision of disciple-making.[3]

b. Teams and groups

Engaging with your friends and neighbours and local community doesn't have to be a solo exercise. (The same is very much the

---

3 Bill Hybels's book *Just Walk Across the Room* has some flaws and omissions, but one thing it does communicate extremely well is how important it is for Christians to get out of their comfort zone and actually start talking and engaging with their non-Christian neighbours; to just walk across the room and strike up a conversation. This book is worth mining for some ideas and teaching in this area. See Bill Hybels, *Just Walk Across the Room: Simple Steps Pointing People to Faith*, Zondervan, Grand Rapids, 2006.

case with evangelism, as we'll see below.) In fact, inviting a group of non-Christian friends to a social event with a group of Christian friends can be a powerful and helpful way of breaking down barriers. The fellowship, love and friendship of Christians for one another and for others is a powerful and intriguing testimony for many non-Christian people. Many conversion stories start with a testimony of people simply being impressed with how Christians live and relate to one another—but that testimony cannot happen if we are not engaging with people around us.

There are two interrelated ways of thinking about this:

- We could make this a goal or value for our existing small groups (or home groups or whatever you call them)—that is, set the expectation that each small group will (say) run a social event with non-Christian friends or family at least twice a year.
- We could set up specific teams or small groups whose focus is to engage with a particular community or subculture, with the aim of not only getting to know and relate to people in that community but over time to move them along the pathway to hear the gospel.

This raises a very significant issue that will be relevant to many of the points in this whole section (about designing pathways)—and that is the place and nature of small groups. We're assuming that if you are reading this book (and have made it all the way to this point), then small groups almost certainly form some part of your congregational life. But what *are* our small groups exactly? How should we think about them? What are they for? And what place could or should they have in the pathways we want to design to move everyone to the right?

These are big questions, and you will need to pause and discuss them at some point during this focus area on pathways—perhaps once you've finished this first section on 'engaging'. We've provided some input and a guide to this discussion in appendix iii, 'Rethinking small groups'.

c. Specialized ministries or groups or events

Many churches run specific ministries or events, either regularly or occasionally, to engage and build relationships with their community. Some of these work because they meet real needs in the community, and others because they are just fun. Examples we've seen include:

- Children's play circles or mother's groups—where the church runs a regular weekly gathering for mothers with young children, usually on a weekday morning. Mothers from the church can get to know mothers from the local community.
- Learning to speak English classes—many churches, especially those in areas with a high proportion of non-English speaking migrants, run weekly classes for community members to improve their English (often using Bible passages as basic texts to read, and so on).
- Sports-related activities—it's common in some areas for churches to run sporting competitions or leagues for young people in the local area.
- Holiday clubs or festivals—some churches put on a week-long program or festival during school holidays, mainly focused around activities for children, to which the whole community is invited.
- Men's shed nights—events that involve some kind of non-threatening activity that men can invite their friends along to, so that they can have an enjoyable night, learn some important life skills (how to cook the perfect steak, how to roast your own coffee beans!), and get to know some Christian people.

The possibilities for these kinds of events and activities are only limited by your imagination. Every community or culture will have contact points and needs that we can connect with.

These sorts of events are best classified as 'Engaging' rather than 'Evangelizing' because (in our experience) they don't often contain very much actual gospel content or conversation. This is not at all a criticism—just a recognition of their nature and purpose. These sorts of activities are a good and necessary first step. They are simple and easy things to advertise in the local community, and to invite someone along to. They will usually have some sort of Christian flavour or message to them—but in most cases this will be a fairly light, easy introduction to some aspect of Christianity, rather than a clear presentation of the gospel and a call to repent. And that's okay. The purpose of these events is to engage, to build a relationship and a connection, to start talking—to actually know and be in contact with the people we want to share the gospel with.

A few points are worth bearing in mind about these kinds of activities:

- They tend to be resource-heavy. They often take plenty of time and energy (and sometimes money) to launch and maintain, and these are resources that can't be put into other areas.

- There is a common tendency in church life to rely on an event or structure to 'take care' of some aspect of our mission, thereby diminishing the sense that it is something that all of us could be thinking about and acting upon as a regular part of our lives. These sorts of engaging activities can be like this—the very fruitful possibilities mentioned above (under 'Personal relationship and 'Teams and groups') are never considered or prioritized because we 'do' our engagement via the annual Winter Festival Community Celebration.

- 'Engaging' events and activities are often very popular and well supported among the congregation. They frequently generate very positive feedback, and are relatively easy to put on. There's a sense of 'outreach' into the community, but it's not as threatening (for the Christians, that is) as something more specifically evangelistic. In fact, we've seen quite a number of churches where engagement has actually replaced evangelism in the church's program. This is worth watching out for.

- By far the most common shortcoming in these sorts of events is that there is not a clear next step for those involved. We tend not to give sufficient thought to how the people who come along to the events are going to take another step to the right—that is, towards actually hearing and responding to the gospel. It's as if the goal is simply to engage, and then hope that somehow something will come out of it sometime down the track.

- As a case study in this, we can't help but think of two playgroups that we know of in churches here in Sydney. Both were well organized by godly mature Christian women, and both succeeded in attracting 20+ non-Christian mothers from the surrounding community to come along to the church each week with their babies and toddlers. Over a three-year period, one of the groups saw none of their non-Christian mothers ever come to church, and no-one got converted. The other group saw a steady stream of the non-Christian mothers come along to Bible study or to church, with around half a dozen converted over the three years. What was the difference between the two? In the first case, the four women who ran the group needed all their time and energy just to organize it and run it each week. There was little time or opportunity for actually connecting with the mothers who came, getting to know them, asking them over for coffee, inviting them to something else, and so on. In the second case, as well as a team of four who organized and ran the group, *another* team of four mothers from the church was recruited and equipped with the sole job of coming to the playgroup, relating to the other mothers, getting to know them, praying for them, and inviting them to read the Bible or attend another gospel event or program of some kind. In other words, some intentional thought, planning, recruiting and training went into how the 'engaging' was going to lead to 'evangelizing'. This made all the difference.

This last point is crucial not just for the 'Engaging' stage but also for every point along our pathway. *What's the next step for someone?* How does someone make the transition from (in this case) engaging to what we're hoping and praying will come next (in this case, hearing and responding to the gospel)?

In all our thinking about specialized ministries and events and activities—particularly with engaging and evangelizing—it's important not to jump too quickly onto the latest bandwagon. You know how it goes: you read or hear about some new idea or innovative ministry that another church is trying with great results, and so you decide to plug it into your own pathway, hoping it will have the same effect where you are. It rarely does.

It's almost always better to build these sorts of ministries around *people* rather than ideas. Look around the room. See who the people are that God has given you—their age and gender and ethnicity, their interests and skills, their contacts and networks—and think creatively about how *this* group of people could engage and evangelize the people around them.

Brad's story

Brad is one of the ministers in an evangelical denominational church in a suburb where people from many nations are settling.

What kinds of questions are you thinking through in engaging with your community?

How can we, as the local church (as opposed to only the individual), be salt and light to those around us? How are we remembering the poor, which Paul made every effort to do, and which the other apostles commanded (Gal 2:10)? Are we ministering in the way presented in James 2:15-16? Are we fishing with a fishing rod, or with a net?

The two key questions to work though are: 'What does our local community need?' and 'What can our local church provide?' Where these two answers meet provides the shape of our community engagement.

What do you mean by fishing with a rod or a net?

I mean not just doing things on my own, which makes it difficult to incorporate the whole church into it. Taking a 'net' approach, I've linked up with community agencies in the area, working out what their clients need and what we as a church can provide. The two key areas have been people dealing with domestic violence, and families that need separate support.

For myself, I have joined a number of committees involving domestic violence, and through these I've answered the above questions.

What does our local community need? Material relief and new relationships for those affected by domestic violence. What can our church provide?

- Emergency relief through our denominational agency in the way of food, toiletries, nappies, clothing vouchers, food vouchers. People can collect hampers at church on Sundays.
- Relationships through belonging to the church community, regular socials, playgroups.

We also run lunches every couple of months, where we invite people who've come through the emergency relief program to lunch, with a program for kids and a place where the adults can have a break and hang out. We're also looking to try and get a playgroup up and running, and from there hopefully we'll also link people into small groups.

What are the overall goals in all of this?

Our outreach ministry has two goals. Firstly, we want people to personally experience God's love through God's people. And secondly, of course, we want people to personally know God's love, in God's Son, through God's word.

At what point do you provide opportunities to learn of Christ?

There's the organic ways, through conversations when they collect some food, but we also want to provide opportunities for these conversations at the lunch (we have a welcoming team who do this), and at the playgroup.

We encourage them to come to church and we also run a series of five evenings on 'Freedom: Answering life's big questions'. I give talks on topics like freedom from harmful desires, from guilt and shame, from religious rituals, from injustice, from despair, and we have discussion time.

So what do your discipleship pathways look like?

Our discipleship pathways now look something like this:

The fishing net > playgroup and socials > freedom talks > small groups and coming to church along the way.

What are some of the challenges?

It is easy in this kind of 'community chaplaincy' work to only make superficial contact, so we are working hard to ensure the church makes meaningful, long-term contact with the community in a way that encourages people to join small groups and other similar programs run by the church.

For instance, the emergency relief works well but we don't want to just fall into a transactional model where we're saying, "All right, here's your stuff, see you later".

We want to keep in contact long term and make sure it has a face and fosters relationship. We're constantly trying to work out how best to encourage people to move along a path to discipleship of Jesus.

What's been the impact on the whole church?

The whole church is more involved in ministry, particularly with the community lunches where we have more than half of our church involved. That's been a good side effect of taking this approach, I think, and there are several easy things that people can do at the lunches to help, no matter how new they are with us. They can sink their teeth in and serve, and I think that also helps people feel more encouraged in ministry.

~

Virginia's story

Virginia is the children's minister at an evangelical church in a culturally diverse suburb.

What programs do you have at your church to connect with new families?

New families come to Children's Church (our Sunday School). We also run Kids Club after school, which is a games-based program for children aged 8-12. And there's also Music and Movement, which is a fortnightly program for 3-4 year old (preschool) children. It's packed full of singing, dancing and music activities. It concludes with a story from the Bible and morning tea.

We also have Playtime for preschool children on other mornings. That's a time when parents, grandparents and carers can come and enjoy a stimulating program of games, music, stories and craft with their child. It's also a place where adults can meet other adults and gain support and encouragement, as well as build friendships. And it's an opportunity for Christians to speak the gospel into people's lives.

Kids Club, Music and Movement and Playtime are all about outreach. And at the moment, across the church there are about 60 ethnic groups represented.

How are you reaching parents?

The midweek teams that have seen the most fruit have been those with an evangelist on their team.

Our pastoral care of the Playtime families has been a bit hit and miss. But when we get it right, it's great. A woman has a baby and somebody from the church turns up with a baby basket and meals. The husband and wife are amazed—for some their own families are not even doing this for them.

There was one lady who came to Playtime and on the second week said, "Don't try and convert me. I'm not here for religion. I like the fact that this is a clean environment and you have quality toys." She was very up-front. Later in the year, she had an operation. The Christians at Playtime loved and cared for her—she received both meals and support. And at the end of that year she happily came along to our Christmas Eve service!

Can you say a bit more about the evangelists?

Everyone is called to evangelize, but we identify people who have shown they have the gift of evangelism. They talk Jesus all the time and they don't even have to think about it.

You try to have an evangelist in each of those programs, is that right?

Yes, it's important that the team leader is not the evangelist. You don't want your evangelist to be the one that has to think about moving the program along, enrolments, making sure things are locked up and set up. You actually want your evangelists to be free to come and just have conversations. They don't need to be chopping the fruit.

How do you inject the gospel into the programs?

In our Music and Movement, there's a story from the Bible for the kids every time. Sometimes this stimulates gospel conversations, sometimes not. What's of primary importance in any midweek ministry to families is that the Christians on the team live and speak Jesus.

Go to **thevineproject.com** for the full interview with Virginia, where she discusses:

- **her vision for children's ministry**
- **equipping highly motivated leaders.**

Sometimes people come because they're curious—"What's on offer for my kids? What is this church on about? Will I feel welcome?"

One Muslim lady came in (as a result of the sign out the front) but was very tentative. She said, "I'm not sure I should be here. I feel like I'm taking the place of someone in your church." The team leader assured her that she was most welcome, and gave her a welcome pack. Inside the pack was a CD of children's songs, *My God is so Big*. Her husband would not let her play it in the house, so instead she played it in her car on the way to and from school. She said it was the only thing her kids wanted to listen to.

The other thing we do in our midweek programs is give gifts. We had an Easter celebration last year where families came together from our Playtime and Music and Movement programs. We must have had about 70-80 there—mums, dads, grandparents and children; it was very ethnically diverse.

One of our leaders read a story that took children from the Easter egg to the empty tomb, allowing them to see Jesus. Then while the children did a craft activity, the adults heard the story of the woman at the well, and were invited to our Explaining Christianity course and our Easter services. The day ended with an Easter egg hunt. As each family left, we gave them a picture book. It cost us about $600 but every family (Muslim, Hindu, etc.) accepted the gift. Our prayer is that these picture books about Jesus will be read in those homes.

DISCUSSION

1. What do you know about your local community? Who lives there? What is the demographic profile for age, religious affiliation, ethnicity, socio-economic background, and so on? (If you've never done this sort of research, now would be a good time to start.)

2. Are there are some obvious contact points between the nature of your surrounding community and your congregation—in the kind of people you are, or in the kinds of needs you could easily meet?

3. What 'Engaging' are you currently doing? What's working well and could be built upon? What new ideas come to mind?

4. Without setting anything in stone, what do you think would be the three most important moves you could make as a congregation to engage more with the people all around you?

Pathway stage 2: Evangelizing

So someone has been 'Engaged'—whether personally or through a small group or via some event or program. What comes next, as they move to the right? How are they going to hear the gospel?

Again, you can think of it happening in different contexts.

a. Personally and in small groups

As with personal engagement, personal evangelism thrives where congregation members:

- personally grasp and embrace the convictions we clarified in Phase 1
- are equipped and trained to know the gospel clearly and thoroughly, and to be able to articulate it for themselves—each in their own way, according to their own gifts and opportunities
- encourage and help each other to keep doing this (e.g. by it being a regular facet or theme of small group or church life).

In other words, personal evangelism is a lot like being on a soccer or football team. There is a basic level of skill and commitment that everyone shares, as well as a recognition that there are different specialties and gifts and roles as you work together as a team towards a common goal.

The basic skill for every member of the Christian team is to know the gospel and be able to articulate it (even very simply) to someone else; the basic commitment is to want to do this, and to seek to do this whenever God gives us opportunity. There are all sorts of different ways evangelism can happen on a personal or small group level—everything from reading the Bible one-to-one with a non-Christian to sharing your testimony or reading a Christian book together or explaining a simple gospel outline.

Again, we're back to 'Equipping'. Teaching and training and encouraging Christians in this area requires that things are happening at the equipping end of your pathway (more on this below).

As with engagement, small groups should have a constant evangelistic hum to them, because they are made of Christ-learners who should be growing in their love for others and their desire to see others saved. And as with engagement, this is something that you could regard as a basic value for all small groups, as well as being a particular focus for some small groups. You could form some small groups whose specific ministry focus or purpose was to promote and practise evangelism.

b. Evangelistic programs or courses

Many churches use gospel courses or programs as a convenient and effective next step for someone to consider the claims of Christ. In our view two of the best are *Introducing God* and *Christianity Explored*,[4] but there are many similar courses available. These sorts of courses have numerous advantages:

- They are enjoyable and engaging, and give non-Christian participants time (over several sessions) to understand the gospel, to talk about it in a relaxed small group setting, to ask their questions, and so on.
- They are the kind of thing that Christians can invite friends to attend with them.
- They can be held in homes or restaurants or on-site at church—at whatever venue would be most helpful for those you're trying to invite along.
- Having them running regularly (say two or three times a year) provides a regular evangelistic drumbeat in the congregational life. We keep praying for it (as each new course rolls around), and we keep being reminded about the challenge of engaging with our neighbours and friends and inviting them to come.

4   They are both very faithful to the gospel and well produced, with the option of using video content. *Introducing God* uses the framework of *Two Ways to Live* to guide participants through the gospel story of the whole Bible over seven sessions; *Christianity Explored* uses the Gospel of Mark to present the claims of Christ.

- They also provide a simple and clear next step for the various people whom we come into contact with at church—whether that's a visitor who doesn't really know the gospel, or an infrequent church attender who has never really sorted out their relationship with God. If the next *Introducing God* course is never more than a few months away, there's an obvious next step for them to take.

- As we equip our people to participate in these sorts of courses (e.g. by teaching them how to invite their friends, and how to answer questions and participate in discussion), we're equipping them for evangelism more broadly in their lives, and motivating them to keep at it. Sitting around a table with non-Christians and talking about the gospel (which is what happens in these sorts of programs) is tremendously exciting and energizing for most Christians.

c. Church

We won't spend much time on this point, since we've discussed it at length in Focus Area 1 ('Make Sunday a flagship'), but if church itself is a constant occasion for evangelism, then this too provides a next step for someone we've engaged with. We can invite them to church knowing that it will be an engaging and accessible experience in which they are challenged with some aspect of the gospel.

d. One-off events or missions

The era of the large-scale Billy-Graham-style mission or crusade seems to have passed, in our part of the world at least. Big events with the big (often famous or international) speakers are much less frequent than in decades gone by.

Without debating all the pros and cons of 'special event' evangelism—whether as a combined church event, or within your own congregation—here's how one-off events or missions can be useful:

- They can serve as a focus and rallying point; something to prepare and train and pray for; something to galvanize energy and activity.

- The success or usefulness of these events depends in large measure on whether they are your sole evangelistic strategy or whether they are part of a broader effort of engagement and evangelism. Churches that are already engaging and evangelizing extensively in other ways (as we've been describing above) can find a high-profile one-off event to be very fruitful. It can serve as a 'harvest point' at which people who have been considering Christ for some time make a decision to repent and trust Christ. Or it can serve as a 'scooping point'—as an earlier step on the pathway, where someone you've been engaging with comes along, is intrigued or challenged, and then decides to find out more. Some churches run some kind of larger gospel event a few weeks before the next *Introducing God* or *Christianity Explored* course is due to start.
- Conversely, churches that aren't already engaging and evangelizing often find the big event or mission to be a let down. The congregation isn't engaging with their friends and so has no-one to invite. There isn't already a stream of people who are considering the gospel, and so no-one is primed and ready to decide for Christ. And we reach the conclusion that 'these sorts of events don't work'.

More of David's story

David is the pastor of an independent church plant in the centre of a large regional city.

What are some of your structures or pathways for evangelism?

Australia Day is a big deal in our city, so at our first meeting as a church we announced we were going to run a stall at the markets and tell people the gospel. Everyone came—it was great for our new church, and people got to know who we are.

From the very beginning we have run an evangelistic program called 'Coffee and Jesus' over five weeks, often at a local cafe. We encourage members to come along with their friends. People hear the gospel at 'Coffee and Jesus', but the real action doesn't happen on the night; it happens in the car on the way home. So I (or someone else) give a talk to generate discussion, with a mix of apologetics and going through the gospel, like *Two Ways to Live* but with different words.

So give us a typical topic for a talk.

Talk 3 is on the cross. We start it with a table question: "Why is it so hard to forgive and forget?" So we discuss love and justice, and how a God who loves can also be just—and that takes us to the cross.

The big thing is that we want them in tables—not one big table but lots of little tables—and we want those tables discussing. That does two things. It makes it really safe for the non-Christian; they aren't thinking that everyone here is a Christian. And our members get real live action in evangelism. It's been a great place where we have seen people become Christians, but it's also where we have won people over to the power of evangelism.

What else happens for evangelism in your church?

'Coffee and Jesus' is always running. Then in terms of the momentum for our year, I want us to have something to set the tone for the rest of the year, something that reminds us all of what we are doing. So, even though some people in church are away in summer, it is really important that we have evangelism at the start of the year.[5]

It really starts in October when we ask everyone in our church to ask family and friends a question. This year it was, "What do you think is the world's biggest problem?" So our members are growing in confidence to have conversations, and we (as preachers) want the answers! We get the answers back, and that becomes the basis of our summer evangelistic series in January. We preach on the four most popular answers people give to that question.

We're actually in the middle of that series at the moment. So two weeks ago we did 'Fear', then last Sunday we did

---

5 Just a reminder for our northern hemisphere readers: summer is December to February in some parts of the world.

'Climate Change'. One person I met on Sunday night, George, was from a Serbian Orthodox background. He was door-knocked by a couple from the mission team who told him we were doing these big questions. He said that climate change was the world's biggest problem, and they said, "Well that is one of the ones we are doing!" He was interested in why a church would talk about climate change so he came along on Sunday. He was very aggressive towards me before church and he was waiting for me to trip up on something. After church he talked to lots of people, and then he came back to me and said, "I really enjoyed it. I'm surprised and I'd like to come back for the next couple of weeks. Would that be okay?"

You've grown up on a diet of expository preaching through books of the Bible. So is this guy going to come back into Judges in February?
We start in February every year with a Gospel. If George keeps coming he will hear the first eight chapters of Mark's Gospel.

How do you avoid a crunch of gears from climate change to Mark?
It's being aware that the people who were there the week before are still going to be there this week, so we need to ease them in. As soon as the preaching series in Mark starts, we also begin our first series of 'Coffee and Jesus', and so we're praying George comes back for the next two weeks, and that he is interested to find out more. Each week we only have one announcement, and that is 'Coffee and Jesus'. That is actually the application point for most of the sermons: you need to look more into Jesus, so you should come to 'Coffee and Jesus'.

1. Look back over your evaluation exercises from Phase 3. What do they tell you about how evangelism is happening (or not) in and through your church?

2. What is working well or has potential to be built upon? What new ideas come to mind?

3. Without setting anything in stone, what do you think are the three most important moves you could make as a congregation to see the gospel shared more with non-Christians?

Pathway stage 3: Establishing

Just to clarify: by 'establishing' we mean that phase in the growth of a learner after they have repented and turned to Christ, where they increase in knowledge and understanding, send down deep roots of faith, and learn to grow in godliness of life as they 'keep all his commandments'. It's the maturation process of the Christian life, and thus it is lifelong. It includes following up a new believer, helping a solid Christian grow further in understanding or deal with a particular sin, encouraging and strengthening believers as they deal with hardship and suffering, and so on. (We've wondered whether 'Encouraging' or 'Edifying' would be better labels for this stage—feel free to choose the descriptor you like best!)

In most churches, this is where the action is. As we've worked through the evaluation exercises in Phase 3 with many pastors around the world, we've found that in the vast bulk of churches, most of the time, energy and effort of church life goes into this area—into groups, activities and ministries that help Christians to persevere in Christ and grow in their knowledge and godliness. (We suspect that you probably discovered this about your own church in Phase 3.)

In one sense, this is understandable and right. What does Paul tell the Ephesian elders?

> Pay careful attention to yourselves and to all the flock, in which the Holy Spirit has made you overseers, to care for the church of God, which he obtained with his own blood. (Acts 20:28)

What are shepherds for, if not to care for and feed and protect the sheep?

All the same, many churches face two significant issues in this area:

- There's a lack of actual fruitfulness or observable results in many of these ministries. The activities and groups and programs exist (and often have for a long time) and continue to trundle along, but we feel less than confident that they are effectively moving people to the right. (Did you come to this conclusion yourself, in Evaluation Exercise 3 in Phase 3?)
- So much effort and time goes into maintaining and growing various 'Establishing' ministries (like small groups or women's ministries or youth groups) that very little happens in the other areas. There's not much engaging or evangelizing actually happening, and this is often because there's not much equipping happening.

These two issues are linked. If the vast bulk of your church life exists in this 'Establishing' area, with not too much happening elsewhere, it actually means that your establishing is failing at a key point. Your people are not in fact becoming like Christ—because if they were, they would be growing in their longing to see other people saved, and to lay down their lives to see it happen. A lack of engagement and evangelism, which is usually paired with a lack of people wanting to be equipped and supported to do this, is usually symptomatic of a spiritually immature, under-developed congregation.

Let's look at three aspects of 'Establishing' ministries, and explore how we could improve them.

a. Establishing new believers

When someone is converted through the ministry of your congregation, what happens next? How are they followed up?

This is a vital question. Spiritually speaking, new believers are like newborn babies. They need constant feeding, they have huge amounts to learn, and they need the protection and care of their spiritual 'parents'. The first 6-12 months after someone has come to faith in Christ are both an exciting and a dangerous time. There is often considerable baggage to be dealt with from their former way of life, and pressures and temptations that most long-established believers no longer have contact with.

This is one area where personal, relational one-to-one ministry is vital. If there is any stage in 'learning Christ' where we need intensive personal tuition and mentoring and coaching, it is this one. We can certainly run special groups for new or young believers, and this can be very helpful in taking them systematically through the foundational truths of the faith. But even in such groups, there needs to be enough mature Christians so that every new believer is paired with someone who can walk beside them and help them learn Christ at this vital stage (that is, 'disciple' them).

This kind of personal follow-up of new believers is something that most mature godly Christians are very capable of doing, with a bit of training and support (back to equipping again!).[6]

In a previous era (and still today in some traditions), catechisms were used for this foundational learning, with formal questions and answers regarding the basics of the faith.[7] This approach may feel outmoded to us but it has benefits worth pondering, most notably in the simplicity of the method (it's not hard to do) and in the way that it standardizes the sound doctrine we wish all Christians to learn.

---

6   Many mature Christians in our part of the world have been equipped to use the *Just for Starters* set of Bible studies as a framework for personally following up new Christians. See *Just for Starters*, 3rd edn, Matthias Media, Sydney, 1996, and the related training resource *Preparing Just for Starters*, Matthias Media, Sydney, 2004—both available at matthiasmedia.com.

7   For a recent attempt to revive catechetical instruction, see http://newcitycatechism.com.

Other churches have a one-year 'basics' program that they require everyone in their church to complete (including all new believers),[8] or adult Sunday School classes that focus on the foundations.

Whatever the method, sound teaching (or 'catechesis', as JI Packer calls it in this quote) is essential to the establishing of Christian disciples:

> The church is to be a learning-and-teaching fellowship in which the passing on of what we learn becomes a regular part of the service we render to each other. Surely this is a realization that today's churches urgently need to recover.
>
> ...
>
> As we contemplate today's complex concerns, hopes, dreams, and ventures of Christian renewal, discipleship impresses us as the key present-day issue, and catechesis as the key present-day element of discipleship, all the world over. The Christian faith must be both well and wisely *taught* and well and truly *learned*! A far-reaching change of mindset about this is called for, without which such well-worn dictums as "American Christianity is three thousand miles wide and half an inch deep" will continue, sadly, to be verified.[9]

b. Establishing newcomers in church

People who roll through our doors as newcomers present a particular kind of 'Establishing' challenge. We have the organizational goal of establishing them as potential members of our church—of helping them arrive, settle in, get to know people, and become part of the fabric of our fellowship, and so on. But

---

8   The very effective *Read, Mark, Learn* set of Bible studies developed by St Helen's Bishopsgate in London is a good example; see http://www.st-helens.org.uk/belong/midweek-bible-studies?ref=nav.

9   JI Packer and Gary A Parrett, *Grounded in the Gospel: Building Believers the Old-fashioned Way*, Baker Books, Grand Rapids, 2010, pp. 15, 17; emphasis original. We're not convinced that Australian or British Christianity is that much thicker!

the more significant goal (although it is not unrelated of course to them joining a church) is working out how to move newcomers one step to the right—starting from wherever they happen to be.

In the majority of cases, newcomers to our congregation will be some sort of Christian person, but just exactly where they are up to, and what they need in order to grow, is immensely varied. Newcomers arrive on our doorstep at all sorts of different stages along the spectrum—from someone who is not a Christian and needs to be evangelized all the way through to a very solid mature Christian who is ready and willing to dive in and be part of the ministry.

In other words, establishing newcomers is another area in which the personal touch is important. Someone needs to spend enough time with each new person to really know them—to know where they're coming from and what they need next. They might need the gospel explained to them; they might need to work through a hurt that has kept them out of every church for the past 12 months; they might have widely diverging views on theological issues that need talking through.

Whatever systems or processes you have for welcoming new-comers, each newcomer ideally needs what one church we know of calls a 'concierge'—someone to stick with them, look after them, introduce them to the church and to other people, and generally guide them to what they need next in order to grow in Christ.

This again requires some organization and some equipping. For example, you could form a small group or team specifically for this purpose. I (Tony) lead a group like this at my local church. We function as a 'normal' small group in one sense—we're a bunch of mature Christians seeking to move each other to the right in Christ through the word and prayer. But our ministry focus beyond the group is following up newcomers. We keep a special lookout for newcomers on Sundays, and work hard to meet them and to get some contact information so that we can follow them up. Each week in our group time, we talk and pray through the names of all the newcomers who came on Sunday (or in the previous several weeks). One of us is allocated to each newcomer or couple (usually on the basis of whether we met them on Sunday), and then we stick with them over the next few months—getting in touch by phone in the first week after their visit, inviting them to our homes (or visiting theirs), introducing them to others, getting to know where they are up to spiritually, and helping them work out what they need next. At any one time, each of us might have half a dozen people that we're praying for and following up.

This kind of personal dimension to establishing newcomers can very fruitfully dovetail with other ministries and activities and structures that help newcomers find their way. For example, you could:

- have a special welcome desk for newcomers on Sunday
- invite newcomers to a special morning tea after church to meet the pastor
- send an email or letter to them early in the week after their first visit
- run special lunches or other social events for newcomers to meet the pastor, other new people, and regulars
- run some kind of special program to orient newcomers to what your church is about, and help them take their first steps towards becoming part of your fellowship.[10]

c. Establishing growing believers

As with engaging and evangelizing, the establishing ministry that moves believers to the right can happen in multiple contexts:

- *One-to-one Bible reading relationships:* this is where people meet regularly for mutual establishing, either short-term (e.g. weekly for three months) or longer-term (e.g. once a month for years). This can be very powerful because it is individual and intensive—we can dig down into issues, and

---

10 The Matthias Media resource *GTK: Get To Know* (Matthias Media, Sydney, 2013) is an example of such a program. It's a flexible four-week course to help newcomers get to know the pastor, get to know some other people, and get to know what you stand for (i.e. the Bible and the gospel).

challenge and admonish one another in a way that is often difficult to do in a small group. Of course, because it is so intensive, it is also inefficient and hard to multiply quickly.

- *Small groups:* small home groups—that is, small clusters of Christ-learners who meet regularly to move each other to the right through the four Ps—remain a basic and important structure for helping believers grow to maturity. The advantages and potential of small groups for this kind of ministry are well recognized. However, as we note in our discussion in appendix iii, this potential is often not realized. In many churches, the small group 'trellis' needs significant work—in the vision of what the groups are and are trying to achieve, in the quality of leaders and the training (initial and ongoing) that they receive, in the quality of the material that forms the basis for study, and so on. Perhaps the most significant step is a commitment to recruit, train and support godly leaders who understand what's needed, and are equipped and mentored to grow in their role. (Again, we'll say more below under 'Equipping'.)
- *Larger groups:* whether in one-off seminars, conferences, teaching nights, short-term courses, or adult Sunday School classes, there are multiple ways in which 4P ministry can take place to help establish the Christians in your congregation. Many churches use these sorts of occasions to address particular hot topics (like social issues, or sex and relationships), or to provide stretching or intensive teaching on a theological topic.

Establishing (or growing) Christian believers is of course not a smooth, rose-petal-covered path. There are plenty of slips, falls and disasters that happen along the way. This is one reason why we don't mind using the word 'establish' to describe the whole process of Christian growth to maturity. As the New Testament repeatedly emphasizes, growth in spiritual wisdom, knowledge, godliness and fruitfulness is in large measure shown in steadfastness and perseverance—in standing firm and not being moved when the storms rage and waves break against us (see, for example, in Colossians 1:9-11 how the outcome of Paul's ambitious prayer for them is endurance and patience with joy). The Christian who is continuing to step 'to the right' is (paradoxically) becoming ever more deeply rooted in the one spot—in Christ.

This raises the question of what is often called 'pastoral care'— that is, looking after one another, especially during the tough times of life. Some churches set up a separate structure or pathway to deal with this so that when something tough happens in life (a bereavement, an illness, or some other hardship), a particular team or group of people swing into action to provide personal support and care.

Ideally, if our small groups were functioning as centres of mutual ministry, then much of this extra or specialized personal care might not be necessary. It's not as if there are two kinds of love and ministry to one another—the Bible study kind that we do on Wednesday nights, and the practical love-in-times-of-trouble-kind, which a different group takes care of at some other point. The cluster of Christ-learners that is a 'small group' should be loving and caring for each other. All the same, many churches still find it advantageous to equip people particularly for this kind of love-in-a-crisis ministry—either as a separate structure, or as part of what every small group learns.

It's helpful to think about pastoral care ministry in the light of our vision to help each person take a step to the right in learning Christ. Times of trouble in life are not the exception but the norm in this present darkness—both for unbelievers and disciples of Christ. And we know that God has a bigger purpose in these trials to produce robust, enduring, joyful trust in him.[11] Growing in character and hope and perseverance in the midst of life's storms is simply an aspect of being established as a Christian, and it happens (as all Christian growth does) through the four Ps.

So when we visit a cancer patient, or pray with a mourning widow, we are not doing anything fundamentally different from

---

11 Rom 5:3-5; Jas 1:2-4; 1 Pet 1:6-7

any other kind of ministry—although the circumstances will require particular patience, sensitivity and care. This leads again to equipping our members (perhaps through small groups or classes) with a basic understanding of how to listen and love and prayerfully open the word with someone in pain, so that they can be comforted and encouraged.[12]

DISCUSSION

1. Which aspects of 'Establishing' do you think you're doing well at? What could you build on or improve?

2. Talk about your small groups (if you have them). What are the issues? What could you do to improve them as effective learning communities? Which new groups might you need to start? How could this central structure in your church be used better to equip disciples who make disciples? (If you haven't yet read and discussed appendix iii on 'Rethinking small groups', now would probably be a sensible time.)

3. Talk about your adult Sunday School (if you have one). How effectively is it teaching sound doctrine? What could you do to improve it? Which new classes might you need to start? How could this structure in your church be used better to equip disciples who make disciples?

---

12 Sally Sims's new book *Together Through the Storm: A Practical Guide to Christian Care* (Matthias Media, Sydney, 2016) seeks to do just this—that is, provide some equipping for everyday Christians in 'pastoral care' within the framework of 4P ministry.

Pathway stage 4: Equipping

As you've been thinking and talking through the various stages that someone might go through (from 'Engaged' right through to 'Established'), you have no doubt noticed and reflected on a constant theme—that nearly everything you might want to initiate or improve at every step of the process requires *people* who are motivated and available and equipped to be involved. "And we just don't have those people", we hear you say.

You're right: these kinds of people—the kind who commit themselves to going to the playgroup to get to know and evangelize the non-Christian mothers—don't grow on trees. Every pastor we've ever talked to feels like he doesn't have enough of these sorts of people, and imagines how different things might be if he had.

In a recent survey of pastors who have been involved in our Vinegrowers coaching ministries, the second most common roadblock to changing the church culture was the difficulty of raising up and developing lay leaders with the vision of disciple-making. Nearly 50% of those surveyed expressed a desire for on-site training of staff and leaders—that is, they wanted someone from outside to come and do this training for them. (By the way, the other two most common roadblocks reported were unwilling-ness to change and the busyness of members.)

Leaders and co-workers don't magically grow on trees, but they do grow. They grow and develop in the same way that all other growth happens—through the work of God in their lives, as his word takes root and bears fruit by his Spirit over time.

This is why the 'Equipping' stage is perhaps the most important in designing pathways to move people to the right. By 'equipping' we mean that phase of Christian growth:

- where Christians embrace the concept of helping to move others to the right—where the penny drops and they realize that the love that God has poured into their hearts pushes them outwards to other people, to long to see other people come to Christ and grow in Christ

- where such Christians are taught and trained and mentored and supported in this outward-looking ministry to others.

The 'Equipping' stage is where we generate and grow a team of fellow workers to move other people to the right—and given how many people there are, and how vast the needs are, we need the biggest team of fellow workers we can get. We should also emphasize that we are not just equipping people to do jobs at church or to participate in our programs; we're equipping people to engage in 4P ministry in whatever context or opportunity God puts before them—whether that is in being a godly parent who loves and disciplines and teaches their children, or a godly worker who seeks to engage and evangelize the person in the cubicle next door.

In many respects, 'Equipping' is an aspect of 'Establishing'— we are only treating them as two stages here for clarity and convenience. It's not a separate stage, like a second blessing, that only some Christians are privileged to enter. It's the normal Christian life—to reach that point of Christian maturity where our Christlike love for others motivates us to want to minister to them in whatever way we can.

This also means that it is *not neatly sequential*, as if you have to have been established as a Christian for a certain probationary period of time before you can qualify to be equipped to minister to others. Many newly converted Christians, for example, should be equipped as soon as possible to be able to share the gospel clearly with their friends—because they will have lots of non-Christian friends who will want to know what on earth has happened.

To understand what 'Equipping' involves, let's think about it as happening at three levels.[13]

---

13 Throughout what follows, we'll point to useful resources that can help with equipping. Nearly all of these resources are from Matthias Media, so for the sake of brevity if it's a resource we haven't already referred to earlier in this book then we'll simply include its author and publication date rather than the full reference details.

a. Level 1: The penny dropping

The first and most basic step is to help Christians make this particular move to the right in their understanding: to grasp that Christ's purpose for me is that I seek with all my heart to move others around me to the right in whatever way I can.

This happens, of course, like any other Christian growth—through some form of the four Ps. The primary and ongoing place this should happen is through the regular teaching of the Bible on Sunday—especially teaching that communicates the sort of mind-blowing, life-changing convictions we sharpened in Phase 1.

In our observation, it is usually helpful to focus on this topic specifically and intensively at some point—through some combination of a special sermon series, Saturday seminars or conferences, blocks of time in which small groups focus on this topic, and so on. Many churches have found *The Course of Your Life* to be a very useful resource in this area.[14]

Equipping Christians to start moving others to the right is first of all a matter of the heart. We need to address people's deep understanding of what their lives are about, and what they perceive God's purpose to be for their lives. Simply equipping people with some practical skills (e.g. how to share their testimony) will not do much if there is not a transformation of the heart.

b. Level 2: Learning some basic skills

Once the motivation and desire to move others to the right is there, some practical help and skills in how to do so can be hugely helpful—especially in giving Christians the confidence that they can do it. Here are some of the basic kinds of competencies or skills that nearly every Christian should have in their kitbag:

- how to speak the word of God to yourself—that is, how to read the Bible prayerfully as a regular part of life[15]

---

14   See also *The Thing Is*, which presents similar content in a short book form.
15   Tony Payne and Simon Roberts, *Six Steps to Reading Your Bible* (six-session course), 2008.

- how to speak about Christ with non-Christians, whether in sharing one's testimony or in providing a simple explanation of the gospel[16]
- how to answer common questions that are raised about Christianity[17]
- how to read the Bible one-to-one with someone else (whether a Christian or a non-Christian friend)[18]
- how to follow up a new or young Christian personally[19]
- how to encourage and minister to others on Sunday (the 'ministry of the pew')[20]
- how to minister to your spouse and children.

c. Level 3: Learning some specialist skills

There are some ministries and some skills that require special training—that is, where someone who is already being equipped at levels 1 and 2 needs some extra training for a particular task or ministry. The most common would be:

- how to lead a small group[21]
- how to lead in children's ministry or Sunday School[22]
- how to lead and minister in youth groups[23]
- how to give Bible talks or sermons.[24]

---

16 *Two Ways to Live: Know and Share the Gospel* (training course); Simon Manchester and Simon Roberts, *Six Steps to Talking About Jesus* (six-session course), 2006; John Chapman, *Know and Tell the Gospel*, 4th edn, 2005.

17 Simon Roberts, *So Many Questions: How to Answer Common Questions About Christianity* (training course), 2008.

18 *One-to-One Bible Reading: A Simple Guide for Every Christian*; *You Me and the Bible: A Reading Guide to the Six Central Ideas of the Bible*; Geoff Robson, *The Book of Books: A Short Guide to Reading the Bible*, 2015.

19 *Just for Starters: Seven Foundational Bible Studies*; *Preparing Just for Starters* (training course); *Christian Living for Starters: Seven Foundational Bible Studies*, 2007.

20 *Six Steps to Loving Your Church* (six-session course); *How to Walk Into Church*.

21 Colin Marshall, *Growth Groups: A Training Course in How to Lead Small Groups*, 1995.

22 Stephanie Carmichael, *Their God is So Big: Teaching Sunday School to Young Children*, 2000.

23 Alan Stewart (ed.), *No Guts No Glory: How to Build a Youth Ministry that Lasts*, 2nd edn, 2000.

24 John Chapman, *Setting Hearts on Fire: A Guide to Giving Evangelistic Talks*, 1999; *The Archer and the Arrow: Preaching the Very Words of God*; *Saving Eutychus: How to Preach God's Word and Keep People Awake*.

In our conversations with pastors over the past six years, we have found—almost universally—a quite remarkable lack of equipping, training and mentoring at level 3. This is especially the case with small group leadership. Very few pastors are satisfied with the nature and quality of the equipping that they provide for their small group leaders (whether in initial training or ongoing support). This seems to us to be (in most cases) a strategic mistake in the allocation of time and resources. Small groups have enormous potential to move people to the right—but their frequent failure to do so is in very large measure due to poor quality leadership. Whatever energy or resources we put into recruiting and equipping small group leaders will pay enormous dividends over time.

d. Getting started with equipping

Overall, our observation is that most churches don't understand the importance of level 1 equipping, and so rarely plan for it. This means that when they do try occasionally to do some level 2 equipping they are frequently disappointed at the response or level of take-up—because there is not the heart or motivation to be involved. This in turn leads to a dearth of candidates for level 3 training.

The result is predictable enough, and common:

- a lack of general involvement by the congregation at various points along the pathway—whether in engaging with non-Christians, evangelizing their friends, reading the Bible with each other, following up new people, or actively encouraging and edifying their fellow believers
- a lack of available leaders for small groups and other ministries, resulting in overly full groups or a lowering of the bar for leadership, or both.

It all starts with 'Equipping', and especially at levels 1 and 2. As you come to design a pathway or structure (below), you will probably find that you need to concentrate your early efforts over on the 'right' (at equipping) in order to make progress in due course further to the 'left' (in engaging, evangelizing and establishing).

Of all the different plans and initiatives that you sift through and prioritize in designing your pathways, this one is critical.

But *how* are we going to achieve this aspect of transformational learning among a growing number of our people? What steps can we take to get started?

We've written on this at some length already in *The Trellis and the Vine*,[25] and you can find further papers and resources at **thevineproject.com**. In the brief space we have here, we would suggest the following:

- Getting started will almost certainly mean initially investing in a small number of current or potential leaders who can help in the equipping of others. Equipping of the kind we're talking about cannot really happen by remote control or impersonally. As we've been arguing all along, the kind of learning that is involved is personal and transformational; it requires content to not only be conveyed but exemplified and practised, prayerfully and patiently over time.
- In practical terms, this may mean spending a year or more investing in the personal, transformational equipping of a smallish group of people, from whom leaders can emerge with the heart and skills to help you equip others. Depending on who these people are, and where they are starting from, your equipping of them might range over all three levels.
- With these better-equipped leaders and 'equippers' in place, your existing 'Establishing' structures (such as small groups) can be very effectively used as a vehicle for level 1 and level 2 equipping. One of the big advantages of this is that the learning can be reviewed and practised over many months, rather than relying on a short course. The equipping gets embedded, and becomes part of the normal group life.
- To improve or supplement this sort of equipping in small groups, you can parachute an 'equipper' (usually one of the pastoral staff) into the groups, one at a time, to provide some inten-

---

25 See especially chapters 6 and 9. (We use the word 'training' rather than 'equipping' in *The Trellis and the Vine*, but the concept is the same.)

sive training. This can really help newer or less confident leaders to learn how to replicate this kind of training in the future.

- For the concrete thinkers among you, the approach we're advocating might look like this:
  o Year 1—gather a small group of (say) ten people, and spend roughly a third of the year each on levels 1, 2 and 3 equipping. The aim by year's end is to have (say) six new or significantly matured leaders who are ready to help you equip others through small groups.
  o Year 2—mentor and support these six new leaders as they start equipping the people in their small groups; meet with these leaders regularly, and parachute into their groups for (say) four-week stints to help them with equipping.
  o Also in Year 2, look for another ten people to work with more intensively.

- As well as working through existing small group structures, many churches supplement this with special training seminars or events or other structures. We know of some churches that put aside a 10-week block where all the small groups come together to focus particularly on level 1 and level 2 equipping. Some churches have an additional structure— a 'school for Christian ministry' or a strand of their adult Sunday School classes—that provides constant opportunities for equipping. There are many ways to do it.

- If your groups are starting to function well, with levels 1 and 2 equipping happening more widely, then new potential leaders will begin to emerge from those groups. At some point, you will need to draw them aside for some more intensive level 3 equipping for leadership. Some churches take potential new leaders out of their normal small group for six months, and provide intensive equipping or training in leadership—that is, this 'leadership training' group functions as their small group for that period.[26]

---

26 This was the genesis from which the *Growth Groups* training material for small group leadership was written.

- Continuing to meet regularly with your leaders is critical. As a minimum you should draw all your small group leaders together for training and discussion quarterly. Better still, gather a group of leaders together monthly in your home to talk and pray about their groups, to be equipped in some aspect of leadership, and to encourage each other (as a team of leaders) to stick with the task.
- We've observed a growing number of churches that ask some experienced leaders to step out of leading a group or class to equip and mentor other leaders. By visiting the groups occasionally, these mentors see the strengths and weaknesses of the leaders and can work on their development.

James's story

James was appointed as the minister to a church within a mainstream denomination in a mid-sized regional city some years ago.

How did you make a start with equipping your members to be part of a mission-oriented church?

It was simply a matter of helping people to see from the Bible that they *are* involved in it. They are where the action is. They have an exciting part in the gospel growing and bearing fruit all over the world. Helping people feel almost commissioned to do it. That was just a whole paradigm shift in how they viewed things. And obviously along with that there was giving them the skills to get on and do the work. We've runs lots of different courses in how to effectively talk to people about Jesus.

What sort of courses did you run?

In the early days we ran specific training courses like *Two Ways to Live*, for how to explain the gospel and how to follow up a new Christian. But I quickly learned that I personally had to get people to come to that. I can distinctly remember turning up at the little old hall we were meeting in for the first evangelism training course: no-one turned up. Because, foolishly, I didn't actually tap anyone on the shoulder, and say,

"Ross, this would be a really good thing for you". So I very quickly learned that it was very important to bring people along in the culture of change, rather than making it a vague all-in sort of invitation.

How important was the pulpit in teaching and re-teaching the Christian life and what church is about?

Absolutely critical. Even to this day, as we sit down at the end of each year and work out what is the ministry goal and focus for the next year, after we've worked through that process, the very first thing we work on is the preaching program. How are we going to work through the Bible, and supplement and support it, and show biblically what we're doing and why we're doing it and what our focus is?

Was it the regular preaching that God primarily used to give people that sense of being commissioned?

I think for me it was. Because I think I'm better at preaching the Bible than doing one-on-one training. But my colleague Steve is really good at one-on-one training, so that was one of the reasons I wanted to get him back on the team and start building a team ministry.

Go to **thevineproject.com** for the full interview with James, where he discusses the process he worked on for changing the ministry culture of a traditional mainstream evangelical church.

Did you choose Steve consciously because he had a different personality and different gifts than you?

Yes, he's clearly better at certain things than I am, and that's why you put people like that on—because they are better at something than you. I was keen to have a team ministry before we started building new facilities. We were nomadic at this time, moving from one location to another.

~

More of Virginia's story

Many churches find it almost impossible to get leaders to commit to training. Do you find that?

You get what you expect. If you have low expectations about people turning up, people will meet your expectations—they won't turn up. But if you value training, if you know it's going to benefit them as an individual and as a team, then you make it compulsory. I said to one young woman who pushed back on this expectation, "At the end of training day, I expect you'll come and thank me for making you go". I was convinced she'd be blessed by the day.

Most people are tentative—they fear if they expect too much of their volunteers, they'll lose them. My experience is the opposite: the more I expect, the more stable my teams have become.

I have higher expectations of my team leaders now than I did years ago, and I've had 100% of them commit again this year. One of them said, "I'll do this until I die".

Now in saying this, we've got holes in our teams across all our ministries. The one constant in kids' ministry is that we're always in flux. We're always in need of more leaders. I'd be worried if we weren't. It would indicate we weren't growing.

What else produces that kind of high-commitment culture?

I've always been clear in my thinking that it's God who changes lives, and his preferred way of working is when his word is faithfully taught and the gospel clearly preached. I am confident in the Holy Spirit, who changes the lives of kids—I personally came to faith at age 10.

But I didn't communicate this to people when recruiting them. So when I asked people to come and help with the kids' ministry, my language was more like, "I'll teach and disciple these kids... I just need you to help them cut and glue, and supervise them safely to and from the toilets".

I realized the way I'd set up kids' ministry was very me-centred. And the hardest thing for me to do was to step out and say, "Actually me teaching... me discipling our kids is not going to grow this ministry". I had to step out of face-to-face ministry with the kids and equip an army of volunteers willing to teach and disciple our kids. I had to let go.

And there's a real grief in letting go of face-to-face teaching of kids. I knew kids' ministry in our church would not grow unless I stepped out and let others step in.

Are you finding it harder to get high commitment from your team leaders and volunteers?

Yes, we do not have the stay-at-home mothers in the numbers we've had previously.

I'm starting this year with incomplete teams across every children's ministry—probably the worst start to the year we've had in a couple of years. That's mainly due to the fact that at the end of last year I had other things pressing in on me at a time when I should have been recruiting my teams.

In years gone by I've had low expectations of my leaders, and the language I've used has reflected that. I now have higher expectations and the language I use for the various roles reflects that—no-one is called a 'helper' any more. Now I have team leaders, leaders and junior leaders.

I do have varying role requirements—it's not just 'one size fits all'. There are lower expectations for some roles than for others, but I do think that it's essential to raise the expectation of what is required. If you expect little, then the volunteers will tend to think, "I'm not doing much. Somebody else could easily step in and do this; it's not that important".

I also remember becoming aware that I was the only one talking about the children as *my* children. I had a very clear understanding that I was responsible for teaching and pastoring our children.

The language used by my teams did not change until my expectation of them changed. I remember asking two women to commit to teaching our preschool kids (3-4 year olds) for a whole term, when previously they'd only been expected to teach one month in every three. These ladies took it on and did ten weeks straight together. They quickly worked out what they were good at and assigned the appropriate roles to the appropriate person. It was quite beautiful to see. At the end of the term I asked them to do a revision quiz with the kids. They were thrilled at what the kids had understood and what the kids could remember.

At the beginning of the next term, both women came to me independently. One asked, "Who's teaching *my kids* this term?" The other said, "I miss *my kids*." I had never heard the language of *my kids* used by anyone other than me. Both women are still teaching our preschoolers to this day.

You increase the ownership of the discipling of children by increasing what is required of each leader.

We don't realize that we rip people off—it is more blessed to give than to receive. To see a kid's life changed because you shared Christ with them—how precious is that! You don't get to see that if you jump in and out of the kids' lives.

And kids give back. Who do the kids seek out during the holiday breaks or at Christmas? Out of all the adults at church, the kids look for those people who've loved them during the year. They make gifts and write cards to thank them for their love and for sharing Jesus with them.

So you think we're afraid of raising the bar?

I can think of one woman with the gift of hospitality who is also a very busy woman. I began to use her gifts in various ways across our kids' ministries. She loved it. Someone commented that they'd not thought to ask her to help in their ministry area because they thought she was too busy.

Sometimes we make decisions for people instead of letting them make decisions for themselves. Our job is to paint the picture of the ministry and explain its importance, but then let them decide if it's right for them in light of their present commitments, the time they have available, and their present capacity. We need to stop second-guessing what we think people will say.

Sometimes people do overcommit, however, and we do need to protect them from themselves. My rule of thumb, particularly when I'm asking a married woman to consider taking on a new responsibility, is to encourage them to pray about it and talk about it with their husband, then get back to me.

e. Equipping leads to exporting

Of the tinkering with models and acronyms there is no end. We've been in churches where extra Es were always being thought of: Edifying, Encouraging, Expanding, and of course Eating.

But before we conclude our look at designing pathways, we would like to commend one additional E for consideration, as a kind of extension to equipping—and that's *Exporting*.

One of the many fruitful consequences of effectively equipping people as disciple-makers is that an increasing number of people want to spend more and more time in 4P ministry. They get frustrated at having to spend so much time working for a living, and will often try to limit their work hours in some way so as to free up more time for ministry. It's from these sorts of people that the next generation of pastors, teachers and evangelists arises.

As we equip people, we need to be on the lookout for 'people worth watching' (as we labelled them in *The Trellis and the Vine*)—that is, those who have the character and gifts to be apprenticed and trained as full-time gospel workers.[27] In fact, if we are to be true to our convictions about God's worldwide plans in Christ, we will long to raise up more workers of all kinds for the harvest, and send them out to do 4P ministry in other places where the need is urgent.

In other words, a natural consequence of all that we have been saying about the gospel and the nature of equipping is that we will constantly be *exporting* people from our fellowship into the ministry of the gospel elsewhere. This is of course painful at one level—not just because it is sad to see beloved friends move on, but because that beloved friend is a key leader who will be very hard to replace!

But to adapt what Paul says about cheerfully giving money, we should cheerfully and generously equip and send our people on

---

27 We don't have a lot to add here to our treatment of this subject in *The Trellis and the Vine*. See especially chapter 10 on 'People worth watching' and chapter 11 on 'Ministry apprenticeship'. For a fuller discussion of ministry apprenticeship, see Colin Marshall, *Passing the Baton: A Handbook for Ministry Apprenticeship*, 2007. MTS (the Ministry Training Strategy) is an organization seeking to multiply gospel workers through ministry apprenticeships throughout the world. For more information, visit http://mts.com.au.

to the work of the gospel in other places, knowing that just as God gave them to us in the first place, so he will continue to give us more people:

> He who supplies seed to the sower and bread for food will supply and multiply your seed for sowing and increase the harvest of your righteousness.[28]

DISCUSSION

1. What 'Equipping' are you currently doing at the three levels mentioned above?

2. Do your members feel that they have a sort of 'ministry career path' in your church, to learn and grow in ministry leadership? Or do they get stuck in the same roles?

3. For level 3 equipping (specialist skills):

    a. For your church, is the leadership bar too low or high?
    b. Do your leaders embody the vision and culture you are creating?
    c. Is leadership in your church seen as a burden or as a motivating challenge?
    d. What will be the main obstacles in your church for training new leaders effectively? How will you overcome these?
    e. Identify by name your *current* level 3 leaders.
    f. Identify by name your *potential* level 3 leaders.
    g. Evaluate the effectiveness of your current leadership training processes. What leadership training programs need to be created? Who will form and lead these?
    h. How will you embed a coaching culture in your leadership development? What will be the benefits?

4. If you had to choose just three important initiatives or improvements to your equipping, what would they be?

---

28 2 Cor 9:10

PROJECT: GETTING STARTED

Having looked through the four stages of building a pathway through your ministries, and no doubt generated lots of discussion and ideas, the task now is actually to bring some order to all the chaos of possibilities, and design some pathways—that is, an aligned, co-ordinated, integrated set of activities, events, ministries, meetings and/or small groups through which each person can make progress towards Christ and towards maturity in Christ (from 'Engaging' through to 'Equipping').

We suggest that you initially design the pathway or structure you'd like to see in place in two years time. There will no doubt be aspects of it that already exist now, and that you can work on improving and aligning. But setting your sights for two years time will allow the space to figure out what sort of equipping you need to do now (and over the next 18 months or so) in order to have the people and leaders in place to make that pathway work—because you will almost certainly lack them at this point in time.

Planning pathways will mean working out:

- which current activities have potential and should be part of the pathway (usually with some improvements or tweaks)
- which current ministries or activities don't really contribute, and should be wound down
- what new ministries or groups are needed
- what equipping and training will be needed for each of these.

Here's an example of the kind of thing you might come up with:

Engaging	Evangelizing	Establishing	Equipping
Community market stall	Church-wide *Introducing God* course twice a year	Improve every member welcoming and newcomer follow-up at church	Train small group leaders to do level 1 equipping with their groups
Playgroup	Team of people trained to read the Bible one-to-one with interested non-Christians (arising out of 'Engaging' contacts)	Run *Get To Know* newcomers program four times a year	Key level 2 equipping skills to roll out through small groups: • relational engagement and evangelism • reading the Bible one-to-one • loving and welcoming newcomers at church
Regular doorknocking (new)		Bible study groups with well-trained leaders; main study curriculum linked with sermons	Run level 3 small group leadership training: • new leaders group • regular in-service training for existing leaders
Small groups run social events three times a year		Quarterly 'mind-stretch teaching nights' for whole church	
Improved church advertising in local community			

(You might also find it useful to map out a separate pathways table like this for particular ministry areas within the congregation—e.g. youth ministry, men's ministry.)

Mapping out pathways like this will generate a set of priorities and actions—that is, concrete things that need to be undertaken now and over the next 12-18 months. As you list down these possible priorities and actions:

- Highlight the key priorities in building your pathway over the next two years; what are the essentials, and what are the desirables?
- Itemize the actions that need to be taken, as well as by when, by whom, at what cost, and so on.

Once you get down the detail of what has to be done, you may well find that your pathway is too ambitious given where you're starting from.

Barry's story

Barry became the minister of an evangelical church in a mainstream denomination about seven years ago. The church is located in the suburbs with a mix of teachers, managers, nurses, tradespeople, and so forth.

When you arrived seven years ago, what was on your heart for this church?

I wanted to make this an outward-looking church. That was my brief when the nominators were talking to me and I was very happy to get on board with that. To my delight, they made good on that. They weren't just talking; they were serious about change. When I came they hadn't run an evangelistic event of any sort for ten years.

I wanted them to be outward looking in terms of getting to know people, inviting them along to stuff, creating ideas, places, venues, things in their home where they initially meet people and where they could share the gospel with them.

I wanted them to view each other as a team and work together and understand that not everyone is a good explainer; some are good inviters and some are really good behind the scenes. So, valuing other members and their gifts especially as part of the enterprise of church and outreach.

Where did you start in setting the vision and culture?

The first place to start was with the Parish Council. They were the obvious group to talk to because they were meeting regularly, and the people who were on it were in Bible study groups; some were leaders. There were only four Bible study groups.

What did you do with the Parish Council to get them thinking about vision and culture?

At the first meeting, I showed them David Mansfield's unpublished 'Discipleship Program'—well, at least my dumbed down version of it. He was saying that people go through different stages in their journey towards becoming mature Christians. They start off as complete outsiders who we need to engage with. There are lots of people who don't know any Christians and they've never been to church, so we want to engage with those people. We want to evangelize those we do know, and then establish them in the faith and equip them to minister.

Colossians 1:28
"Him we proclaim, warning everyone and teaching everyone with all wisdom, that we may present everyone mature in Christ."

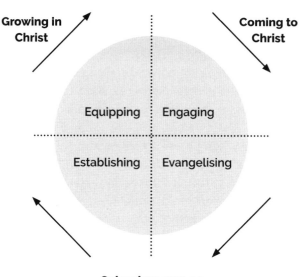

Colossians 1:13-14
"He has delivered us from the domain of darkness and transferred us to the kingdom of his beloved Son, in whom we have redemption, the forgiveness of sins."

I showed them this diagram, and talked through it at the first meeting. And I asked them whether they thought our church was good at all four of these stages. They just shook their heads.

I said, "Okay, just think of churches you know. Forget theology for a minute. Let's just brainstorm: where would you put that big charismatic church down the road? What are they good at?"

They said, "They're very good at advertising, they have a big front door, lots of people know about them—so I guess they're good at the first E (Engaging)."

"So what about the church where they get a two-hour sermon on some doctrine like the Trinity? Where would you put them?"

"Well, they're all Christians, they've got a solid understanding, but they haven't understood that they're supposed to be equipped for ministry to serve other people, so it's sort of category four ('Equipping'), but failing."

I said, "Where do you think our church and the normal suburban church fits?"

They said, "We don't know. What do you think?"

I said, "I'm convinced everyone is stuck in zone three ('Establishing'); they became Christians years ago, maybe in their youth as young adults, and they've been marking time ever since. They've never understood that the Christian life is about glorifying God, serving him however you can, reaching out to the lost and getting on with the job."

So after one meeting they were all fully persuaded and the whole thing changed?

They were fully persuaded about the problem I was identifying. They agreed that the vast majority of people at church were stuck in stage three—that most people didn't serve in any capacity. The people at church were probably Christians, but with a weak understanding.

So, that was our first Parish Council meeting. I said, "Whatever we do, we've got to try and be the church that's good at doing all four! No church has ever pulled it off, but I want us to be the church that gives it a good crack." They all laughed at that and said, "Well, that sounds right".

And so at the next Parish Council meeting, I came back and said, "Here's my plan. There are four terms in the year; so let's devote each term to one of those four stages of evangelism and growth."

So you did engaging in term 1, evangelizing in term 2, establishing in term 3 and equipping in term 4. Are you still doing that now, seven years later?

Yes. I think in the first year they were ambivalent—they thought, "Yeah it's a plan, but we'll see if it can work".

It shocked them having a three-month mission across term 2. That's caused quite a bit of a stir amongst the local ministers. When I've showed them the plan, they've said, "That's ridiculous—you should be evangelizing all year round. But you're doing more evangelism than we're doing!"

How have you worked on the equipping?

In 2010, I started a thing called 'Prepared to Serve'. It's 'one year with Barry'. I got the idea from Richard Coekin in the UK; every leader had to spend two years with him in his kitchen. So I pulled people, men and women, out of their Bible study group for a year's training with me.

We have spent a term on doctrine (God, Trinity, Scripture, humanity, atonement, eschatology); one on serving (using our gifts, the ministry of the pew, men and women in church, money, prayer, Bible reading); one on evangelism (*Two Ways to Live* training on steroids); and one on growing Christians (understanding the 4 Es, how to teach the Bible, home visiting, one-to-one ministry, and so on).

It's like a glorified Bible study year with me. The first year was with young adults. In the five years since I've started, about 56 people have now done it across all ages.

Many of our people find *Two Ways to Live* too hard, so we use ABC: Admit, Believe, Commit. They found it refreshing to

For more interviews with pastors on how they've structured their church's ministries to keep moving people forward, go to **thevineproject.com**. There you will find the full interview with Barry, where he talks about some of the obstacles he faced in changing the church culture.

be able to explain the gospel in simple terms and remember it—even the elderly can do it.

Explaining the Es (I call it 'The Wheel') in term 4 is the crux of it all. The Christian life is a journey, and you never get to the end. Make it a priority to keep growing, keep learning, challenging yourself, trying things. But also understand that different people you encounter will be at different stages on the wheel, and that you can be useful in their life in helping them take the next step from where they are. If you meet someone, get to know them, engage, invite them to your house. Start getting Jesus into the conversation with friends you already know.

Addendum: Equipping parents for ministry at home

As we noted at the end of Conviction 5 in Phase 1, the home or household is a key context or location for disciple-making—that is, a place in which the word is spoken and has its powerful transformative effect on our relationships. In one sense, we could think of ministry in the home as being a 'pathway' all of its own, with family members engaging with each other, sharing the gospel with each other, and encouraging each other on to maturity in Christ.

More of Virginia's story

Here is another excerpt from our interview with Virginia, in which she discusses what they've done at her church to equip parents to help their children 'move to the right' in Christ.

Do you do much to equip parents to disciple their kids in the home?

I find it's like exercise: we think we're doing more than we really are. My experience is that parents think they're doing a lot more than what they really are. I surveyed our kids two years ago. Parents think they're reading the Bible and praying with their kids regularly, but from the kids' perspective it's happening a lot less, and in some cases not at all.

But some of our parents are doing brilliantly, and you can tell. You can tell from the way kids talk, the questions they ask, the way they pray... you can tell whether they are being discipled well at home.

Leaders can tell which ones are being helped at home?

Yes, it's very evident. The most telling sign is the way the kids pray.

Our kids are encouraged to pray in their small groups every week. The under-7s pray twice—first a repeated prayer about what they've learned, and then their own prayer. It's when they pray individually that you hear maturity in their prayers. And you can hear it from a very young age.

Are the mothers more active than the fathers?

Yes, the majority of mothers are talking to their kids at home.

I can think of one boy who was being discipled well by his dad (the dad had become a Christian but his wife hadn't). I remember saying to the boy, "You pray with your dad every night, don't you?"

The boy looked stunned and asked, "How do you know?"

I responded, "I can hear it in your prayers".

He'd stopped praying 'me-centred' prayers. He was praying for God to be glorified in everything. Dads who pray with their sons have a big impact, particularly on their boys.

What are your hopes for parents reading the Bible and praying with their kids?

I hope parents will think intentionally about using the time they have and making more of the opportunities they have. So don't waste your trip to and from school... don't waste that break during the TV commercial (talk about what you've just seen)... don't waste bath time...

Parents think, "I don't have time to read the Bible and pray with my child".

But you can use bath time to retell or read stories from Scripture. A great routine we encourage our parents to establish with their children from infancy is: *Bible, bath, bed.*

We've just started Bible reading plans for children aged 3-11. The first Sunday these were introduced a mother said, "I've been so convicted lately about how slack I've been at reading the Bible with my kids. I was praying just this morning that God would help me start this year afresh with my children. I turned up to church and my child came out with this Bible reading plan."

It's a really simple idea, but so helpful for families. This mother just was so excited that her church had a plan for her child.

Parents who have been regular with these Bible reading plans now report that their children refuse to go to bed if the Bible hasn't been read. Routines for children are very important and critical for the ongoing discipleship of children. It generally takes one month of doing it intentionally every day before a routine like this is established in the life of a child.

Focus Area 3: Plan for growth

In many ways, what we're trying to do in the Vine Project is produce growth—growth in people and growth in numbers, as more people are engaged, evangelized and established in God's church through the 4P ministry we do as his fellow workers.

This leads to a key question that we need to face now at this point of the process, because it will shape some key decisions along the way: *What if it works?*

Thinking about growing

What if, under God, the work you do in the Vine Project over the next few years sees significant growth in your congregational numbers— more people converted and established, more people in groups of all kinds, more people on Sundays, more people to follow up and work with? What if your congregation numbers doubled (say) in the next seven years?[1] How would you cope with that growth? Do you have the facilities? How would it change your staff requirements? How would it change the way you organized and ran things?

---

1   Which they would if you managed an average growth in numbers of around 10% per year.

"Well," you might say, "that would be a great problem to have!" And so it would.

But here's the thing: the more that you and your congregation dream of that level of growth, pray for that level of growth, organize yourself around that level of growth, and plan for that level of growth, the more likely you are to see it happen.

We need to be clear: this is not because of any 'positive thinking' effect, nor even because big numbers and plans tend to inspire and motivate people to get involved. Real gospel growth comes through 4P ministry (and no other way); you can't market your way to it with a glossy brochure.

However, if your aspiration and godly expectation is for growth it will change the way you plan, and thus what you actually do. You will build structures and pathways and various trellises to facilitate and drive the growth that you aspire to.

For example, you might say to yourselves, "Under God, we'd like to aim to see 100 people converted in the next two years; so that means we'd need to be meeting and engaging with (say) at least three times that many people in our community". That goal would then lead you to consider what plans or initiatives you could launch, what resources you'd need, and what equipping and training of your people would be required in order to meaningfully engage with 300 non-Christian outsiders in the next two years.

And in turn, you would end up having to make some tough decisions about what other ministries or activities you might have to de-prioritize or close down altogether in order to be able to put the effort and resources into engaging 300 new people.

The goal you set shapes the way you plan and what you end up actually doing—which in turn makes it far more likely that you will in fact get within sight of your goal.[2]

---

2   None of this is to deny the sovereignty of God in salvation, and in all things. We can't force God's hand, nor can we ever think that ministry operates via a simple cause-and-effect formula. However, as we've argued above, the sovereign God uses created means and human agents to do his sovereign work. In particular, he has chosen to use the four Ps as the means by which people come to Christ and grow in Christ. In that sense, the four Ps are the cause, and conversions and growth in Christ are the effects. If the effects are not (cont)

One of the big questions will be around people. Who will lead these evangelistic initiatives? Who among us has the gifts and vision to build a team to reach a particular people group in our community? Who should we recruit into our fellowship to drive these ministries?

The same of course goes for the mundane but vital infrastructure that supports 4P ministry throughout your congregation—things like buildings and meeting spaces, administrative staffing, fundraising, and so on. If you aspire to double your numbers in seven years, but you have buildings and facilities that won't accommodate those numbers, you have four options:

- plant one or more new congregations in a new location
- plant one or more new congregations at another time in your own building
- extend the size of your building (or move to a bigger building)
- give up on your goal of doubling in seven years.

It's as simple as that.

Now some readers may be thinking, "We're a long way off from doubling in seven years. I'd just be happy to stop declining! Or to see some actual growth and people converted."

And this may be quite right. You may be starting a long way back, and need to put in quite a bit of work just to get 'moving to the right' ministry happening among a decent number of your people.

However, we suggest that you don't leave it too long before raising the eyes of your people to the fields all around them that are white for harvest. A longing for gospel growth—and lots of it—springs from our convictions: that millions are lost in this present darkness all around us, that Christ alone has the words of

happening very much (i.e. people are not being converted or growing), then it's reasonable to stop and evaluate whether we are in fact faithfully and energetically using God's means (the four Ps). And accordingly, it is also reasonable to plan and think in advance about how we might employ the four Ps more widely and effectively, so that we might see more gospel growth.

eternal life, that he has commissioned us to 'make learners' of all nations, and that he himself is driving the process by his word and Spirit.

If we live in a community of 20,000 then we should desire to bring the gospel to everyone, and work and pray to that end. We may well start with people groups we are best placed to reach—whether a local school community, or an ethnic subculture, or whatever—but our burden will be to see our whole town, suburb, city and nation covered with effective gospel ministries. We know God will use other churches and ministries as well (not just us), and there will be times when we should work together to achieve more than we can as individual churches. But in our view, one of the culture changes that many churches need is a revolution in their level of gospel ambition. Putting it baldly, we need to think big.

There are of course dangers in thinking big. There's the credibility danger of creating disillusionment in the congregation by setting some pie-in-the-sky goal that we'll never achieve. And if we talk big but act small (like not providing for more people on Sunday, or not equipping ministry leaders), then no-one will believe us.

There are also spiritual dangers in having ambitious plans:

- you might begin to lust for the glory and reputation that accrues to the minister of a large and growing church
- you might be tempted to build a feel-good, people-pleasing ministry in order to attract the crowds
- you might start to treat people like objects, and lose the compassionate inefficiency that leaves the 99 in order to seek after the one
- you might start exaggerating or fudging the facts to protect your credibility (i.e. by making out that goals are being achieved when they're not)
- you might fall into the unprincipled pragmatism that follows any ministry method that 'gets results'.

All these dangers need to be recognized and avoided.

But the alternative spiritual danger is often even more perilous: that we retreat into a loveless inward-looking smallness that has no compassion on the lost multitudes all around us.

More of Barry's story

Barry became the minister of an evangelical church in a mainstream denomination about seven years ago. The church is located in the suburbs with a mix of teachers, managers, nurses, tradespeople, and so forth.

What are your plans for growth?

In 2010, we set the goal of having 1500 regulars by 2020. That would require five weekly church services, two new church plants, 50 growth groups,[3] a staff team of ten pastors plus admin staff and apprentices, and a budget of $1.5 million. We launched the vision at a big prayer breakfast with a '2020 Vision' booklet.

How will you keep the momentum going till 2020?

At one of the churches in our city, there's a map of 100 church plants that grew out of the church's ministry over 100 years as the suburbs sprouted.

I showed our leaders that map and we talked about our church being on the edge of a massive population expansion. Soon there will be 300,000 new people five minutes from us. We have to take responsibility for Christianizing these suburbs.

I'm not experienced in planting churches. I'm not sure I can hold a network of churches together. I am a major limitation to the vision. We're now at a size where people can't know me very well. I will have to change as much as anything else. I only really know how to grow from a small base to whatever we are now.

We have choices to make. To reach 1500, will we go for three large congregations of 500 each or 30 congregations of 50 each? Both are costly and difficult in terms of property. Anyone can run a church of 50, but church venues and housing will be hard. Then again, how many preachers can speak

---

3   The term 'growth group' is simply another way of talking about a small Bible study group—a distinctively Christian group where Christians can grow, and which is also a catalyst for the growth of the gospel. See Marshall, *Growth Groups*, pp. 5-6.

effectively to 500 people? In a small church people tend to say you're a good preacher, whether you are or not, based on how much they have a personal relationship with you. I get "You're a good preacher" all the time, but I don't know if it's true unless I preach to bigger group.

We've agreed we should be a hybrid and so develop a bigger building and hall—and plant churches. More are coming here than ever before, so we need a bigger facility.

In being a project manager, I have a skill problem with planning backwards from a goal. All my ideas are small ideas. And our Parish Council is financially conservative. So we have some challenges!

DISCUSSION AND PLANS

1. Where are the greatest needs and potential for engagement and evangelism in your local community or context? Which groups of people do you think you could most effectively connect with and reach?

2. Toss about some stretching but achievable numbers for your congregation in some of these areas:

   a. the number of non-Christian people converted in the next five years
   b. the number of Sunday attenders at church in the next five years
   c. the number of congregations in your network
   d. the number of small clusters of learners (i.e. small groups)

3. What would be the implications of these sorts of numbers for:

   a. your physical property and resources?
   b. the possibility of planting new fellowships or churches to reach your goals?

4. With these larger longer-term growth goals in mind, look back over your priorities and plans for improving Sunday and for your ministry pathways:

    a. What would you change or prioritize differently? Does that change the mix?
    b. How do these growth goals affect your plans at each stage of the pathway—engaging, evangelizing, establishing, equipping?
    c. What's missing?

5. Having looked back through your other plans, come back to the rough numbers you were tossing around in question 2. Settle on some numbers that you want to pray about, that you think are stretching but doable, and that serve to finalize and drive your plans and actions in the other areas.

6. Now go back again through all your plans and actions in Focus Areas 1 and 2, and finalize the priorities and actions you're going to put into effect.

If you need help...

The discussion questions and suggestions above are an accurate but brief guide to the steps involved in planning for change and growth. And for some of our readers, they will be all that's needed.

However, from our conversations with many pastors, we know that Barry is not alone when he says, "I have a skill problem with planning backwards from a goal." If that's you, then don't be shy about seeking help and support. Here are three suggestions:

- God may well have blessed you with people in your church who have a high degree of professional skill in this area. Spend time with some of these people; help them to grow in conviction and in having a heart for the gospel, and draw on their experience and wisdom in effective planning.

- Get hold of a copy of Craig Hamilton's *Wisdom in Leadership* if you have not done so already. It's the best single-volume compendium we've seen of wise, practical help on a huge range of everyday ministry issues, all within an excellent Reformed-evangelical theological framework.
- Make the most of the online support community at **thevineproject.com** to ask questions and to get ideas and resources for effective ministry planning and implementation.

Focus Area 4: Create a new language

L anguage shapes culture.

If we want to change 'the whole way we do things around here', we'll need to change the language people use and the categories in which people think about 'the way we do things around here'. We'll need to teach our congregations a new way of talking—one that our people can understand and relate to, but which signals and communicates the direction in which we're trying to head.

In other words, you need to work out a plan for comprehensively communicating the vision that you have crafted for becoming a 'transformative learning community', or for 'moving to the right', or whatever terms or descriptions you have come up with.

You've already done some of this work back in Phase 1 in clarifying your convictions, and writing some basic communication pieces (e.g. a simple statement, a manifesto, a vision presentation).

Now you're a bit further down the track. You've made progress in drafting some plans. You have more of an idea of the key priorities you want to work on over the next few years, including some major goals for gospel growth.

It's time to start *communicating* all of this—the convictions and the new way of thinking about 'learning Christ', the pathways to move people forward (from engaging through to equipping), the bigger long-term goals that you're dreaming and praying about reaching, and so on.

Let's look at how that communication can happen both explicitly and implicitly.

Explicit communication

Do your eyes ever glaze over when people start talking about visions and missions and values and purposes and goals and strategic priorities? Do you sit quietly hoping you're not the only one in the room who doesn't really understand the difference between all these important sounding words? If so, you'll be relieved to know that we're not about to get into a theoretical discussion of management terminology.

But if you are going to shift the whole culture of your church in the direction that we've been discussing then whatever labels or terms you end up using, there are several key messages that you will need to communicate explicitly, memorably and often. You need to create a new (or renewed) language that becomes the normal, default way in which you talk as a congregation about who you are, what you're on about, and what you see in your future.

In particular, you need to craft some clear communication that answers four key questions. Fortunately, everything that you've done to this point should help you answer these questions pretty quickly:

a. *What sort of church does God want us to be?* (This is often called 'vision', and is driven by the theological convictions we sharpened in Phase 1.)

b. *Under God, how are we going to get to that future?* (These are the broad means or strategies that we are going to use, and again flow out of our convictions from Phase 1 about the four Ps of ministry, moving to the right, and so on.)

c. *What are our specific goals for growth in the next (say) five years?* (These are the specific goals for growth that you have just worked through in Focus Area 3.)

d. *What are our specific priorities or plans for reaching those goals?* (These are the other focus areas you've worked through in this phase—i.e. 'Making Sunday a flagship' and 'Designing pathways'—as well as any major practical steps that are required, such as employing staff or making property decisions.)

Your answers to 'a' and 'b' are your own way of expressing the theologically driven convictions that should shape and change your culture. Taken together, they should give a rationale for pretty much everything you do as a congregation. Whenever someone in your congregation pauses to wonder why we are now doing X rather than Y, the answer that should pop straight into their minds is, "Oh of course, I see why—because God wants us to become *this* kind of church, and the way we're going to get there is by doing *that*".

How can you effectively communicate your answers to 'a' and 'b'? Here are a few thoughts:

- Boil your answers down to short, clear, memorable statements that you can repeat over and over again, in as many different ways and contexts as possible. You could even combine your answers to 'a' and 'b' into one sentence: "Under God, we want to become [this kind of church] by [doing this]".
- Try to make the way you express them distinctive and penetrating ("We all want to learn Christ and help others to learn Christ by engaging, evangelizing, establishing and equipping"), rather than generic ("We want to give God the glory in all things by loving him and other people"). Strive hard for *clarity*.
- Share these memorable summaries wherever you can: on every piece of paper you print, in every email and on every web page, on bookmarks and t-shirts, on your PowerPoint

presentations on Sunday, in your regular newsletter, as a constant prelude to announcements about what is happening, and so on. Your congregation should get to the point where they know it's coming, and could finish the sentence for you.[1]

- Regularly unpack, explain and expound your answers to 'a' and 'b' in sermons, on 'vision days' to the whole congregation, in meetings with key leaders, in membership classes, in booklets and other documents, in Bible studies, and in any other way that communicates and persuades your people of the truth of these convictions.
- These short vision-type statements are directed to your congregation, and won't necessarily feature in your public advertising about your church in the local community. Don't feel you have to craft them so that they are appealing to a non-Christian who sees your church sign as he drives past. How you advertise your church to the community is a separate question.

When you combine your answers to 'a' and 'b' (your big vision of the future and how to get there), with your more specific answers to 'c' and 'd' (specific goals for the future, and specific plans for getting there), what you magically have is a 'strategic plan'. This document should be detailed enough to provide a road map for most of your weekly and monthly decisions and actions, but short enough to be digestible and usable. A 60-page bound plan will sit unused in someone's bottom drawer. A 6-page PDF, with some good summary tables and charts, can be a constant presence on the desktop and the discussion table.

---

1   See Craig Hamilton's chapter 'Your people should be able to do a good impression of you' in *Wisdom in Leadership*, pp. 421-8. Of repeating the vision over and over again he says, "...when I'm starting to be bored by it that's probably when people are starting to vaguely remember it". His chapter on the nature of vision is also very useful; see 'The point is clarity, not labels', pp. 337-44.

Implicit communication

As well as communicating your vision explicitly (and often), you also want it to become a constant note—like the sound of a tuning fork—that resonates through your congregational life. Here are some ideas for how you can achieve this:

- Give some thought to changing the names of some of your ministries or elements in your 'pathway', so that they reflect the vision you want to communicate.
- As you plan the weekly corporate prayers in your main church gathering, use some of the main categories or labels or language of your vision to shape your prayers. If the four Es were part of your language, for example, you could focus on praying for engaging, evangelizing, establishing and equipping ministries on different weeks.
- Keep relating the preaching to aspects of the vision, when the Bible passage takes you there.
- When you're announcing or advertising or reporting back on church events or activities, keep using the language of your vision to describe them, to show how they fit into the larger picture of what you're all doing together.
- Share stories of how people are becoming Christians and growing, how they are learning to be Christlike day to day, how they are being persecuted for standing up for Christ, and so on (see Gary's story below for an example). The telling of stories is perhaps the most important form of implicit communication. Whether in testimonies or interviews during the Sunday gathering, or in email newsletters or video clips or other documents, there are few things more powerful than hearing real people talk about how they are beginning to live the disciple-making culture you are wanting to see grow.

More of Gary's story

Gary leads an evangelical Anglican church in a multicultural community with a rapidly growing population.

How do you keep setting the vision and culture you want?

I'm really big on the principle that vision rides on stories that capture our vision and values. So whenever I hear a story of someone witnessing to someone, or someone making a big call for Jesus, I either email it out or interview the person in church.

For example, just recently one woman told me a story about getting her growth group to hold her accountable about going to visit an Afghani lady in her street. The two women are now meeting up regularly with their respective husbands, having 'Jesus talk'. It was just a really lovely story. So (with her permission) I'll shoot that out in an email to everyone. Most weeks there are stories going out.

And personal interviews—just getting ordinary people to tell of opportunities they have. We use the phrase 'Making heroes out of ordinary people'. As a pastor they kind of expect me to evangelize, you know—I'm paid to, and I went to Bible college. But I'm forever trying to find that person who's not going to be the classic show pony, to bring them up the front and let them tell their story of evangelizing.

More of Richard's story

Richard was appointed as the minister of a mainstream denominational church in a large regional city a few years ago.

What about symbols or artefacts that helped change the culture?

Changing the church sign was a great moment. The church was on a large block, and early on they sold the front half to a motel to pay for the building. From the road, all you can see of our church is a driveway. So there was this massive great big white arrow, with conservative blue writing and this 1970s photo of a family.

Someone suggested we change the sign and increase our visibility and do something fun. I suggested we make it green and bright. Two conservative elders said, "Let's paint a big green arrow". So I stayed hands off, and let the two elders paint the sign. If anyone asked me about the sign, I said, "You'll have to ask Barry and Ian about that!"

Immediately people in the community started talking about the big green arrow. We put a banner across the top, and we had a new website. It gave us a presence. It was fun.

Another massive thing was the carols. We used to sing carols every year in the church building.

"Why do we do that?" I asked.

"Because it's Christmas."

I suggested we invite the community. So we formed a team, did letterbox drops, printed and wore green T-shirts with our slogan, and did face painting. It was a big thing, and people were a bit nervous about it. But it was packed (about 400 came) and it brought people onto our patch. It was crazy. We had the kids crowded in down the front, some of them being rough—and I'm trying to separate these kids with my feet to stop them from having a punch-up, while I'm playing *Hark the Herald Angels Sing* on my guitar.

As you engage in innovating and implementing, we encourage you to make the most of the support available at thevineproject.com.

But God honoured all that, and from then on we realized we had to go outside with the carols. So since then we've had an outdoor carol service, led from the back of a truck parked in our driveway.

We also remodelled the church bulletin and made things more professional. We worked on our website and on our audio-visuals. We wanted people not to be embarrassed if they came.

Every week I sent out an email that included news from the bulletin as well as a short piece that I wrote—commending the congregation for being welcoming to newcomers and reinforcing that, or responding to the sermon. All this helped to reshape the culture—small things that together become very powerful.

PROJECT: DEVELOP A COMMUNICATION PLAN

1. Look back over the draft manifesto you put together at the end of Phase 1. Is there anything you'd like to change or improve?

2. Boil down the manifesto to some simple statements that answer the two big-picture questions about your church culture:

   a. What sort of church does God want us to be?
   b. Under God, how are we going to get to that future?

3. Devise a communication plan for how you are going to:

   a. explain, expound and persuade the congregation of the truth of these statements through sermons, web presentations, video clips, vision presentations, meetings with leaders, and so on
   b. keep repeating and disseminating these statements as widely and often as possible.

   You could use a planning template like this:

Form of communication	Medium or channel	By when?	Person responsible
Summary statement	Opening PowerPoint slide, bulletin	April 1	Jim
1-hour vision presentation	Whole church celebration dinner	June 20	Warwick

PHASE 5 //
MAINTAIN MOMENTUM

Maintain momentum

Perhaps you're thinking that the hard part is over. There's no question that Phase 4 is time-consuming and demanding—so much thinking and rethinking, so many options and possibilities, and so much talk, talk, talk about what we're actually going to do.

However, as we've noted once already, strategic planning is actually the easy part. Execution is where nearly everyone falls down. The truly challenging stage in driving any deep culture change is actually executing your plans—persistently, flexibly and effectively over the considerable period of time that will be required for any real change to take place.

This final phase of the Vine Project is all about that challenge. In this phase we'll talk about the inevitable obstacles, challenges and difficulties that will come, and plan for how to maintain the momentum not just for this year, or the one after that, but for many years into the future. We'll look at five topics:

1. Understanding the obstacles
2. The pressure on pastors
3. The pressure on our people
4. Leadership, staffing and governance
5. Practical skills in maintaining momentum

As we do so, we're very aware we are covering topics that deserve whole chapters or books of their own.[1] Our aim is to give you the contours of the landscape and a map for navigating your way through it, but then point you to where more detailed directions and guidance can be found.

1. Understanding the obstacles

Changing 'the way we do things around here' never happens quickly or easily. Our shared language, practices, habits, structures, activities, traditions, accepted wisdom, symbols, rituals and relationships have all been bedded down over a considerable period of time—sometimes centuries.

Every culture has a certain weight or inertia to it, like one of those roly-poly wobbly man toys that you can push over but which always rights itself and returns to its former position. As we've already noted more than once, changing a culture takes some persistence. It's not a commando operation; it's more like an extended land war in Asia.

But there is also the inherent difficulty of implementing any plan successfully in our world, given the natural forces of chaos and entropy. People are fallible; they make mistakes or fail to follow through on their promises. The world is complex, and we can't factor in every circumstance or variable in our plans. The future is unknown to us, and may bring an unexpected change that wrecks our plans entirely.

All of this is just the ocean we sail on. Any attempt at 'culture change' in any organization in our world—whether a business or government agency or school—will face these headwinds.

But as we seek to bring culture change to churches, we face an additional primary-level obstacle: sin. I suppose we might say that the general entropy and frustration of doing anything in the

---

1   Even more so than in the many other sections of this book of which the same could be said!

world is a result of sin and the fall, but in church culture-change the presence of sin is more acute. This is because what we're seeking to do is move our whole church culture, and the people who inhabit it, in the direction of godliness and maturity in Christ. If our convictions are right, the kind of change we're talking about is not just an organizational realignment or a new strategic approach—*it's a repentance towards Christlikeness.*

In other words, the fundamental reason that church cultures are not more aligned with the convictions we clarified in Phase 1 is not historical or circumstantial—it is spiritual. It is a lack of trust in the word of God, a lack of dependence on the Spirit of God, a lack of Christlike love for those around us, a lack of hope in the eternal kingdom of Christ that is our true home, and so on.

This is the basic reason that church cultures, and the people in them, will resist change in the direction we're talking about. It's the same reason our own hearts resist this change. As I (Tony) write this paragraph, I'm looking out my study window at my non-Christian neighbour working in his yard. There is part of my heart that is glad I am busy here at my desk writing about evangelism and growth, because it is easier than being out there talking to him about Christ. And this is just how all of us are. Our sinful hearts have a bias to the 'left', even as the word and Spirit of God urge and lead us to the 'right'.

Culture change is even more difficult than a land war in Asia. It's a spiritual battle against forces that we cannot even conquer in ourselves, let alone in our congregation—not with our own resources. We can only do it with the weapons that God provides, like the armoury of truth, righteousness, gospel, faith, salvation, Spirit, word and prayer in Ephesians 6.

In particular, we must keep praying and depending on God to wield the sword of his Spirit in the hearts of his people.

As you engage in maintaining momentum, we encourage you to make the most of the support available at **thevineproject.com.**

DISCUSSION

1. Look back over the list of roadblocks or obstacles to change that you talked through in Phase 3, Evaluation Exercise 7. Would you change your rating now as to which ones are likely to be the most challenging?

2. Would you *add* any other major obstacles to the list (following the planning you did in Phase 4)?

3. Looking again at the most significant obstacles you have now identified:

   a. See if you can reword each one as a spiritual problem, with a Bible passage that warns of this problem or commands us to be otherwise.

   b. What could you do to spot and defuse or avoid each one of these obstacles?

4. Here is a different list of obstacles—a list of reasons that churches have given, looking back, as to why their efforts to initiate growth and change have failed.[2] Which of these do you think are most likely to jeopardize your own efforts to reshape your church's culture?

   a. The project was not really brought to God in prayer; we talked about praying, but ended up not praying much at all.

   b. We failed to enlist a core group of passionate lay leaders or advocates to help model and lead the change.

   c. We underestimated the power and inertia of the existing culture.

   d. We didn't do enough to foster a sense of urgency for the changes.

---

2   Adapted from J Herrington, M Bonem and JH Furr, *Leading Congregational Change: A Practical Guide for the Transformational Journey*, Jossey-Bass, San Francisco, 2000.

e. We didn't give people enough time and space to make the emotional transition to some of the new structures and initiatives we introduced.

f. We bought someone else's solution. We attempted to 'bolt on' new programs and strategies to the existing work, rather than rebuild the culture from the ground up.

g. We backed off some key decisions because we didn't want to face the fallout or awkwardness of putting them into effect.

h. After a while we could not see the benefits of the changes, so we reverted to the status quo.

i. We did not really demonstrate the new ministry culture in such a way that people could see what it was all about.

j. We did not effectively communicate the reasons for change and what it would all mean for reaching more people with the gospel.

k. We were not willing to make changes to our organizational structures in order to remove obstacles to change.

l. We did not work out how to translate the vision into understandable and achievable implementation steps.

m. We tried to do too many new things at once. The process suffered death by a thousand initiatives.

n. We got started on the change process but lost momentum. We didn't have any plans in place for keeping ourselves going.

2. The pressure on pastors

In *The Trellis and the Vine*, we wrote briefly about the different ways that pastors see themselves and their roles. We talked about the pastor-as-service-providing-clergyman and the pastor-as-CEO and the pastor-as trainer. We might add to that recent calls for pastors to be missional leaders,[3] shepherd-leaders,[4] and who knows what else.

Not all of this is faddish (although some of it is). As we've talked personally with many hundreds of pastors, there is a widespread feeling that traditional views and expectations of the pastor's role are outmoded and have been for some time.

One hugely significant shift is simply in the changing patterns of regular social churchgoing. Many of our traditions and expectations of pastoral ministry belong to an era in which a sizable proportion of the population went to church regularly. Of the situation in England, Derek Tidball writes:

> In the days prior to the upheavals produced by the industrial revolution it seemed an adequate approach to divide England into a number of parishes and to ensure that through adequate staffing in each place the spiritual needs of the nation would be well met. That, at least was the theory! In support it could be claimed that, whatever the reality of personal belief, most people would be found at church and virtually everyone was within its orbit. The industrial revolution imposed severe strains on the parochial system and subsequent shifts in population have made it even more problematic, so much so... that the parochial system is now entirely inappropriate.
>
> This conclusion... should not be reached on the ground of management studies alone. More significantly, the parochial system is inappropriate because it is built on the presupposition that the nation is a Christian

3   Alan Roxburgh and Fred Romanuk, *The Missional Leader: Equipping Your Church to Reach a Changing World*, Jossey-Bass, San Francisco, 2006.

4   Timothy Z Witmer, *The Shepherd Leader: Achieving Effective Shepherding in Your Church*, P&R Publishing, Phillipsburg, 2010.

nation and all that needs to happen is that the sheep need to be penned... Today any pastoral theology, if it is to be adequate to meet the needs of the contemporary church, must take into account the missionary situation in which it exists... Pastoral theology must concern itself not only with the penning of existing sheep but with the birth of more sheep.[5]

Perhaps the most cataclysmic change has been in the way many churches approach evangelism. In the era where large numbers of nominal 'Christians' came to church, there was more than enough 'missional' work to do in simply evangelizing the non-Christians who came to church or brought their children to Sunday School every week. The idea of having to go out to the community, make contact with the unbelievers who were out there, and share the gospel with them—this simply wasn't on the agenda. There was no need, and no time, come to that.

This is no longer the case almost anywhere in the Western world (and hasn't been for decades). There are some pockets of the United States where it still may be like this, but even there it is changing rapidly.

However, even though the landscape has changed drastically, many churches still have expectations of ministry and of the pastor that belong to this bygone era. And many pastors themselves grapple with what their role is in the rapidly changing, increasingly spiritually hostile climate they inhabit. Is my role to protect and guard and feed the sheep? Or is it to go out into the world and find the lost sheep?

This is a massive subject. For now, these brief points will have to suffice:

- We don't need a new model of pastoral ministry so much as a return to the New Testament vision of pastoral ministry— for that was a ministry conducted in the furnace of a largely hostile, pagan culture.

5   D Tidball, *Skillful Shepherds: An Introduction to Pastoral Theology*, IVP, Leicester, 1986, pp. 15-16.

- In the New Testament, we don't see any hard, fast line drawn between the work of pastors, elders, overseers or evangelists. All undertake ministries of the word and prayer, preaching and teaching the gospel, publicly and from house to house, so that people might be saved.[6]
- The convictions we clarified in Phase 1 about the nature of all Christian ministry show that the role of the pastor or overseer is no different in essence from the role of every Christian—to move others to the right through 4P ministry, whether non-Christians down at the 'Engage' end or mature Christians at the 'Equip' end of the spectrum.
- The role of the pastor, under these convictions, is largely to be a model Christian. It is to serve as an exemplar, leader, mobilizer, teacher, guardian and guide for the whole congregation, as they together seek to move each other and everyone around them to the right.
- If we want to mash together biblical language with our metaphors, the pastor is a shepherd who is leading his sheep to the right—which means he is constantly teaching and helping and equipping his sheep to go back down to the left to bring others with them. In other words, it is something of a false dichotomy to say we need mission leaders, not pastors. Pastors who feed and lead their sheep according to the convictions we have outlined above will themselves have a heart for the lost, and will build and grow evangelistically active, outward-looking churches.
- The pastor's role, then, is not primarily therapeutic—although this is frequently a pressure point for many pastors. They are the ones who are expected to be there at the hospital bedside, to counsel the broken-hearted, to comfort the bereaved. And of course pastors can and should take the lead in providing this kind of love and care to those who are in need. However, as we have noted earlier,[7] this

---

6   See Paul's famous charge to Timothy to preach the word and discharge all the responsibilities of his ministry, including doing the work of an evangelist (2 Tim 4:1-5).

7   In Phase 4 (Focus Area 2).

sort of pastoral care is not a separate or alternative responsibility, somehow removed from being a learner in Christ who seeks to make other learners. As we grow in love and Christlikeness our hearts will go out in compassion to those in any sorrow or need, and we particularly long that they would be encouraged to persevere and put their faith and hope in Christ (by the prayerful ministry of the word of God). The pastor leads and exemplifies this sort of pastoral care ministry, but he can no more do it all than he can do all the evangelism or all the engaging with outsiders. Here too there is a 'pathway' to be thought through, and co-workers to be trained.

In other words, pastoral leadership flourishes and is effective when pastors are constantly seeking to invest in and deploy new pastors and co-workers to serve alongside them, whether as volunteers, part-timers or full-time staff. We need more pastors (not less) who can teach the faith, nurture spiritual maturity, and take responsibility to lead and equip the saints in all aspects of Christian living and 4P ministry.

DISCUSSION

1. How would you characterize the key expectations that your congregation members currently have of the pastor or pastoral staff?

2. Which of these expectations are likely to be obstacles to your plans for culture change? How might you address these through teaching, communication and conversation?

3. One common way that the pastor *himself* can be an obstacle or bottleneck for growth and culture change is in the fullness of his diary. If there is no time for the pastor, for example, to be closely involved in the equipping of

new 'learners who help other learners', then culture change is unlikely to get off the ground.

It's worth pastors doing a careful audit of their time. Where is the time actually going? What could be rescheduled or delegated? What priorities and time allocations need to change?

3. The pressure on our people

It's not just pastors who are feeling the heat. In fact, as we've talked with pastors about building a disciple-making culture in their churches, many have commented that their people are under massive pressure—in demanding or hostile workplaces, in struggling marriages, with sick children or ageing parents, with chronic health problems, and with all the other troubles and complications of living in this fallen world. Pastors have said to us, "It's all very well to talk about training our people to be disciple-makers, but I feel like our people are just struggling to survive from one day to the next. We have a hard enough time just getting people to turn up most Sundays—let alone starting anything new or extra!"

The first and most important thing to say is that we must understand and respond to the pressure our people are under *theologically*, in terms of what the Bible says about this fallen world. The kind of pressure we're talking about is situation normal in this present darkness, and its most significant effect is the temptation it brings to abandon Christ, to retreat into the darkness, to give up our hope, to yield to despair.

In other words, learning Christ (as we described and defined it in Phase 1, Conviction 2) is not an academic or theoretical exercise that we make time for after we get life sorted out. Learning Christ means precisely learning to trust in him and put our hope in him in the midst of all the complications, troubles and pressures of life. And just as growth in Christlikeness in the midst of life's pressure is *exactly* what being a disciple is about, so helping people do this through 4P ministry is *exactly* what being a 'transformational learning community' is about.[8]

As we hope we've made clear often enough already, we must not compartmentalize disciple-making as a certain set of activities to be undertaken by the truly committed or by those who have their lives together. The kind of transformational learning we have been talking about invades and changes every facet of our lives, including how we deal with the trials of life.

Having said all of this, there is an obvious need to be realistic about what our people can cope with in terms of time, energy and effort, given the stage of life they are at. There's no point setting your whole project up for failure by embarking on plans that bear no realistic relation to the amount of time and energy that your people have available. It's a recipe for guilt, burnout and discouragement all round.

4. Leadership, staffing and governance

In a landscape where both shepherd and sheep are under considerable pressure, building the right kind of leadership team will be critical. At some point, if you are going to gain any sort of momentum in your Vine Project plans, you will need to address three related questions:

- *Who should be on the team that leads the growth of 4P ministry in our congregation?* (This is the really the outgrowth of your Vine Project Team—the group of people who understand the culture you're wanting to build, and who take the lead in helping to build it. For the sake of this discussion, let's call this 'the leadership team'.)

---

8   In fact, it's striking how often the New Testament speaks about the Christian walk in terms of perseverance and endurance in the mist of trial. Hebrews 10-12 is a good example.

- *What full-time and part-time paid staffing is required to support and lead the growth of the ministry?* (Very often, the staff team would overlap significantly with the leadership team, although in most churches they wouldn't be identical.)
- *How does all this relate to the official governance structures of our congregational life?* (The church committee, the session, the parish council, the eldership, the deacons, or whatever labels these structures have in your part of the world—we'll refer to this below as 'the governance team'.)

This is a difficult subject to write about, because we know the circumstances of our readers are very diverse. Some of you will be in churches where the answer to all three questions could simply be 'the elders'; others will be in churches where there aren't any 'elders' at all (not by name, at least).

However, most churches have these three identifiable groups or levels of leadership in some form or other. There will be considerable overlap between them, but they are not identical. Not everyone who is a key leader in the growth of the ministry will be on staff, or necessarily be an elder or governance person. Not every member of the governance team will in fact take on a key ministry leadership role. And the paid staff, while probably exercising key ministry leadership, may or may not be part of the official governance structures.

We don't intend to enter into any discussion at this point about polity and church structure—not because these issues are unimportant, but because it is simply beyond our scope.[9] We can, however, offer some brief guidance about each of these levels of congregational leadership.

---

9   Such a discussion would require a book all to itself—besides which, we earnestly hope that Reformed-evangelical churches with a variety of convictions on these matters will take up the challenge of the Vine Project, and adapt the ministry principles we're discussing to their own situations.

a. The leadership team

This team will be made up of some combination of ordained pastors, elders and other lay leaders, depending on your church's tradition and polity. Its key role is to reshape and lead the whole culture of your congregation in the direction that we've been discussing—towards making disciples who make other disciples (or, if you like, towards 4P ministry and moving everyone to the right).

This, in other words, is the team that will take active responsibility for implementing the plans you've been putting together (in Phase 4), and maintaining the momentum for change over time. (It would be strange if the senior pastor of the congregation was not also the leader of this team.)

Is this leadership team identical to the Vine Project Team (the people who are working through this book together)? We might say that the leadership team is what the Vine Project Team becomes, together with others who are persuaded of the vision and drawn into leading and equipping the congregation (whether other lay leaders, or other paid staff, or other governance people).

Humanly speaking, one of the key factors for the success or failure of the Vine Project is how well you choose and equip and support the people you draw onto the leadership team. So choose people carefully. Avoid people who are charming, gifted, keen, influential or otherwise outwardly impressive but who do not share your convictions, or who lack faithfulness and spiritual substance.

b. The governance team

In some church contexts, the kind of leadership team we're discussing (above) may be subordinate to the elders or parish council—to those who have formal authority and responsibility for all the affairs of the congregation, including the management of its finances and property. It can be very efficient and helpful for one team to be focused on the nuts and bolts of money and infrastructure and IT and property and the like, while another group is driving the ministry plans.

Whatever the relationship between the two, it hardly needs to be said that the degree of fellowship and like-mindedness between the leadership team and the governance team will make or break the effectiveness of your disciple-making vision. One of the first steps in your communication plan should be to spend plenty of time making sure that all levels of leadership in the church are on the same page, and pulling in the same direction.

Over time, you may find that your clarified convictions about ministry, and the plans you are implementing for cultural change, end up exposing some inadequacies in your current structures of governance and leadership—or some previously unexposed problems with the people who currently inhabit those structures. We can only say the obvious: on the one hand, don't burn down most of what you've achieved by having a massive internal fight over leadership structures or personnel; on the other hand, it would be very unusual to achieve real growth and change without some tussles or conflicts with existing leaders (who very often have an investment in things staying the way they are).

c. The staff team

Just as different churches have different governance structures, so the way that churches appoint and deploy paid ministry staff varies hugely. Whatever staff structures you have in place, however, we'd like to suggest that as you rethink Sunday, and design new pathways for seeing people move to the right, it is almost inevitable that you will run up against limitations in your current structures or staff mix. You may be able to fudge along for a while with the people and structures you have, but eventually— if momentum is going to be maintained—you'll have to bring some new people on board, or redeploy some existing staff.

This situation is often the result of the departmental or 'org chart' approach to church staffing that has become common in recent decades. There's a ministry that needs doing (men's, women's, youth, children's, etc.), and so we appoint a staff member to drive it. The result can be a collection of 'silos' (as they are called in business): different ministries running under their leaders, without much communication or common vision.

For example, having read *The Trellis and the Vine* or become otherwise convicted of the need for disciple-making or equipping or similar concepts, some churches respond by appointing a 'discipleship pastor' whose job it is to take care of this new disciple-making emphasis while the senior pastor, the youth pastor, the men's pastor and the various other pastors get on with what they were doing before. But as the Greeks say, "This no work".

What are the alternatives?

Some key members of your staff team will always be devoted to the public exposition of the word through your Sunday gatherings and other mission events. These are primary teaching roles for able and godly preachers, who teach sound doctrine for the spiritual health and direction of the whole congregation. Through their regular teaching, all other leaders and ministries are shaped by the true gospel and genuine discipleship.

Other pastors or leaders on the team can be either generalists or specialists. For example, a women's pastor could have a 'generalist' responsibility for engaging, evangelizing, establishing and equipping among the women of the congregation. She would train leaders who exercise these ministries and activities under her care. This could be the same for a senior's minister or youth minister, or for the pastor/s of a new congregation that is planted out of your existing one.

Another way forward is to employ staff with more 'specialist' roles. For example, those with particular gifts for evangelism could oversee all the engaging and evangelizing pathways across the whole church. They could focus on making all these ministries effective in every sphere. On this specialist model, you could have a leader (staff or lay) overseeing each major point on the pathway: engaging, evangelizing, establishing and equipping.

In whatever way you select and deploy the staff team, and the volunteer or lay leaders who work alongside them, it needs to be clear how each person is responsible to lead and nurture 4P ministry in their particular area, to see people take a step to the right towards Christ and maturity in him. So when the staff member in charge of men's ministry is asked what his job is, he should say something like: "to engage unbelieving men in relationship, to bring the gospel to them, to establish them in the faith and the church, and to equip them to make disciples of others". That's very different from the more common answer: "To run the men's ministry".

5. Practical skills in maintaining momentum

a. Make the right sort of plans

A key aspect of maintaining momentum is to make sure you have the right sort of plans to start with. If your plans are vague, unrealistic, poorly expressed or waffly, it is very unlikely that they will gain much traction or have much longevity. It's difficult to make much progress when people aren't sure exactly what to do and when, or when they don't know even know if progress is being made or not (because there's nothing in the plans to indicate what progress might look like).

If your plans are going to be understood, embraced and put into effect over time, they need to:

- be clearly and simply expressed in plain English
- be sufficiently well-defined and specific that everyone knows what they are, and could say whether or not you've made progress in achieving them (one way to test this is to ask whether any sort of measure or metric could be applied to aspects of the plan)
- be exciting and fresh but realistic in scope—that is, you need a small set of priorities or critical factors that you want to put your energies into; if the plan is too vast and has too many 'priorities', they cease to be priorities and become a wish-list
- be applicable to as many aspects of your congregational life as possible—a key factor in building and maintaining

momentum is to have plans that everyone can grasp and be part of, whether in the men's ministry or youth or women's Bible study or whatever; good quality plans help everyone to work together towards the same goal

- have someone assigned to each step or action, who is responsible for driving it forward
- have realistic time frames attached to the different steps or actions.

Making good quality plans and following through on them is a practical skill that some of us are better at than others, and the above points are only a very brief introduction to the subject. Don't be proud—get some help. Look for people in the congregation who are good at this.

DISCUSSION

1. Which of your current ministries and programs are not aligned (or will be difficult to align) with your new disciple-making vision and culture? What can you do about this?

2. Take some time to look back over the plans you made in Phase 4, and see how they can be improved in light of the six bullet-points above. Come up with a revised set of plans that:

   - are crystal clear
   - have well-defined and specific goals
   - have a small number of key priorities
   - apply to all your ministries
   - have someone responsible for them
   - have a realistic time frame.

b. Review, learn, adapt

The plans you made in Phase 4, and have now revised and improved, are no doubt first class. But if normal experience is anything to go by, within the first 12 months you will face some surprises—some things will flop, others will unexpectedly take off, unavoidable delays or problems will sidetrack you, and so on.

In other words, unlike the laws of the Medes and the Persians (which can never be changed), your plans need constant monitoring and review and adjustment. You will need to pause at regular intervals and check how things are going, talk honestly about progress, and make changes to your plans where necessary. You might find it useful to have a regular monthly meeting to keep things on track and to co-ordinate and deal with spot fires, as well as a more major 12-month review to adjust the plans for the following 12 months.

You may also need to repeat parts of the whole Vine Project process in (say) five years time. You may need a fresh clarification on your convictions, in case you've wobbled off course. You may need to look again at your own lives, do a fresh re-evaluation of the ministry, and conduct a major revision of your plans.

c. Identify gaps in practical skills

The following practical skills are more important for leading in culture change than we might think. And it's worth being honest about what capabilities are missing in your context. If you can look back at a repeated cycle of making plans that are never implemented effectively, there might be a skill deficit.

It's not hard to work out what practical skills would be valuable in leading and managing our ministries, especially if we are trying to make significant changes. For example:

- personal management and controlling the diary
- leading teams and team meetings
- managing ministry projects
- developing and running training programs
- coaching skills and delegating skills.

These kinds of gaps can be addressed in various ways:

- by attending to the personal development of team members (there are many resources, books and programs available, both Christian and secular, which can help pastors or other team members improve their practical skills in these areas)[10]
- by adding new members to your team with particular strengths in these areas
- by using the gifts and experience of current church members.

The support community at **thevineproject.com** will also provide resources for developing practical skills in leading and managing disciple-making ministries.

DISCUSSION

1. Work out a monitoring and review process for your plans over the next 18 months.

2. What gaps do you see in the capabilities of your leadership team? How will you fill these gaps?

More of Gary's story

Gary leads an evangelical Anglican church in a multicultural community with a rapidly growing population.

How have you personally had to change since you got bigger? (I mean, as the ministry got bigger.) What have been some of the challenges for you in your gifts and personality?

Well, I'm highly intuitive and relational, and I can't afford to be that intuitive any more. I need to make more evidence-based conclusions whenever I make a decision! I need to think

---

10 One useful secular online resource is Manager Tools: see http://manager-tools.com. We've also mentioned Craig Hamilton's *Wisdom in Leadership* numerous times already. As a theologically astute one-stop compendium of practical wisdom and leadership tools, with many suggestions for further reading, it is hard to beat.

'structure' more; I need to know where I'm weak and let others step in.

There's a phrase that comes to mind: 'There's not a well-rounded leader, there's only a well-rounded church'. So it's about using the gifts of the church rather than trying to be the jack of all trades, which is what our heroes were, and then realizing you know, I'm only good at three or four things—so I ought to spend more of my time there. So I don't run staff meetings now—the executive pastor does that.

When I started the church plant, my philosophy was to teach Jesus from the Bible in the context of loving relationships. But as things grew they became more complicated, and I had less time to do what is my first love. Part of having a growing staff team is that you have to spend more time with them. I always remember you (Col) saying, "You think putting on a staff worker is going to save you time, but it actually takes more time".

Obviously you've got to still meet up with people around the word—otherwise you lose integrity—but you don't do it in the way you did when you had 40 people.

And how many are on the staff?

Ten people, mostly full time. We've got a new guy for next year who is going to be a church planter for us the year after that.

So the model of growth is to do some church planting?

We have goals for the next ten years, and one is to church plant every two years. Each plant will be a satellite ministry for five years and then they will get to decide if they want to go independent or not.

But we want to make sure they get our DNA. And also we want to plant with a minimum of 70, because there has been a lot of burnout in churches that are small and are trying to do everything.

In a way, we're doing it slower. The old me would have jumped at moving more quickly! And sometimes you've got to do that, but maybe I'm getting too old or I just want things to last, survive and thrive.

～

Dan's story

Dan is the pastor of a Bible church in a medium-sized semi-rural town.

What have you learned about keeping the momentum for change going?

One key lesson is that there has to be a commitment to the change even as people are moving through the learning curve. There is a moment when things seem to lose momentum and it could be tempting to stop. Since most in the church are not early adopters of a new idea, you have to give the new idea time to take shape so that the late adopters can see it and embrace it. Change is hard for people. Staying committed to the change is very important, even as people are taking time to adjust to the church.

One of the things that I did personally was to make sure that I set reasonable goals in assessing the change. I did not expect the entire church to embrace this vision, but I was hoping that at least 20% would embrace it. I have found that the best way to keep the 20% interested is by spending time with them, following up with them and then giving them space and time in the service to talk about their experiences with the new mission. As people were encouraged by the change I would give them opportunities to share how the change impacted them for the better. As much as I would like the world to be driven by conviction and principle, some people cannot commit to a change until they have observed that it works. Testimonies are essential in giving people confidence.

The other thing I have experienced is that if I reach out to people personally by taking the time to walk them through the change, it makes a difference. I recently did this—I called about 25% of the church to alert them to a change, and after spending the better part of four days calling people I felt as if a core of people were ready and prepared for the change.

When I call people, I tell them that change for the sake of change is not always good. Yet change for the sake of mission is always great. When you take the steps to advance the mission, things get messy. If the apostle Paul had never left

Antioch there would have been no uprising of the religious establishment in Galatia, no Judaizers leaving Jerusalem to spread their teaching in Antioch and Galatia, no persecution of the apostle, and no need to write the majority of the New Testament.

But God works in the mess and uses the mess to make the glory of Christ known to the world. Change will create a mess, but as long as that mess is created for the sake of the advancement of the gospel then it's a mess God will use to carry out his mission. The best way to manage change, in my opinion, is to acknowledge that change for the sake of the mission makes things harder, not easier—and that is okay; it is what God uses to do his work.

Allowing people to acknowledge the mess is what keeps the mess from taking momentum away. In fact, I find excitement when the change creates a mess. It shows that we are walking the pattern of Scripture.

Epilogue

Perhaps your emotions upon arriving at this final page of *The Vine Project* are similar to ours as authors.

At this point we are feeling exhilarated, excited, exhausted, overwhelmed, anxious and hopeful all at once. We are all too aware of our inadequacies and imperfections, and of the gaps and mistakes that are bound to exist in what we've written (even though we can't see them at the moment). And yet we're confident in the truth and power of God's word to bear fruit and to change lives, and we look forward to what God will do through this particular example of 4P ministry in the years to come.

Because that's what this book essentially is. It has been an exercise in doing the kind of ministry that we've argued all Christian ministry is about:

- We've shared the word of God with you, and sought to clarify and sharpen from the Bible what discipling, disciple-making, ministry and church life are really about (Phase 1).
- We've patiently applied those convictions to your own heart and life (Phase 2).
- We've then sought to help you think through what your convictions mean in practical terms for those around you— for the whole culture of your church, and for the lost world that is waiting to be reached (Phases 3 and 4).

- We've talked about the challenge of patiently and persistently keeping at the whole process of culture change in the face of many pressures and difficulties (Phase 5).
- And through it all, we've been praying, and will continue to pray, that God will work by his Spirit through these very human and imperfect words of ours to help you make progress, one step at a time.

In other words, we've been trying to move you and your whole church to the right by the word of God.

Your privilege and challenge now is to go and do likewise.

The task is simple enough to describe, but of course impossible to do—save for the transforming power of God, who alone makes us competent for such a ministry, and who shines his glorious light in the hearts of those to whom we proclaim the gospel of his Son.[1]

To him be the glory.

---

1   2 Cor 3:4-6, 4:3-7

Feedback on this resource

We really appreciate getting feedback about our resources—not just suggestions for how to improve them, but also positive feedback and ways they can be used. We especially love to hear that the resources may have helped someone in their Christian growth.

You can send feedback to us via the 'Feedback' menu in our online store, or write to us at info@matthiasmedia.com.au.

APPENDICES

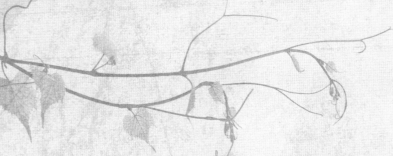

i. *The Trellis and the Vine:* What did you miss?

I n many ways, you could describe *The Vine Project* as the practical, what-do-we-do-now sequel to our earlier book, *The Trellis and the Vine* (*T&V*). However, if you've not read *T&V* there's no real need to go back now and do so. The theological and ministry convictions expressed in the two books are the same—if anything, we feel that the way we've expounded those convictions in Phase 1 of this book is sharper and clearer, although we will leave that to those who have read both to judge.

The one aspect of *T&V* that may be helpful to understand is the metaphor on which it is based, and which will keep cropping up from time to time in this book as well.

As we say in both books, the basic work of any Christian ministry is to preach the biblical gospel of Jesus Christ in the power of God's Spirit, and to see people converted, changed and grow to maturity in that gospel. This is where the life and power of all ministry is to be found: in the prayerful, Spirit-backed speaking of the message of the Bible by one person to another (or to more than one).

In *T&V*, we likened this vibrant, dynamic, gospel growth to a spreading, fruitful vine, taking our cue from the imagery that

Paul uses in Colossians 1:5-6. And accordingly we described the essential work of ministry—of making disciples of Jesus through the prayerful speaking of the word—as the 'vine work' that all Christians are called to take part in, each in our own way.

However, just as some sort of framework or trellis is needed to help vines grow, so Christian ministries also need some structure and support. It may not be much, but at the very least we need somewhere to meet, some Bibles to read from, and some basic structures of leadership within our group. All Christian churches, fellowships and ministries have some kind of 'trellis' that gives shape and support to the work.

These trellises may be administrative and managerial in nature (e.g. finances, infrastructure, organization, property, governance) or they may be 'ministry trellises' (e.g. organizational structures, events, activities or meetings in which vine work can happen). In this sense, the church database and the finance committee are 'management trellises' that support the growth of the vine; and the youth group and women's coffee morning are 'ministry trellises' that provide an organizational structure in which people can get together to grow the vine.

One of the main contentions of T&V was that in many churches the 'trellises' have become disconnected in some way from the 'vine work'. There is a multitude of 'stuff' happening around the church, with many people working hard at organizing and maintaining things, and running various activities and events, but *without a lot of vine work actually taking* place—that is, without the word being prayerfully taught and spoken so that disciples are made and grown. In fact, perhaps the only time real vine-growing work happens is during the regular Sunday service in the various activities that happen up the front (especially as the pastor preaches his sermon).

And so, very often, the pastor feels overworked and frustrated. He keeps working away energetically, but is a little discouraged that his faithful vine work each Sunday doesn't seem to bear much fruit. In fact, he often feels he would like to do more to help and equip others to be involved in vine work, in the work of watering and planting and helping people to grow in Christ. But the sad truth is that a lot of the trellis work also seems to fall to him to organize—rosters, property and building issues, committees, finances, budgets, overseeing the church office, planning and running events. There's just no time.

And that's the thing about trellis work: it tends to take over from vine work. Perhaps it's because trellis work is easier and less personally threatening. Vine work is personal and requires much prayer. It requires us to depend on God, and to open our mouths and speak God's word in some way to another person. By nature (by sinful nature, that is) we shy away from this. What would you rather do: go to a church working bee and sweep up some leaves, or share the gospel with your neighbour over the back fence? Which is easier: to have a business meeting about the state of the carpet, or to have a difficult personal meeting where you need to rebuke a friend about his sinful behaviour?

The problem that T&V tried to name, and which struck a chord with many of its readers, is that it is very possible for a church to be busy and active, and to have all the usual programs and apparatus of church life in place, but for the basic common task of disciple-making through the prayerful speaking of the word of God to have drifted to the margins. It is very possible to have a well-built, well-maintained trellis on which a bedraggled vine is struggling to grow.

ii. Thevineproject.com

Sign up for your free membership

Thevineproject.com provides online support for you and your Vine Project Team as you progress through each phase of the project.

Online resources

The team manual

The team manual (available in PDF and MS Word formats) contains every discussion question, activity, evaluation, and mini-project that appears in this book. Your team members will be able to use them to prepare and write or type individual responses prior to your team meetings.

Pathway resources for disciple-making

Here you'll find links to a wealth of resources developed by our publisher (Matthias Media) and others, which will help move your people through the four Es. Whether you're seeking to engage, evangelize, establish or equip, you should be able to find the resources you need.

Overcoming potential roadblocks in each phase

These FAQs, articles, and audio and video resources address common roadblocks in building your whole church culture around disciple-making.

Full interviews with pastors

You can download our full interviews with all the pastors we introduced in this book. These interviews provide valuable insights, as real-world case studies, from pastors who are leading their churches toward a disciple-making focus.

Templates to get you started

We'll provide you with numerous templates to help you communicate *The Vine Project* to your church leaders, congregation, and potential team members.

Connect with others working on the Vine Project

Online forum

Through our online forum we're seeking to build a community of members who ask questions of us and of each other, and who share their insights and experiences while benefiting from the experiences and insights of others.

Blog

You will be able to follow our blog on the practicalities of disciple-making.

Connect with others in your locality

If you are interested, we will connect you with other churches in your area and provide ideas for how you might learn from each other as you embark on the project.

Go to thevineproject.com for more information

iii. Rethinking small groups

To grow a transformative learning culture in our churches, the priority of everyone learning together and moving to the right needs to drive every activity and program of church life. That's what we're trying to rethink and redesign in Phase 4 of *The Vine Project*.

Where do small home groups or Bible study groups fit into this?

Nearly every evangelical church has them. And they can be a powerful ministry structure for shaping and reinforcing the culture that we'd like to see take hold throughout the church. Much like our main Sunday gatherings, if our small groups don't express and practise and demonstrate the culture we're wanting to foster, the whole project is unlikely to succeed.

In our observation and experience, however, many small groups in many churches are stuck. Even in groups where Bible study and prayer are still the core activities, it often feels like there is little progress in our Christian maturity, fellowship and evangelism. Members can go from one year to the next without any significant change in dealing with sin and living for Christ.

Many groups seem to have evolved into book clubs in which the book under discussion happens to be the Bible. Especially among middle-aged adults, we have heard many stories of small groups that have been meeting for ten-plus years, but with little happening that is new or engaging, and with no new members joining (which is hardly surprising given how tight a ten-year-old group culture would be). It's a Groundhog Day version of Bible study. Attendance is patchy, no-one prepares for the Bible study discussion, prayers are perfunctory, and members are disengaged, and every week is the same.

But even if many of our groups are like this, we still feel compelled to have them. Small groups are just part of our expectation. It feels like we're not a proper church if we don't have them.

Now, we are not anti-small-groups—far from it. We have been in small groups and leading them for a combined total of something approaching 80 years! We have seen God at work producing genuine faith, hope and love in his people through these groups. We've been in churches and seen churches where small groups meeting around the word of God have been fundamental to growing godly, mature, sacrificial disciples of the Lord Jesus. Small groups have been a mighty movement of Christian discipleship.

All the same, everywhere we go, pastors are concerned about the quality of their small groups, and whether they are really achieving anything. Sharpening the diagnosis a little, we see three common symptoms:

- Blurred vision: in many churches, the purpose of small groups is confused, with competing expectations for both members and leaders. When we ask pastors or group leaders why they have small groups, we generally hear one or more of the four Cs: Care, Content (Bible and prayer), Community, and Commission (disciple-making). Then we ask what they would fear if one of these dominated. This question exposes the confusion. If pastoral care dominated the purpose of the group, it might be no different from (or even inferior to) a secular support group. If the Bible and prayer dominated group life, then relationships and love for each other may be superficial. And so on. There is rarely a clear, all-encompassing vision for what small groups are designed to achieve.

- Sheep-pen mentality: small groups in many places have become a safe haven for pastoral care and community building. Pastors tend to herd their people into small groups, almost like holding pens. These are not groups that purposefully and effectively move people to the right towards maturity in Christ. They function as somewhere to put people so that hopefully they will stay with us. Often, pastors don't really know what is happening in the groups because they operate quite independently, with leaders having little accountability to anyone. These groups can be quite disconnected from the vision of the church. If this pattern continues, small groups can become seedbeds of discontentment and factionalism.
- Deficient leadership: small groups don't make disciples; *disciples* make disciples. If we give the leadership of small groups to people who are not learning Christ themselves, the group members will have no shepherd to follow. In many churches, we have lowered the bar of small group leadership in order to generate more groups—and then we wonder why the groups and members stagnate.[1]

This brings us to what a small group essentially is—if we apply our convictions to understanding them. A small group is simply *a cluster of Christ-learners who have committed themselves to move to the right together through mutual 4P ministry* (Proclamation, Prayer, People, Persevering).

A small group then, if it is functioning properly, will always have these characteristics:

- It will be led by a mature Christ-learner who understands that this is the purpose of the group, who is committed to this vision personally in his or her own life, and who is being equipped to lead the group in this common task. In fact, a well-equipped group leader will understand that his

---

1   At one very large and well-known North American church at which we were running a workshop on these issues, the leadership team confessed (rather sheepishly) that for many years, small group leaders had been recruited by sending round an email calling for volunteers.

or her role is not to lead a group, but to lead people—to help each person step to the right, not only through the group time but also through personal contact, prayer, phone calls, and so on. It's important to underline that the essence of small group leadership (and all Christian leadership) is not technique but character. Leaders must model the life of learning Christ in order to teach others.

- The circumstances of its meeting (who is in the group, how often they meet, etc.) will be shaped by the goal of moving to the right, rather than by personal comfort or friendship.
- Likewise, the content that the group members share with one another will be focused on the Bible, including the disciple-making convictions (that we have clarified in this book) that spring from the Bible.
- Because growing to maturity in Christ will always mean a love and concern for others, every healthy cluster of Christ-learners will have a focus and purpose beyond itself; that is, the group will inevitably be thinking and praying and acting to see others they know (outside their group) move to the right as well. At the very least, a healthy small group will constantly be praying for non-Christian friends and family, and helping and encouraging each other to make progress in seeing those people take some steps towards Christ.
- This outward focus means that it will be common for a healthy small group to be equipping its members to help others learn Christ. Some of this equipping might be done in the group time using various training resources on answering questions about Christianity, explaining the gospel or reading the Bible with a non-Christian neighbour or colleague. Small groups are an ideal setting for this kind of mutual equipping because as the members take their first steps in 4P ministry, they have the support, wisdom and prayers of the group to keep them going.

This final point—about healthy small groups having a focus beyond themselves—is a vital one to think through as you consider the various structures or pathways you want to design for moving people to the right.

In most churches, everyone is supposed to be in a small group, with other structures or groups or ministries being an additional commitment. The small group is considered to be a kind of default weekly time-block that everyone has to find time for, and then anything else you do to minister to others (to reach out, or serve, or evangelize, or be involved in any sort of ministry) is an extra thing on top. This makes many people's lives very full—and often makes it difficult to find people with the time to be involved in ministry.

This is worth rethinking. If we are right that the very nature of any small group should be outward looking, why not use the small group itself as one of the basic building blocks for the pathways you want to design?

For example, rather than starting a new ministry or team to focus on engaging with your local community, make this a goal of some or all of your small groups:

- You could make it a normal expectation for every small group to do some community or local engagement every year, and provide resources and training to help them do this.
- Or you could form some small groups whose particular mission or focus was to engage with the local community— for example, you could form a small group of people who all live in the same neighbourhood or apartment building, and make it their focus and goal to get to know as many people in that neighbourhood as possible; to become known as 'that Christian group' that is always putting on community events, helping people out, and talking about the significant issues of life.
- Or you could mix and match these two emphases—that is, try to get as many groups as possible involved in engaging, while also having one or two groups for whom it is a special focus.

One objection we have heard to this notion of the small group having a focus beyond itself is that it loads up small groups and leaders with too many expectations. If we expect the small group to do everything, or to achieve everything, we will just be setting ourselves—and especially our hard-working group leaders—up for failure. Just let the small groups focus on 'Establishing' Christians in godliness, the argument goes, and let other aspects of the church program take care of the other Es.

There is a truth to this objection. If we overburden one particular ministry 'trellis' (like small groups) then we are likely to see it sag, and its leaders become discouraged. And other structures for supporting or enabling different aspects of the pathway will be necessary and important (such as centrally organized evangelistic events, and so on).

However, if our convictions about Christian growth are correct, then it's not really possible for small groups just to focus on 'Establishing'—because we will not be establishing our people in Christ if they are not learning a Christlike love for the lost, and longing to be equipped to serve others. The small group cannot (and should not) seek to do everything. But if our small groups never think outside themselves to consider the multitudes living in this present darkness, then we will never change the culture of our whole congregation towards reaching the nations with the gospel of Christ.

Col's story: Reinvigorating small groups as gospel teams

A few years ago, in collaboration with Phil Colgan, the minister of our church, I (Col) invited ten men aged between 30 and 50 to be in a team with me for a year. They were all married, and all faced the usual pressures of growing families, work responsibilities and insecurities, midlife questions, and the constancy of juggling too many balls. They were mature, godly men, serving faithfully in the church with a variety of gifts and personalities. Most had been in small groups for years, and some had led groups.

We felt they would be refreshed and challenged if we injected some outward-looking ministry into the team.

We introduced the language of being a 'team' and explained how this was different from being a 'group'. That in itself was an interesting discussion. There were suggestions of team caps and jerseys! But at that early stage, I wasn't really sure what they thought of the idea. I suspect there was a little humouring of me going on, hoping I would get over it soon.

We did some Bible studies on 1 Corinthians following the sermon series, and I introduced the Swedish Method of Bible reading as a way they could read with their families or other blokes.[2] We prayed for each other and our wives and children (we produced a sheet with the names of their kids and ages), talked about our job situations, shared how we came to know Christ, ate junk food (unless our wives sent supper), and joked around a fair bit. We started using emails to keep in touch during the week with news and prayers. We wanted to be a band of brothers who would back each other no matter what.

In our studies we talked about how 1 Corinthians 1-4 applied to us as a team. I confessed to them that I had a definite agenda—like the apostles, we are entrusted with the gospel, and like the apostles this will take us out of our comfort zone (scum of the earth sort of thing).

So we talked about some of my wacky ideas about being a team. Let's move the team meeting to a club instead of my lounge room, I said, so we can meet other men. Let's get rid of the ghetto mentality. How about we run *Simply Christianity* for our mates? We could do some doorknocking in the parish or set up a stall in the local shopping precinct. It was all a bit overwhelming for most of them.

So what happened?

We started by agreeing to hand out leaflets at the train station before Easter—team bonding and gospelling at the same time.

We did some work on the 'ministry of the pew',[3] and I gave them the assignment of talking with one of the older women at church, because we tend to stick with each other. The older

2   See Peter Blowes, 'The Swedish Method', *The Briefing*, no. 364, 1 January 2009, pp. 16-21, available online (viewed 26 February 2016): http://matthiasmedia.com/briefing/2009/01/the-swedish-method/; and Peter Blowes, 'Motivated, reproducing, applied Bible teaching: The Swedish Method', GoThereFor.com, 23 May 2015 (viewed 26 February 2016): http://gotherefor.com/offer.php?intid=28725.

3   Using an early pre-publication version of the material that became *Six Steps to Loving Your Church*.

women were delighted, if not a little bemused. We worked at connecting with men at church who seemed on the fringe—to get to know them and offer to meet with them one-to-one. We learned how to read the Bible one-to-one with another Christian bloke, practising with each other for a few weeks.

All of this made our Bible study and prayer more urgent. So when were in 1 Corinthians 5 and 6 and reading about the excommunication of the unrepentant brother, we got talking about how we could simultaneously welcome the sexually immoral, the greedy, slanderers, drunkards, swindlers and idolaters to church to hear the gospel, while disciplining brothers in the church who were tempted back to these sins. We thought of our non-Christian mates, and what they would make of our church. Would they feel welcome? Would they hear the gospel? Wrestling with this sharpened our Bible study and took it from intellectual theory to how we run our church and team in practice.

We did some Bible study on God's big plan in Christ to build a people for himself, so that we saw our mundane lives in the light of what God is doing.

At some stage we had a look at the 'moving to the right' diagram.

My initial hope was that each team member would be helping to win or grow one other bloke as a disciple, as well as leading their families in Christ. This is still a work in progress. A few have started one-to-one Bible reading with someone else at church.

We ended up with 35 men on our prayer list, some on the fringe of church and lots of unbelievers. What to do with them? Do we invite them to church, the team or what? We found a space we could book in a local club, and during November we moved our Wednesday night team meeting to the club and we invited guests. Sometimes we just had a meal, and other times one of the guys gave a testimony or short talk relating the gospel to men. It worked well. We worked as a team, inviting, meeting each other's mates, and praying hard. We're still following up some of those who came along.

At the end of the year we decided to continue for another year with a similar pattern, including about four 'club nights' throughout the year.

What did I learn from the experiment?

It's not too hard to rejig a regular Bible study group into some sort of disciple-making team. It's important to teach a big vision of what God is doing in the world, redeeming a people for his Son. Pray hard for others. Talk about how you could help others take a step to the right. Work at personal encouragement of others on Sunday by prayer and sharing in the word. Focus especially on disciple-making in the home. Give some practical training in reading the Bible with others. Do some kind of engaging and evangelism work as a team.

By working at helping others to take steps to the right, we inevitably talked about our own struggles and needs for deeper repentance and faith. It was a pretty honest fellowship. Over time many of the groups at our church—men's, women's and mixed—have tried different ways of becoming a gospel team. Starting with one team infected the other groups.

It's hard to think of each day as an opportunity for making disciples. But when we are in a team like this, we stick at it. We need each other. Personally, when I'm not in this kind of team, I get slack in praying and working at personal evangelism and following up people at church.

DISCUSSION

1. How would you rate the small groups in your church? Do any of the worrying symptoms mentioned above resonate with you?

2. Jot down your own profile of the 'ideal' small group for your church. What would you like to see small groups become?

3. What are the key steps in moving small groups in your church towards the ideal, from where they are now?

matthiasmedia

Matthias Media is an evangelical publishing ministry that seeks to persuade all Christians of the truth of God's purposes in Jesus Christ as revealed in the Bible, and equip them with high-quality resources, so that by the work of the Holy Spirit they will:

- abandon their lives to the honour and service of Christ in daily holiness and decision-making
- pray constantly in Christ's name for the fruitfulness and growth of his gospel
- speak the Bible's life-changing word whenever and however they can—in the home, in the world and in the fellowship of his people.

Our resources range from Bible studies and books through to training courses, audio sermons and children's Sunday School material. To find out more, and to access samples and free downloads, visit our website:

www.matthiasmedia.com

How to buy our resources

1. Direct from us over the internet:
  – in the US: www.matthiasmedia.com
  – in Australia: www.matthiasmedia.com.au

2. Direct from us by phone: please visit our website for current phone contact information.

> Register at our website for our **free** regular email update to receive information about the latest new resources, **exclusive special offers**, and free articles to help you grow in your Christian life and ministry.

3. Through a range of outlets in various parts of the world. Visit **www.matthiasmedia.com/contact** for details about recommended retailers in your part of the world.

4. Trade enquiries can be addressed to:
  – in the US and Canada: sales@matthiasmedia.com
  – in Australia and the rest of the world: sales@matthiasmedia.com.au

Also from Matthias Media

What if **every Christian** in your church understood clearly who they are **in Christ**, and saw their purpose not just as being a disciple of Jesus Christ but being a **disciple-making disciple**?

It's an intriguing question, and exciting to imagine the impact it would have for the kingdom.

But don't leave it hanging there as just a nice theoretical question: "What if…?"

Ask the next question: "*What would it take* for every Christian in my church—no, what would it take for *me* to change my life and make decisions and choices firmly based on Christ's Great Commission?"

The Bible's answer: it would take the Holy Spirit applying the life-changing truths of the gospel in a way that deeply affects both my heart and my way of thinking about the course of my life. It would need me to prayerfully soak in God's word and its revolutionary message, thinking carefully about its practical implications. And it would definitely be helpful to have the assistance and prayerful encouragement of a group of Christian brothers and sisters who were doing the same thing alongside me.

Enter *The Course of Your Life: A personal revolution*, a video-based resource from Tony Payne and Matthias Media. For more information, sample videos, PDF downloads, and more, visit: **www.thecourseofyourlife.info**

Related…

The Thing Is, written by Tony Payne, is a short book that conveys the same fundamental ideas as *The Course of Your Life*. What is the point of it all—the purpose, the real reason you get out of bed in the morning as a Christian?

FOR MORE INFORMATION OR TO ORDER CONTACT:

Matthias Media
Email: sales@matthiasmedia.com.au
www.matthiasmedia.com.au

Matthias Media (USA)
Email: sales@matthiasmedia.com
www.matthiasmedia.com

Also from Matthias Media

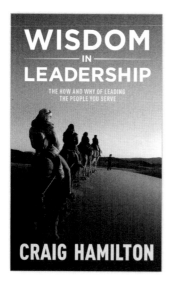

In *Wisdom in Leadership* Craig Hamilton shares what he has learned through many years of being a student of the Bible and theology; a discerning reader of books on leadership; a keen observer of life and the way things work; and a loving leader of the people God has placed around him.

This book is a goldmine of helpful insights for pastors and anyone else with leadership responsibilities in their church. With 78 chapters covering an extensive range of topics, this may well be the only book on church leadership you'll ever need to read.

"Reading this book won't make Christian leadership easy. But it will make it easier. The strategies and principles here won't remove all frustration from Christian leadership. But they will make it less frustrating. This book won't solve every problem. But it will help you solve a whole bunch of unnecessary problems that you really don't need to face."

—Craig Hamilton, author

What people are saying...

"Craig Hamilton's book *Wisdom in Leadership* fills a significant and costly gap in Christian circles, and does so with verve, wit and wisdom… This book could be a game changer for many Christian leaders and, as a result, a blessing to many churches and Christian ministries. Highly recommended."—**Rory Shiner**

"It's a while since I've been as excited about a book on leadership as I am about this one. Craig Hamilton's *Wisdom in Leadership* is a treasure chest of wisdom. It's set to become my go-to book for Christian leaders and I've already pre-ordered copies for each member of our church's leadership group."—**Dave McDonald**

"I'm reluctant to give commendations for books unless I actually think they are not only true, but also well written, worthwhile reading and a needed contribution. Craig's book is all three. It's the book on leadership I'd want to write if I were to write one."—**Mikey Lynch**

FOR MORE INFORMATION OR TO ORDER CONTACT:

Matthias Media	Matthias Media (USA)
Email: sales@matthiasmedia.com.au	Email: sales@matthiasmedia.com
www.matthiasmedia.com.au	www.matthiasmedia.com

Also from Matthias Media

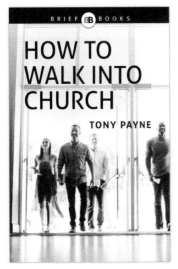

If you've been a churchgoer for more than just a few Sundays, walking into church probably doesn't seem like it deserves its own how-to manual. Right?

In fact, it most likely seems like a pretty straightforward and trivial weekly activity.

But things are rarely as simple as they seem, and how you walk into church reveals a great deal about what you think church is, what it's for, and what you think you're doing there.

In *How to Walk into Church*, Tony Payne helps us think biblically about church. Along with giving plenty of other practical advice, he suggests a way to walk into church that beautifully expresses what church is and why you're there—a way that every Christian can master.

If you go to church, this Brief Book is for you.

What people are saying...

"This book is a great idea. It's wonderfully practical, helpful, and relevant. I hope we can give it away to our new members. Tony has given us a necessary reminder on the importance of walking into church with the right heart, the right head, and the right spirit."—**Kevin DeYoung**

"This outstanding book is packed with profound reflection on what church is and practical application of what it means to 'go to church'."—**William Taylor**

"*How to Walk into Church* is so clear, so simple, so straightforward, so practical—and so eternally important! As such, it is a brief must-read for all Christians." —**R Kent Hughes**

"Sometimes the simplest things are the easiest to overlook—things like walking into church. How do you walk into church? If you read this little book, I believe you will think about it a lot differently and you will do it a lot better."—**Tim Challies**

FOR MORE INFORMATION OR TO ORDER CONTACT:

Matthias Media
Email: sales@matthiasmedia.com.au
www.matthiasmedia.com.au

Matthias Media (USA)
Email: sales@matthiasmedia.com
www.matthiasmedia.com

Also from Matthias Media

Growth Groups is an acclaimed training resource that has been widely used to train Bible study group leaders throughout Australia, the UK and the USA over the past 20 years or so. The training material has a number of objectives:

- to equip leaders with the vision, attitudes, knowledge and skills to initiate and lead a small group (or 'growth group' as it is called)
- to train leaders as Bible teachers and pastors, not simply small group facilitators
- to develop an understanding of small-group ministry shaped by the Bible
- to impart a big vision of the ministry of growth groups—a long-term, expansive strategy.

Growth Groups consists of a manual for each person being trained, plus a book of notes for the trainer. The manual falls into two sections:

- Section 1: a set of 15 'training topics' about small groups; these are like discussion papers that are read and discussed as part of the training.
- Section 2: 10 training sessions that utilize the training topics, along with other exercises and activities.

Growth Groups can be used either as a 10-week training program for future Bible study group leaders, or to provide ongoing training for current group leaders. Whatever way you end up using the material, *Growth Groups* provides everything you need for the vital task of training small-group leaders.

FOR MORE INFORMATION OR TO ORDER CONTACT:

Matthias Media
Email: sales@matthiasmedia.com.au
www.matthiasmedia.com.au

Matthias Media (USA)
Email: sales@matthiasmedia.com
www.matthiasmedia.com